Through the keyhole

Manchester University Press

Through the keyhole

A history of sex, space and public modesty in modern France

Marcela Iacub
Translated by Vinay Swamy

Manchester University Press

Published by Librairie Arthème Fayard 2008

First English-language edition published in 2016 by Manchester University Press
Altrincham Street, Manchester M1 7JA

www.manchesteruniversitypress.co.uk

British Library Cataloguing-in-Publication Data
A catalogue record for this book is available from the British Library

Library of Congress Cataloging-in-Publication Data applied for

ISBN 978 1 7849 9151 7 hardback
ISBN 978 1 7849 9152 4 paperback

Typeset in 10/12 Sabon by
Servis Filmsetting Ltd, Stockport, Cheshire
Printed in Great Britain by
Bell & Bain Ltd, Glasgow

Contents

Acknowledgments

First and foremost, I would like to thank Radu Florinel, who, in December 2006, invited me to the School for Engineers and Architects in Fribourg to deliver a lecture, which became the inception of this book. Without that invitation, the so-refined and so-secret question of the relationship that our culture has woven between architecture, sexuality and law would never have aroused my curiosity.

Yet without my editor, Sophie de Closets, this work would never have seen the light of day. It was through her encouragement, intelligence and kindness that I could complete the most unpredictable task that is the writing of a book.

I thank my colleagues in the historical Demographics Laboratory at the *École des Hautes Études en Sciences Sociales* (EHESS), in particular, Hervé Le Bras and Maurizio Gribaudi, whose helpful comments, and the interest they showed in this project allowed me to improve and deepen my research.

I thank Mathieu Lindon and Arnaud Esquerre for their encouragement and friendship.

Finally, I would like to thank Lola, who accompanied me day and night during the difficult period of the writing of this manuscript, making all kinds of effort and sacrifices to render those times more cheerful.

Marcela Iacub

Abbreviations

Bull. crim.	*Bulletin of the Criminal Chamber of the Court of Cassation*
Cass. crim.	Criminal Chamber of the Court of Cassation (Supreme Court)
D.	*Recueil Dalloz (post-1945)*
DH	*Recueil hebdomadaire Dalloz (pre-1941)*
Dr. p.	*Droit pénal*
GP	*Gazette du Palais*
JCP	*Juris-classeur périodique (Semaine juridique)*
RSC	*Revue de science criminelle et de droit pénal comparé*
S.	*Recueil Sirey*

Translator's foreword

A remarkable book-length study by a dynamic and prolific author whose work has not been previously available to an Anglophone readership, Marcela Iacub's *Through the keyhole* is a significant contribution to what, since Foucault, has been called the history of sexuality. It traces the history of the word *pudeur* (modesty, often translated as decency in the legal context) as a specifically legal term used in Article 330 of the old Napoleonic Penal Code, which regulated "modesty" in public space and thus sexuality in general. Having held sway over French society for almost two centuries, the term *pudeur* was finally taken out of the French legal code during the 1992 reform. Iacub shows how this shift occurred and explores not only the impact of the prolific jurisprudence produced by Article 330 on the ways in which France (and by extension, Western culture) constructs sexuality but also the consequences of such a construction on our understanding of important notions such as public and private space, consent and morality.

Marcela Iacub is of Argentinian origin, and received her law degree in Buenos Aires, where she was admitted to the Buenos Aires Bar as one of its youngest lawyers. She moved to France in 1989, where she completed her doctorate at the *École des Hautes Études en Sciences Sociales* (EHESS). A prolific author of over a dozen substantial works, and a currently a researcher at the CNRS (*Centre National de la Recherche Scientifique* or the French National Center for Scientific Research), Iacub has made a noticeable impact on the field of sexuality and legal studies both in France and abroad.[1] An Italian translation of this book (*Dal buco della serratura, una storia del pudore pubblico dal XIX al XXI secolo*) by Graziella Durante was published in 2010 by Edizioni Dedalo. In addition, several of her books have been translated into Italian, Portuguese and Spanish.

Yet, for lack of much-needed English translations, none of her work is available or even known to those in the English-speaking world who cannot read French. The present translation seeks to fill this important lacuna.

Iacub uses various significant public debates from different periods of Post-Napoleonic French legal history to frame her analysis. For instance, in 1857, the author tells us, a group of young people who had engaged in an orgy in the confines of a private mansion was sentenced for contempt of public decency because a curious voyeur was able to watch them from the outside through a keyhole. In 1893, Iacub explains, students who organized the second annual Arts Quat'z' ball in Paris declared a "war of the nude" against the courts by demanding that certain forms of public nudity be considered "chaste." Or, from the 1960s, she excavates a passionate public debate that ensued on whether women bathing topless on French beaches constituted indecent exposure. Iacub shows us that in each of these historical moments, the crux of the debate hinged on the following questions: where does the public end and the private begin? What can we reveal and what ought we to hide?

Today, this old word *modesty* (or *decency*) has disappeared from the French legal code and been replaced by the term *Sex*.[2] But, far from an epic tale of a hard-won freedom, Marcela Iacub's analysis demonstrates how the techniques used by the State have transformed our sexuality into a spectacle in the last two centuries, and have conditioned our spaces, our clothes, cultural practices and even some of our mental illnesses, thus allowing the author to call for a politico-legal history of the gaze.

The 1992 revision of the French Penal Code to no longer include the term *pudeur* was more than just mere updating of legal vocabulary. It represented not only a semantic shift but also an epistemic rupture, which Marcela Iacub explores in this work through an analysis that blends the fields of law, architecture, literature and psychiatry. We discover how the law has long divided the visible world between domains that are considered legal and illegal with regard to certain acts and behavior, thus transforming real (and sometimes indistinguishable) spaces into institutional and political spaces. In this context, for Iacub, the final erasure of the term *pudeur* in 1992 does not in any way imply that French (and by extension Western) society has moved away from moralistic definitions and means of shaping and adhering to social mores. Rather than read this final disappearance of *pudeur* from the French legal, and perhaps cultural, lexicon as a liberation (and thus progress), Iacub shows how anxieties of the post-Napoleonic period that produced the very concept of decency allowed for the construction of a sexuality that was controlled through spatial dispersion. Yet, over time, this control of sexuality through a tight regulation of space gave way—through a series of legal judgments from the nineteenth into the mid-twentieth century—to a sexuality that is now articulated through what she calls the politics of Sex. Thus, Iacub's text lays out the underlying stakes for contemporary French society of this semantic and indeed conceptual shift from *pudeur* (decency) to Sex.

Much of our understanding of this shift is predicated on a careful consideration of the concept of public and private space and the ways in which different interpretations of Article 330 in fact constituted that crucial difference. Iacub elaborates on how in the nineteenth century the definition of the public came to depend not so much on physical space but rather on the relationship between the actors in the given space. The meticulous examination of the different developments in the jurisprudence of Article 330 allows Iacub to trace the ways in which modesty was defined, regulated and even imposed on society. This juridical contextualization proves key to comprehending why in contemporary French society the regulation of sex and sexuality has taken on great significance while the seemingly quaint idea of modesty is thought to be no longer current or even viable.

One can quite clearly trace key elements of Iacub's work back to Michel Foucault's influential thought. As is well recognized today, Foucault changed the shape of scholarship in many disciplines in the Anglophone world, ranging from history and literature, to sociology, anthropology and, of course, gender/sexuality studies. The key to understanding the shift signaled by Foucault's important work is engaging with the way in which he studied the dynamics of power (*biopower*) and its operation in order to comprehend the construction and maintenance of various socio-political structures in our society. Iacub undoubtedly follows Foucault in her approach to studying French society.[3] She, too, is clearly attuned to the immanent power dynamics, especially of the post-revolutionary judicial system, that have produced and upheld certain (if evolving) ways of conceiving morality and ethics since the early 1800s. She inherits from Foucault his particular vein of discourse analysis, which pays attention both to what Foucault, and scholars after him, have called governmentality—which also invokes the psycho-social dimensions of administrative and justice systems—as well as to the way in which it has become reified in our very understanding of culture and society.[4] But the interest of Iacub's work to non-Francophone scholars goes beyond mere Foucauldian influence: she provides a model of how historians and scholars of intellectual history can deploy key concepts such as archeology and genealogy,[5] first developed by her illustrious predecessor, to productively call into question the ways in which French society conceived of regulating sexuality. Her method is in fact deeply archival and evidence-based, consisting of discourse analysis of legal cases that were tried in various French courts.

Like Foucault, much of the basis for Marcela Iacub's scholarly work stems from her insistence that, despite its singular syntax and position, Law is not a pure and objective "positivist" text created outside social discourse. Rather, the formalism she ascribes to this discipline ought to be understood as arising only from a reading of its rationale within the context in which it is produced. Thus, rather than provide an apology (*une démarche apologétique*) that seeks to justify the law in place, or denounce its shortcomings, Iacub's approach takes as its starting point the possibility of comprehending Law as akin to other social sciences. This allows her to employ an archeological method of interpretation of the jurisprudence in order to understand the genealogy of the regulation of sexuality in the twentieth and twenty-first centuries.

In so doing, Marcela Iacub's own scholarship is inspired by the work of the preeminent Austrian legal scholar of the early twentieth century, Hans Kelsen,[6] and more recently, the thought of Yan Thomas,[7] both of whom have influenced her approach to legal studies and the place of analysis of case law in comprehending or even constructing the related social history. In commenting on Kelsen's demonstration that "positive law" was not to be thought of as separate from or as a pre-condition to the "doctrine" that arose from its interpretations,[8] Iacub points to the crucial building block of her intellectual project in general, and in *Through the keyhole,* in particular. In this work, she exposes the nature of the successive and sometimes paradoxical development of jurisprudence, the effects of which, as her analysis clarifies, in fact account for a seemingly astonishing move. From the nineteenth-century vision of sexuality, which needed to be regulated through spatial structures—and in which the State's purview only extended to public spaces—she brings us to understand the inception of a new late-twentieth-century position on sexuality, indicated by the changes in the 1992 reform. This view, for Iacub, depends on an understanding of sexuality as a "flaw" (*une faille*) that renders the individual forever vulnerable and exploitable at any moment, thus making the State a necessary mediator and protector, no matter the space.

The interest in this book-length essay for an English-speaking reader is far-reaching. First and foremost, Iacub's contribution is instructive to the non-Francophone reader precisely because she pursues an approach that lays bare in a simple yet nuanced manner the complex and often hidden articulations of State power which construct and shape our understanding of morality through the necessarily "activist" interpretations of law provided by the judicial arm of government. Thus, Iacub's argument reposes on the bedrock of an analysis that brings to the fore the imbricated nature of the relationship between legal and moral discourses on sexuality, which extends far beyond French borders. In so doing, Iacub puts pressure on our implicit notions of progress and their moral underpinnings. The attention paid to case history—ranging from unknown "private" individuals and theater productions to the appearance and the public acceptance of the feminine "topless" bathing suit (monokini)—could serve as an important model for those wishing to examine the way modesty/(in)decency has been treated in other judicial systems.

Both Iacub's subject and method will surely appeal to the same audience as those interested in Foucauldian approaches to interrogating history. They shed new light on matters surrounding sexuality and identity within social institutions—such as marriage or other forms of cohabitation—and in the fields of performance and art. Furthermore, Iacub's discussion demonstrates how France's notions of public/private, decency/indecent exposure—as enforced through Article 330—all impacted public policies of the time. For instance, she accounts for how twentieth-century France came to tolerate (semi-)nudity in certain public spaces such as beaches and nudist camps.[9]

The implications of Iacub's project are especially important for those of us who work on historical approaches to the construction of gender and sexuality. Even though Anglophone nations do not have the same judicial systems as in France, the methodology that

Iacub has developed will resonate with those wishing to further our inquiry into the import of jurisprudence in shaping culture, politics, and even ethical definitions of the society in which we live. In the United States, for instance, a whole patchwork of laws on public decency still exist (varying by state both in wording and reach),[10] all of which call for an underlying definition of what "the public" is and what constitutes decency. It is in the context of these still-extant laws that gay bathhouses or sex-positive events such as New York's well-known Chemistry Party,[11] use similar strategies as their counterparts in France of creating a membership-based attendance in order to avoid legally constituting a "public," and thus be spared from coming under the heel of the law. Thanks to Iacub, readers will discover in this translation of her work that such techniques in fact have an interesting, if complicated, legal history,[12] which Iacub parses out to show how the very definition of the public (and thus our definition of permissible sexuality) has been transformed.

Iacub's training as a legal scholar (a *juriste*, which, in France, is a more academic and research-oriented profession than an *avocat*, or lawyer, who practices law), and her analytical approach based on a thorough study of case law, allows her to distill the underlying import of a wide variety of decisions that refer to Article 330. Iacub's careful study of such cases gives her the authority to make bold claims about the catalysts for the shifting definitions of public modesty, and thus gendered behavior and sexuality. The importance of this book, then, stems equally from its content as its method: clearly, Iacub both demonstrates the link between such juridical decisions and the ways in which the ethics and morality of (French) society have evolved, and offers us a mode of interrogation that might prove productive for other legal systems and societies.

In this sense, Iacub's perspective on the power dynamics at play in the construction of gender and sexuality resonates with the work of several Anglophone scholars in the fields of sexuality and gender studies.[13] Our debates about acceptable (sexual) behavior often rely on unarticulated definitions of private and public. Whether or not the construction of those spaces differs significantly in the Anglophone world, Iacub's critical and legally-grounded framing of such questions as what constitutes such divisions, and how they impact our understanding of sexuality, lends scholars in these fields a clearly tenable method to approaching the construction of gender and sexuality within our own societies.

In Part I, entitled "*Constructing and demolishing the wall of modesty*," Iacub traces the use of modesty to separate two supposedly distinct worlds of the private and the public within society. She leads the reader from its inception in the Napoleonic Code through its heyday in the late nineteenth century—when even the mere presence of a keyhole rendered an otherwise enclosed space potentially public—to comprehend how the various iterations of subtly, but firmly, interpreted judgments through the twentieth century finally led to the erasure of the term modesty in 1992.

In Part II, "*The visual liberation of public spaces*," Iacub analyzes the parallel progression of the "liberalization" of public space as the hold of modesty over legal discourse waned. This liberalization of course is not to be understood as progress in the evolutionary sense of the word. For Iacub, the change that was introduced in many ways "repackaged" French society's spatialized treatment of sexuality. By closely analyzing various theater performances (including *Hair*), and considering public debates about vestimentary prohibitions (of the monokini for instance), Iacub brings us to appreciate how various juridical moves not only paralleled the social mores current in the day but were also perhaps instrumental in shifting the grounds on which those very mores were founded.

Part III, "*The politics of spaces in the era of sex*," demonstrates how the control of sexuality through spatialization, in which the old Penal Code was master par excellence, has perhaps reached its limits. With the 1992 reform, the semantic shift has ushered in a new moral order in which the stakes are very different. Iacub shows how the decline of marriage as an institution that governed sexuality[14]—along with its attendant spatialization—is intimately linked to the rise of the reign of "consent." Her analysis leads us to comprehend why present-day France, like much of the Western world, has paradoxically become obsessed with regulating so-called sexual perversions while it has moved towards celebrating various forms of sexuality previously forbidden through the enforcement of marriage as the guiding model for sexuality.

Much of Iacub's astute analysis depends on a trenchant parsing of the terse language with which legal discourse cloaks itself. Thus, each word itself becomes a carrier of great weight and meaning. To that end, I will end this short foreword with a few words on the mechanics—and the challenges—of the translation itself. Throughout this book Iacub develops a distinctive conception of socio-spatial and institutional relationships playing out in public and private to organize the history of French laws regarding modesty and public decency. Terms from the original French that may need no unpacking in other academic contexts appear here with meanings that sometimes shift explicitly according to context. These include *lieu* ("place" in the physical sense, e.g., a beach or street, or "space," as conceptualized by judges and legal scholars; e.g., a bedroom may be designated a closed private space); *technique* (often simply "technique," signifying an active effort by legal officials or scholars to reform the spatial order of Sex; it is also occasionally rendered as "mechanism" to describe the articulation of the link between a subject of the law, his/her actions, and the judicial system); and *vue* ("spectacle," as imposed by a participant in a sexual scene or visually experienced by a witness thereof, or as in the capacity for potential witnesses to see, or "visibility" of a space from an outside vantage point).

In addition, I have also chosen to retain "publicity," the cognate of the term *publicité*, whose rare connotation in the French refers to the nature of an act or a space that renders it "public" in the eyes of the law, which often resulted in consequential interpretations of Article 330 of the Napoleonic Code, and its successors. Finally, the word *exhibeur* (exhibitor), rarely used in current French, is sometimes employed by the author to distinguish from the more current form, *exhibitionniste* (exhibitionist). In the context of this discussion, the former can be understood to designate culprits under the old law (Article 330) who did not necessarily seek to derive pleasure from transgressing the law itself (i.e. render it into an object of sexual pleasure). Rather, they were held in contempt of public decency for having (in)voluntarily exposed themselves. In contrast, exhibitionists, as will be explained in detail in Part III, especially as understood within current framework of the new law, are those culprits who do derive pleasure from transgressing the law itself and as such render it into a sexual object. To help the reader, the first occurrences of these latter terms in the main text have been signaled by a translator's footnote.

In closing, it must be said that, as with other publications of this nature, this translation is not the result of a solitary project. For generously giving her time to respond to my questions, I am most thankful to Marcela Iacub. My sincere thanks goes to Lane Kisonak, my research assistant in 2012–2013, for his help and to the Gabriel Snyder Beck Research Fund established at Vassar College, for the generous support at various stages of this project. I wish also to express my gratitude to Emma Brennan of Manchester University Press for her patience and for believing in the project and to Michael Janes for the meticulous copy-editing; to Louisa Mackenzie, whose encouraging yet critical eye I have long benefitted from, and last but not least, to Tilde Sankovitch, mentor, friend, whose support has been most invaluable.

Vinay Swamy
New York
July 2015

Notes

1 In February 2013, Iacub also published her second short work of fiction, *Belle et Bête* (Paris: Stock), which caused a furor in France for allegorically recounting a brief liaison between the author and the erstwhile IMF director, Dominique Strauss-Kahn. The French politician sued in court and won monetary reparations from the author and publisher. Nevertheless, the book was allowed to be published by the judge on 25 February 2013, albeit with an apology inserted (http://bit.ly/19ZEdSQ, accessed 4 January 2015). It must be noted however that this encounter with the highly charged polemical world of media, sex and politics engendered by Iacub's fictive work should not—and does not—erase Iacub's tremendous output of serious scholarship (over ten full-length works and many more contributions to the academic world and beyond) that has been acknowledged and constitutes a significant corpus with which the foremost intellectuals in France have engaged.

2 When discussing this newer ideological construct, Iacub capitalizes the term "Sex" in order to distinguish it from other more practical connotations (sex, the act, or a person's assigned sex, for example).

3 For her position on the relationship between legal discourse and the social sciences, see Marcela Iacub, *Le Crime était presque sexuel et autres essais de casuistique juridique* (Paris: Flammarion, 2002). In its introductory chapter, Iacub explicitly acknowledges her debt to Foucauldian thought, in particular to his concept of pastoral power and his approach to thinking about "a history of the present" (pp. 11, 21).

4 For more on governmentality, see Tony Schirato, Geoff Danaher and Jen Webb, *Understanding Foucault: A Critical Introduction* (London: Sage, 2012), pp. 67–102; or Lisa Downing, *The Cambridge Introduction to Michel Foucault* (Cambridge: Cambridge University Press), pp. 17–18.

5 Both archeology and genealogy take on specific valence as Foucauldian terms. As Schirato et al. explain, if Foucault's concept of archeology was developed to analyze discursive practices at the local level, "genealogy [for Foucault] works through the relations of power generated from [such] localized discursive practices and regimes" (p. 51).

6 Most well-known for his work entitled *The Pure Theory of Law (Reine Rechtslehre)*; Iacub cites the French translation (*Théorie pure du droit*. Trans. Charles Eisenmann (Paris: Dalloz 1962)) of Kelsen's revised second edition of this work in her *Le Crime était presque sexuel*.

7 In explicating the conceptual framework of her intellectual project that she delineates in *Le Crime était presque sexuel* (pp. 7–24), Marcela Iacub cites several of Thomas' works, including "*Fictio Legis*, L'empire de la fiction romaine et ses limites médiévales," *Droit*, no. 21, 1995: 17–63.

8 Iacub, *Le Crime était presque sexuel*, p. 13.

9 See in particular Chapter 5.

10 For a list of current US laws on public decency listed by state, see HG.org "Nudity and Public Decency in America" (www.hg.org/article.asp?id=31193, accessed 11 January 2015).

11 http://chemistry-nyc.com/info.php (accessed 15 March 2015). In an interview with the *Huffington Post*'s Carina Kolodny and Noah Michelson, Kenny Blunt, a co-organizer of the Chemistry Party, has publicly acknowledged that membership is needed so as to avoid the transformation of the party space into a public space (http://huff.to/18EjIJO, accessed 15 March 2015). For an in-depth discussion of this technique of avoiding transforming an enclosed place into a public space, see Part II of Iacub's work.

12 See for instance her discussion of the case of Frédéric de Chirac in Chapter 6.

13 See for instance the work of Heike Bauer, Lisa Downing, Anna Marie Jagose, Peter Cryle, Leslie Hall among many others. See also Mary Ann Case, "Disaggregating Gender from Sex and Sexual Orientation: The Effeminate Man in the Law and Feminist Jurisprudence," *Yale Law Journal*, vol. 105: 1–105.

14 It is no doubt clear that, with the recent near-hegemony of marriage equality as the signal issue of LGBT rights in both the European Union and North America, marriage has still very much retained its disciplinary–regulatory function. It must be noted that Iacub's book was written before the marriage equality laws were instituted in France (May 2013) and the USA (June 2015). More importantly, her broader argument that marriage is no longer used as the sole way to regulate sexuality would certainly support some of the critiques leveled at marriage equality from the left.

Introduction

What is a history of public modesty?

In some Barbarian cultures, it is deemed disgraceful to be seen naked
Herodotus, Histories I, chapter X

Modesty (or decency) is a term that has disappeared from the French Penal Code.* It seems as outmoded as corsets, virginity before marriage, catching women in the act of adultery, and unwanted pregnancies. The word evokes a bygone world in which Victorians used to fit their pianos with trousers to hide their nudity; a world in which people worried about seeing women ride bicycles, or one in which Prosecutor Pinard wrote his famous diatribe against *Madame Bovary*. Rather than being nostalgic, our contemporaries express a sort of irony mixed with indignation, relieved that the term is obsolete.

In criminal law from those times, the term "indecency" referred to two types of infractions. The first kind encompassed assaults committed against individuals. The old Penal Code punished violent indecent assault [*L'attentat à la pudeur avec violence*], which covered forced sexual acts that could not be categorized as rape, such as sodomy and fellatio. The code also punished nonviolent indecent assault [*L'attentat à la pudeur sans violence*], which targeted sexual relations with minors who were too young to give consent. In both cases, the perpetrators undermined their victims' right (not) to consent to sexual relations. Though the law used the word "indecency" to evoke the nature of the violation to which

* Translator's note: There is no exact translation for the French term "*pudeur*." While modesty possibly comes closest in many cases, legal definitions in English tend to use the term (in)decency. Thus, in this text, in keeping with usage in English, the French offense of *outrage public à la pudeur* is translated as *contempt of public decency* or *indecent exposure*.

the victims were subject, it was not a question of a psychological wound, as one would understand such violations today. Indecency referred to a moral order, which the perpetrators of these infractions forced their victims to transgress, despite themselves, thus risking impoverishing their sense of morality and corrupting their instinct.

Article 330 of the old Penal Code—made famous by Georges Courteline's eponymous play[1]—also punished *contempt of public decency* as a misdemeanor directed not against a particular individual but against society as a collective. The law sought to protect society from the sight of certain sexual scenes. According to nineteenth-century legal scholars [*juristes*], the repression of this misdemeanor was aimed at avoiding an over-sexualizing of social life as well as fighting libertinage and debauchery, which risked undermining a moral order founded on the institution of marriage and the sacrifices that it entailed.

Thus, thanks to public modesty, yesterday's society could veil things of a sexual nature in order for them not to perturb the social order. However, for the world of sex to stay covered, like those Victorian pianos, it was not sufficient to avoid unbridled exhibitionism. Public modesty implied a most serious policing of one's very behavior and gestures.

In order not to be convicted for indecent exposure, one needed to be vigilant and zealous, with no room for error. The smallest negligence could prove to be fatal. One needed to watch out for windows, the wind, flies of trousers, cracks or breaches in walls and improperly closed doors. These interfaces that allowed private sexuality to come into contact with public space could, in the blink of an eye, transform nudity and benign pleasures into a misdemeanor. Thus, public modesty became paradigmatic of a society that rendered sexuality into a threat, a shameful and dangerous activity from which one needed to be protected.

Not only did this crime permit the confinement of nonviolent sexuality to secrecy and darkness but it also symbolized a pitfall of the past. Feminists have long denounced a practice that was current up until the 1960s: too often in punishing rape, judges re-categorized it as contempt of public decency.[2] The metaphysical violence of rape was thus reduced to a simple public scandal, drastically lessening the supreme crime against women to a minor and almost ridiculous infraction.

Thanks to this infraction, the courts not only veiled bodies and pleasures but also the most serious crimes of a sexual nature. By its intent to cover up, to silence sex, this misdemeanor ought to have done the same with its criminal manifestations. For, by condemning the evil of which Sex was capable, by describing the acts and gestures and speaking of the ravages it produced on its victims, did it not also underscore the very power and scandal and trickery of this demon that the society of the past sought so much to weaken and block?

The moral revolution

The reform of 1992 erased all trace of the word "decency" from the Penal Code, permanently sealing off the present day from the world of the past with this semantic change. In the early 1970s, a "revolutionary" movement, which is still underway, was launched. It brought about the legalization of contraception, abortion, the equal rights of illegitimate and legitimate offspring, the abolition of adultery as a crime, as well as divorce by mutual consent. This movement has engendered a veritable explosion in the number of convictions for sexual violence and has also created an institutional framework close to marriage for same-sex couples. In short, with its semantic makeover, the 1992 reform set in motion this on-going process, in which it stood as a milestone, and toppled Napoleonic marriage from its monopoly over sexual and family life.*

Henceforth, it is the term "Sex" that organizes the ensemble of crimes and misdemeanors against morality. Freed from its Victorian shackles, Sex, whose destructive as well as affirmative power we don't cease to recognize, now takes the place of marriage as the source of rights and destiny. And its thunderous victory pushed the term "modesty," which used to *hide* it, out of the present and into this form of forgetting we call history.

However, the old world did not bring down indecent exposure with it. Article 330 of the old code morphed into the new Article 222–32, and this change in numbering (which saved it from

* Translator's note: the passing of the 1999 civil union law (Pacte Civil de Solidarité, also known as PaC*S*) and the 2013 Loi Taubira, which permits any two citizens to marry, regardless of their sex, have further put pressure on traditional notions of marriage.

Courteline's ironies) was accompanied by a modernization of vocabulary. We no longer use the term "indecent exposure," but *sexual exhibitionism*. The sentences meted out for this new misdemeanor were reduced and the list of banned acts was further shortened. So, women are no longer banned from wearing monokinis, nor are people convicted for failing to cover up keyholes before engaging in indecent acts. Rather, this misdemeanor comprises a more specific behavior that consists of imposing sexual exhibitionism on others in a space accessible to the public eye. But the precise meaning of the notion of public decency did not disappear with the new infraction. Even though we no longer use this expression, the exhibitionist is still seen not just as a threat to the individual but to the collective, conceived as an undifferentiated sexual and moral entity, that is to say, exactly that which the Napoleonic codifications of public modesty were supposed to protect.

Although the penalty for the new infraction is so miniscule in comparison with the heavy sentences for other sexual aggressions, it is so precise in its definition and conviction is so rare that, by its insignificance, the new infraction only evokes its past splendor. Technically, if the infraction continues to protect public modesty, it seems to exist only as a vestige, like a river emptied of its waters or a bomb that has been carefully defused.

The spatialization of sexuality

If one envisages public modesty as a product purely of the past whose only interest lies precisely in being out of fashion—if one analyzes it as the negation of the world that we have ended up creating after long and bitter battles—one loses sight of the most important aspect of this story. By desiring to bury that past, one is neither interested in the forms that it took, nor in the tactics that it deployed, nor the manner in which the past inscribed itself into a system in order to draw its significance from it.

In the moral domain, social scientists are so eager to glorify the present, so hounded to denounce the past and to transform it into a narrative about the fight between Good and Evil, of Justice against Injustice, of Progress versus Reaction, that they do not take the time to reflect on the positive aspects of those past institutions. In so doing, they deprive themselves of the possibility of comprehending the present they are looking to glorify, the institutional procedures that came to structure it, and the way in which this present is still very much a declension of that despised past.

Of all the institutions that organized morality, none has been more neglected and less understood than the one charged with protecting public modesty. It is called upon only to denounce the tool used by judges to censure artists, persecute homosexuals who openly flaunted their sexuality on the street, humiliate rape victims and make life difficult for "libertines" and wayward individuals [*des distraits*]. Such an approach has allowed us to be attentive neither to the juridical rationality of such an institution nor to the specific practices that it employed to do the work that it is accused of doing.

Nevertheless, what the history of this infraction teaches us when we consider it less from an ideological point of view and allow our curiosity to lead us is that it did not "repress" sexuality, did not bury or condemn it to silence. Rather, sexuality was distributed in space. Instead of trying to make it disappear, sexuality was made answerable to two opposing regimes of visibility, the first private and the other public, defined according to the nature of the space. In private, one could enjoy sexual liberties allowed for by the Code, while, in public space, it was imperative to hide oneself.

In this sense, one can see how Article 330 of the Penal Code, which organized this double regime of public and private in which sexuality could be expressed, in fact constructed a wall. The wall of modesty was a way to separate the two spaces by a physical frontier. Article 330 did not aim to judge sexual behaviors in the absolute. It was content to define them according to the space in which they were enacted. And if the article censured the public expression of sexuality, such behavior was left completely alone when it was enacted in private.

The wall of modesty incarnated the promise made by the Napoleonic State not to intervene in the peaceful sexual life of individuals. Thus, it sought to break with the older invasive and violent practices of the previous centuries. The wall of modesty was the solution found by the Napoleonic State to separate forevermore penal law from religion, to no longer use legal punishment as a tool for purification and salvation. With Article 330, the new State had invented a mechanism with which to curb itself without having to recognize the sexual liberty of citizens, who were, in principle, required to organize their intimate life around marriage. Sexual liberty was a precious and shameful thing to which one could only have access away from the public gaze, in the twilight zone that the State had organized for the benefit of citizens, in this region called *private*, to which it had decided to turn a blind eye.

Invading private space

But, just a few years after its construction, the wall of modesty began to engender profound regret. The courts started to doubt its legitimacy, and to question the State's promise not to intervene in private sexual behavior. If this infraction has an intense history of jurisprudence, it is because, since it was constructed, the wall of modesty has not ceased to be challenged, to be displaced and breached, so as to extend the boundaries of public space to private space, until they were erased altogether. It was as if, as soon as it was constituted, this wall had authorized something intolerable, a harbor for vice, a school of corruption; as if it had been a structure unworthy of a civilized society, one that would have allowed people to hide, rather than be governed.

The displacement of the wall's boundaries constituted a veritable challenge to a certain way of governing sexuality: the expression of a more and more insistent desire to see what was invisible to the eyes of the State, not to rely upon this arbitrary barrier that had given such power to the configuration and stature of space.

Slowly but surely public space began to infiltrate private space until in 1877, at the zenith of this process, the totality of visible space became potentially public. This spatial technique of controlling sexual behavior, which had originally left those at home in peace, began now to function like a tool to moralize private space. Article 330 was used to punish sexual behavior with the claim that it had been seen by others; not because those who let themselves be seen had committed some wrong against those who had seen them but because they had produced *a public uproar in a private space*.

From then on, it was sufficient to have more than two individuals in an enclosed, and even locked, space to make it public. It was consent, and not the nature of the space, or its visibility from the exterior that became the principal criterion for the space to become public. If one of the witnesses was nonconsenting to a scene that took place in an enclosed space, invisible to the exterior, then the space in question was transformed into a space that was as public as a street or byway. The private–public distinction no longer had the clarity of a line that separates two countries on a map. It was unstable to the point where lovers could be punished for forgetting, in the heat of the moment, to lock the door, even if they had closed the shutters and the door of their bedroom. But it was not only these consensual behaviors that the courts punished based on Article 330. They also censured those alleged acts of violence for which they did not desire to impose the full weight of punishment provided for by the code.

Thus, Article 330 served two opposing goals: to soften the punishment provided for crimes and to transform behavior that the Code did not foresee into misdemeanors. Thus, this infraction seemed most to be able to express sexual evil, which was manifested through this curious grammar of space and scandal.

Liberalizing public space

But if private space was subject to increasing control during the last quarter of the nineteenth century, it was also in that period during which public space began to be liberalized in reaction. This phenomenon seems completely rational. Given that the wall of modesty had been virtually demolished, it seemed natural to homogenize the rules of the two worlds. Thus, starting from the end of the nineteenth century, French society sought to soften the rigidity of the Napoleonic Code governing public space and declared war on judges, who ended up giving in gradually. Not only artists, producers, and directors but also nudists, "débauchés," and even the most respected legal scholars employed different means to achieve their goals.

First there was the theory of the "chaste nude," which claimed that nudity was not always synonymous with obscenity or sexuality. The so-called war of the "nudes" began at the turn of the twentieth century, culminating only in the 1930s with the relative triumph of the liberal groups.

The other move, more radical than the first, sought to play with the notion of consent, which had been used until then toward an inverse goal: extending the public to private spaces. If the public consented to a particular performance, why could the theater in which the event took place not be considered private space?

During the period before the moral revolution, the liberalization of public spaces was not so much due to the courts but to the indulgence of public prosecutors and the open-mindedness of certain administrations. Thus, after the late 1960s, under the watch of benevolent administrations, one sees a veritable explosion of performances with sexual content, as well as the organization of open-air practices, like nudism on certain beaches.

It was in this period that a movement began to radically transform the ways in which sexuality was governed. Judges, who found it more and more ridiculous to sentence women for having simply worn a monokini on the beach, began progressively to be stricter in applying sentences for sexual crimes provided for in the criminal code. Slowly, but surely, Article 330 was used with decreasing frequency, either because it was deemed to be too repressive, or because it was not stringent enough. This movement became more radical in the 1970s, culminating in the moral revolution, which fundamentally changed the institutions that organized family and sexual life in their entirety.

Sexual exhibition

The process by which private life was "dematrimonialized" and made subject to the empire of another, more powerful, master called Sex, marks a veritable turning point in the history of public modesty. Sexual life was no longer organized by either marriage or space. Hereafter, it was Sex, and its psychologizing and juridical techniques, that was going to take charge with a penal legislative arsenal that was the most repressive in the history of French Law since the *Ancien Régime*. Indecent exposure was no longer going to be charged with softening crimes or creating new infractions. Nothing would seem serious enough to punish those who transgressed sexual interdictions, while no intimidating, corrupting, harassing or violent behavior would be ignored by the penal order.

The new crime of sexual exhibition, which replaced the old Article 330, has very specific functions, which aim to censure certain forms of public sexual exhibition thought to be aggressive or deviant. It is forbidden to impose sexual exhibition on others in a space accessible to the public gaze. Those who seek to satisfy their desires in spite of that gaze are no longer punished. Rather, the legislator seeks to track down those for whom the public gaze is an object of pleasure.

Indeed, the law admits that one can revel in the public gaze under certain specific circumstances. Erotic spectacles, swingers clubs and gay saunas have all become legal. The law leaves such "debauchés" alone while pursuing "perverts", and particularly exhibitionists: those strange creatures, who had been previously considered by the courts to be innocuous and who aroused the greatest curiosity among psychiatrists in the late nineteenth century.

Public space is no longer synonymous with the absence of sexuality. If the distinction between public and private spaces continues to exist, it is to limit a particular and specific form of eroticism that allows for observation and self-display.

This visual liberalization of public space goes along with a penal regime that increasingly affirms its grip on the individual's sexuality. Never before has the penal system pronounced as many sentences for sexual crimes and misdemeanors, and never has public space been so eroticized. This evolution no doubt signals the very failure of the mechanisms that spatialize sexuality, according to which sexual desires are to be contained/controlled by a system of external walls and borders. In the world of Sex, these walls have been replaced by an internal surveillance of the desires of each individual, in a system that tends to confound legal transgression with mental malady. Spatial borders have become psychological/mental frontiers.

Moreover, imposed sexual exhibition, the only remaining technique of spatializing sexuality, is itself an imprint of this way of exploring psychological depths. The guilty exhibitionist is punished in the eyes of the law, less for having affected the public by transgressing the frontiers of the visible than for having shown dangerous desires. These desires are not those of criminals, like rapists, who enjoy sexual pleasure outside the law. Nor are they those of decent people who find their pleasures within the law. The penal order places the exhibitionist in this strange liminal space that separates two psychological universes, for s/he is said to gain pleasure from the law itself.

A history of the gaze

The history of public modesty conceived as one of the spatialization of sexuality is also a history of its "visibilization." It posits the examination of the ensemble of practices that transformed sexuality into a spectacle, that is to say, into an event whose specificity is to *expose oneself*.

Article 330 of the 1810 Code instituted a type of "original fiction" according to which all public space was under surveillance by the gaze of the State's eye. This gaze was supposed to see all obscene acts that took place in such spaces, whether by day or night. It was not necessary for an individual to embody such a gaze. This eye saw even into deserted streets, unlit byways and even into places where no human being might venture. And in private spaces, into which this all-powerful eye could not penetrate, the State turned a blind eye to sexual scenes, even if a crowd witnessed them.

The function of this fictive vision, which was brought into being in public spaces, was to anticipate all possible gazes and to protect the individual from sexual spectacles that s/he was not supposed to see.

But, in order to widen the field of vision for this all-seeing eye, the judiciary began quite early to depend on human eyes. So, it was decided that under certain conditions, the individual's gaze could incarnate the symbolic gaze of the State. This extension was brought about in two different directions. First, the State employed human eyes to render public spaces not only into spaces in which everything was supposed to be seen but also as kinds of watchtowers thanks to which the public eye could penetrate into private space. So, the fact that human eyes are parts of bodies that can be displaced from one space to another allowed for private spaces to be rendered public: it was sufficient for these eyes to penetrate that space. Thus, thanks to the mobility of the human gaze, private places not visible from the exterior became spaces deemed object of the watchful eye of the State. For, as I will explain in detail, the true subject of the gaze was the State, and not the individual who saw. No doubt, for this reason, the act of seeing was never simply the obverse of the act of revealing oneself [se montrer], for only the former could become the exercise of a kind of public charge. Unlike the act of revealing oneself, apprehending a sexual scene is an act that one can exercise in the name of the State.

Thus, the history of public modesty is the history of complex and polymorphous techniques by which the State's gaze rendered the population's sexuality into spectacle. It is therefore not only the history of the way in which the State appropriated its own power to see but also of the forms by which the State harnessed human eyes to quench its "scopic desire" and how it came to realize that its fictive gaze became the object of desire of those it was supposed to monitor. The most recent reforms did not transform this institutional production of the gaze according to and in the frame within which we see and are always seen. In this sense, the history of public modesty is a kind of genealogy of our visual perceptions, a way in which to comprehend the notion that to see is less an act by which the world discovers itself within consciousness than an event that engages us as political subjects.

Producing spaces

But the history of public modesty/decency is also the history of those practices that the judiciary undertook in order to produce spaces, that is to say, techniques by which they succeeded, thanks to sexuality, in transforming physical places into institutional spaces.

Between the 1810 Penal Code and the reform of 1992, by appealing to fiction or to forms of analogical reasoning, judges transformed the nature of places in which sexual scenes used to be enacted. In order to endow themselves with the capacity to transgress the rules that obligated them to respect the frontier between the public and private worlds, they made believe that an act in a specific space in fact took place in another. So as to displace the wall's frontiers, they pretended that the wall displaced itself on its own, for it was truly necessary to justify the quasi-magical operation in which they were engaged: the metamorphosis of space. Was it not a task befitting the Titans to rule that a room under lock and key, invisible to the exterior, was a public space comparable to a voting booth or a church during mass, using only the logic that, of the three people present, one had not given consent to witnessing a sexual act?

Indecent exposure made it permissible to unify distinct places—a street and an apartment, for example—into one single space and to pretend that an opening existed even in a wall with no physical cracks, to presume that closed theaters were in fact open. It considered scenes that took place in locked bedrooms as if they had occurred on the street, and those that occurred on deserted streets as if they had occurred in a theater full of people, but spectacles performed in front of hundreds of people to be private.

Far from having obeyed an arbitrary subject, this ingenious, constant and cumulative jurisprudence was promoted by a careful and never-failing logic. The courts took recourse to comparisons, analogies, fictions, that were stabilized, widespread and commonplace, and were not devoid of foundation.

These practices eventually not only constructed sexuality as an ensemble of comportments but also as a matrix of production of institutional spaces, which were substituted for real places—as it so often occurs in legal texts. And it is in this institutional space constructed by the courts over the last two centuries that our sexuality is always situated. Despite the 1992 reform the distinction between the spaces has remained intact. Thus, we live in a sexual space that judges have incrementally constructed since the beginning of the nineteenth century without ever having raised, during the last reform of the Penal Code, the issue of either its artificiality or its relationship with the society that we sought to leave behind.

In this sense, the history of public modesty can be seen as an archeology of contemporary sexual scenography. This history allows us to comprehend how the law has constructed the sexual spaces that we still inhabit, in ignorance of what we owe it—as much in understanding the limits the law imposes on us as being aware of the pleasures that it affords us.

Notes

1 Georges Courteline, "L'Article 330," in *Théâtre contes, romans et nouvelles, philosophie. Écrits divers et fragments retrouvés*, Paris: Robert Laffont, 1990, pp. 169–181.

2 See, among others, Michèle Bordeaux, Bernard Hazon, Soizic Lorvellec, *Qualifié viol*, Geneva: Éditions Médecine et Hygiène, Paris: Méridiens-Klinckseck, 1990.

Part I

Constructing and demolishing the wall of modesty

> Wall: Anything that serves as a partition, barrier, or separation; an obstacle constituted by persons or things in order to oppose and resist
>
> *Grand Dictionnaire Encyclopédique Larousse*

Great walls, such as the one built by the Chinese, have had the objective of protecting those who constructed them from the assaults of enemy troops. Other walls were built to protect from foreign diseases and were conceived of as quarantine lines (*cordons sanitaires*). We have sometimes raised walls so that residents do not escape, transforming the territories they encircled into prisons. The fall of these walls was the symbol of liberty finally reclaimed. The virtual wall that the Napoleonic Code erected in 1810 created two separate worlds within a single society. But, far from having caged society, this wall had the strange and distinctive feature of having sought to protect it against the will of its own architects to control and punish. The justification that the jurists of the nineteenth century gave to Article 330 of the Penal Code of 1810, which had created the wall of modesty, was in essence the following: on the one hand, there was the world of public space, which was required to be stripped of any manifestation of sexuality; on the other, the private world in which everyone could enjoy the greatest of liberties because the State had promised not to interfere with it. Thus, the wall of modesty guaranteed citizens a peaceful indulgence in their sexuality, as long as their activities remained hidden from the public gaze.

This manner of establishing private space was a negative technique by which the protection of personal liberties was assured. These liberties existed not because the State recognized them in an explicit or specific manner but rather because it delineated an enclosed space within which the State could not penetrate. The jurists were proud of it, for they perceived in it the sign that their law—unlike that of the *Ancien Régime*—had freed itself from religion, was able to distinguish sin from crime, and limited itself to punishing acts that disturbed social order. Gone was burning at the stake for acts of sodomy, incest or bestiality; commissions convoked to measure the erections of impotent husbands were a thing of the past and nonviolent sexuality that took place in the secrecy of private space was no longer a matter for the State.

Conversely, on the public side of the wall of modesty there had always been a very negative view of sexual desires, which were deemed to be uncontrollable and dangerous forces that the State sought to contain using a system of walls and barriers. Among these, the State did not differentiate sexualities as natural or against nature, legitimate or illegitimate. All sexuality had to be hidden, for even sexual acts that were framed within marriage could, if they ever took place in the public space, awaken base instincts and lust that could make the population susceptible to debauchery.

In this way, the wall could be seen as a sort of compromise between the protection of recently acquired private liberties and a past that the new order sought unsuccessfully to bury altogether. The wall not only transcended the old law, which had given sexuality a central and almost magical place, but *also what remained of it* in a post-revolutionary present that had rendered sexuality almost irrelevant. The wall was there to remind us that, as a result of Napoleonic codifications, this secularized sex was not a trivial matter. At the very least, it required for sex to be hidden, in order not to break with this long history that no revolution or guillotine could eradicate from the collective conscience.

But this fragile equilibrium could not hold up against its own contradictions. Very quickly, the private side of the wall came to be perceived as a hideout that virtue had granted vice and corruption. This is how, toward the middle of the nineteenth century, as the judges launched their great moral crusade, they gave themselves every means possible to bring within their reach the sexual behavior that the permissive Code had allowed to thrive with perfect impunity. They eventually won this battle in 1877, when all visible space became potentially public. For this reason, the history of the wall of modesty is one of long regret.

1

The construction of the wall of modesty

As Article 330 of the Penal Code of 1810 states very tersely, "[a]nyone who is in contempt of public decency will be punished with imprisonment of three months to a year, and a fine of 16 to 200 francs." Until the reform of 1992, which transformed Article 330 into the current offense of sexual exhibition, only a few legislative provisions increased the severity of punishment prescribed for this infraction, and did so without actually changing its definition.

The first was the law of 20 April 1825, known as the law "of sacrilege," (repealed on 11 October 1830[1]), which established that the punishment provided for by Article 330 could be extended from three to five years of imprisonment when the act had been committed in a church. On 13 May 1863, a law raised the maximum punishment provided for by the Code of 1810 from one year to two. This change allowed for individuals previously sentenced for public indecency to receive punishments for recidivism.[2] In 1885, public indecency became an offense eligible for, in case of repeated infringement, the punishment of relegation.[3] But this provision was repealed in 1982. Thus, between 1810 and 1992, it was the courts that (re)shaped this infraction, redefining its meaning and indirectly attributing to it new functions within the penal framework.

But, before we analyze the fundamental place of jurisprudence in the history of Article 330, it is important to understand the nature and significance of the legislative gesture that created this provision in the 1810 Penal Code; this law, which divides visible space in two by forbidding the public expression of sexuality, did not exist in the legal framework of the *Ancien Régime*.

Apart from the novelty that it introduced with regard to the past, and even before the courts charged themselves with the task of transforming it, the law contained in Article 330 had the unique characteristic of appearing exogenous to the juridical order that had invented it. The logic of the law against public indecency, in contrast with other offenses against morality, made it seem as if it was an institutional innovation that emanated from another world of norms.

Unlike laws that targeted other moral offenses, this curious legislative invention conceived of sexuality as a behavior whose main trait did not have to do with consent, legitimacy or normalcy. Public indecency rendered sexuality into a *spatial* event the legitimacy of which depended on its visibility or invisibility to the public. Sexual behavior was thus conceived as a *spectacle*, and was deemed legal or illegal, depending on what the perpetrators, these "actors despite themselves," chose as their stage. In the logic of Article 330 it was important to discern whether this act took place on the right or the wrong side of the wall of modesty.

I Sexuality in the Criminal Code of 1810

The Penal Code of 1810 had confirmed the major changes in definitions of sexual crime that the French Revolution had initiated. As the spokespersons for the Penal Code of 1791 had declared to the Constituent Assembly, "You will see that this bevy of imaginary crimes that stuffed the old law books will soon disappear."[4] This revolutionary heritage, which the Code of 1810 did not repudiate, meant that all crimes related to heresy, such as so-called acts against nature, incest and debauchery, would no longer be under the jurisdiction of the criminal court.

The State did not seek, as in the past, to punish what was considered a *vice* in the eyes of the moral law or a *sin* in the eyes of the religious law. It refrained from intervening in those spheres unless such acts were considered to harm to social order.

This clear separation between criminal law and religion made France at once an example and an exception among Western nations. Thus, in the same period, and for a long time to come, in Germany or England sodomy, bestiality and incest continued to be punished. In England, sentences by hanging were pronounced against sodomites until 1861. Towards the end of the nineteenth century, a Swiss-German law still punished couples living under common-law marriage.

The Penal Code of 1810 had gotten rid of God, but it gave itself a new master that was certainly less terrifying but still quite despotic. Indeed, the Napoleonic codifications had rendered the institution of marriage the center of the political organization of the private sphere. By the type of constraints that it instilled, this entirely secularized institution appeared to be the most able to ensure simultaneously the policing of urges, the distribution of gender roles and the reproduction of citizens.

Given that criminal law depended on marriage, its provisions were less intended to ensure freedom to consent or not to consent to sexual relations than to reinforce the hegemony of the institution in the matter of morality. Thus, it is this sexuality, dominated by marriage and cut off from any transcendence, that criminal law was responsible for organizing.

Sex, marriage and criminal law

Unlike the law of the *Ancien Régime*, marriage from the Civil Code of 1804 subjected sexuality to its control: the validity of marriage did not depend on the possibility for spouses to maintain normal sexual relations. In contrast to the past, impotence was no longer a cause that justified annulment.[5] Moreover, for the marriage to be valid, it was not even necessary that the spouses have "normal" sexual organs. According to a famous case of 1903,[6] it was sufficient that a couple had the appearance of a man and a woman.

The right to legitimate filiation was also marked by the slight contempt for things sexual. Presumption of paternity and the difficulties in ruling it out meant that children who were born to a married woman were required to have been born of the marriage, even if the legal husband was not the father. It was the same for children to whom women had not given birth.[7] It was very easy for a married woman to pass off a child born to another woman as her legitimate son or daughter. The couple enjoyed a fairly broad power when it came to managing appearances and the consequences of their sexual relations.

Marriage as institution rendered sexuality as a type of exclusive service that spouses owed to each other. Engaging in sexual relations was a duty that could be exacted by force. Not only could you call the police to compel a recalcitrant spouse to return to the marital home but it was also possible to use physical violence to obtain favors from her.

The courts had decided that there could not be rape between

spouses, as long as the husband had engaged in forced vaginal penetration of his wife. Other forced sexual acts could be classified as *indecent assault*. One could only complain of sexual crime (other than rape) when there was no penetration of the "appropriate vessel" or when there was vaginal penetration under exceptional circumstances. Thus, in 1919, the Supreme Court handed down a verdict of indecent assault in a famous case, in which the husband had violently engaged in sex with his wife in the presence of their children while his brother had helped force apart his sister-in-law's legs.[8]

But unlike under the old law, the couple had the right to decide by mutual agreement to engage in "unnatural" sexual intercourse. However, since it was not a duty they owed one another, each spouse had to explicitly consent to each of these "unnatural" acts—as if they were not married.

Both criminal and civil law fought against extramarital sexuality. Adultery was a crime that was described and punished differently depending on whether the husband or the wife was unfaithful. Adulterous filiation could not be established even after the dissolution of marriage.

Thus, marriage had rendered sexuality into an exclusive service, an obligation which, whether one fulfilled or not, had no influence either on the validity of the marriage, or—barring exceptional cases—on filiation, and even less on the happiness of those concerned. Matrimonial sex was really the only kind that was constructed in law. Napoleonic codification had created "sexual rights" as attached to marriage, returning to a tradition that dates back to the Middle Ages.[9]

Vaginal intercourse between spouses was the legal ideal of the new moral law. In essence, this meant that, in order to promote this ideal, all other forms of sexuality had to be discouraged, by means of negative incentives.

Consent and sexual acts outside marriage

Sexual relations outside marriage were tolerated by the criminal law to the extent that they were consensual. Civil law considered them with great disfavor and, as such, they did not give rise to any right.

Attempts to establish paternity were banned and it was only toward the mid-nineteenth century that the move to contact "seduced" women—even just to compensate them for the dishonor caused by an extramarital pregnancy—began to be accepted in a very small way.[10] It was not until 1912 that the attempts to establish paternity were allowed in specific cases.

Procreation, for either men or women, did not, in and of itself, give any rights. Although attempts to establish maternity were authorized, it was very easy for women who so desired never to be the subject of a verdict that found them to be the legitimate mother of the child to whom they had given birth. And, if abortion was forbidden, secret abandonment of children was very easy and very common in the nineteenth century.

Extramarital sexual relations were divorced from their consequences in terms of parentage—unlike today, when they are, and only for women, separated from procreation. Rather than distinguishing sexuality from procreation (abortion was illegal after all), Napoleonic law separated sexuality with ease from the creation of a legal relationship of filiation, equally for both sexes.[11]

To acquire the status of a parent, the progenitor had to manifest his or her consent. But the Napoleonic Code did nothing to encourage the recognition of children born out of wedlock. They had, moreover, a very diminished legal status compared to that enjoyed by legitimate children. In this light, even outside of marriage, the truth of sexuality was as subject to one's will as to the law.

Violent sexual acts were prohibited by the Penal Code, as were, from the mid-nineteenth century, acts performed in the absence of conscious and manifest consent. Following a ruling of the Court of Cassation of 1857,[12] the definition of rape included sexual acts on women who were hypnotized, asleep, or had fainted.[13]

But consent was only taken into account when qualifying those acts that were different from the ones that the Code favored. Thus, it was assumed that the mere fact of having been united by the bonds of marriage meant that one had given consent in advance and forever more to accept any "normal" sexual acts, as well as any children that were to be born of this union.

A violent extramarital sexual act only qualified as rape if it included vaginal penetration. All sexual acts other than rape were punished as violent indecent assaults. In the latter case, the act in question could be a source of corruption, while in the former, the sexual act, which was held to be the monopoly of marriage, had been forced upon the individual.

The Code also prohibited nonviolent acts that took advantage of the minor status of the partner. Such was the case with *abduction* and *incitement of minors to debauchery*. In 1832, the category of nonviolent indecent assault was created to punish sexual relations with minors under the age of 11 years.[14]

As part of a logical break with the law of the *Ancien Régime*, the 1810 Penal Code does not punish incest, even as an aggravating circumstance in offenses against minors. If kinship was taken into account in such cases, it was only if abuse of authority was suspected. Thus, abuse by a teacher was considered in the same manner as that of a father.

The role played by marriage, seen as the ideal of moral order, created two types of distinctions relevant to classify sexual relations in criminal law. The first was the physical techniques employed in the act (vaginal intercourse and all other sexual acts) and the second depended on the type of relation between partners (marital, extramarital but consensual, extramarital and nonconsensual).

Thus, vaginal intercourse was the sexual act par excellence, compared to which other types only remained diminished versions. Marriage constituted consent par excellence, whereas extramarital consent was only a pale shadow of this ideal, and the absence of consent meant the very denial of marriage.

Article 330, which was also part of the chapter on *indecent assault*, introduced new criteria for judging sexual behavior. From this perspective, the only important question was whether those acts were perpetuated in *private* or in *public*. But before examining the strange peculiarities of Article 330, we should return to the circumstances of its inclusion in the Penal Code of 1810.

II The invention of public modesty

> It is [at the very least] superfluous to highlight these offenses in detail. Besides, is it not easy to recognize such familiarities that civilization excuses, such speech that gallantry allows, the liberties that fashion permits without confusing them with crude expressions, unprincipled attitudes and exhibition of corruption, the absence or licentiousness of clothing, the forgetting of principles and the aims of Nature and all of the affronts to modesty and public integrity?[15]

Nineteenth-century jurists all agreed to affirm that the offense of contempt of public decency did not exist under the *Ancien Régime*. Unlike other penal infractions regarding customs such as rape or adultery, public indecency only became a legal concept with the legislative revolution.

In the treatises by Jousse[16] and Muyart de Vouglans,[17] which give us a very complete idea of the last stage of the old law, we cannot find any similar infraction. To be sure, prostitution was severely reprimanded, and very broad police ordinances could punish certain forms of what was called "shamelessness."

Cultural historians who have delved into the appearance of new rules aimed at protecting modesty have found, starting at the end of the sixteenth century, some police measures that forbade for the first time certain public behaviors that were allowed until then. However, such measures, which can be identified as relating to modesty, targeted isolated situations and very specific behaviors.

In this way, an ordinance of the Provost-Marshal of Paris stipulated that the act of bathing while nude in the Seine put one at risk of being chased after ["couru sus"] and beaten with canes at the location where the scandal took place. A ruling with such a sentence was handed down on 4 July 1736, even if, in fact, it seems rather to have been linked to the fact that the men, apart from their nudity, had begun to fight on the banks of the Seine. Other, older provisions forbade the mixing of sexes in public baths, and another, dating from the end of the eighteenth century, forced female dancers to wear leggings.[18]

From the sixteenth and seventeenth centuries, as behavioral historians show, these isolated rulings focused on the visibility of the body, while older bans sought to prevent actual contact. It was for this reason that administrative measures from the sixteenth century shut down the famed steam rooms that were so popular during the Middle Ages.

But the *Ancien Régime*'s legislation prohibited persons in *a specific place* from engaging in *specific behaviors*. The protection of modesty in public was therefore limited only to *some places* and *certain specific behaviors*; there was no law that standardized public space and considered forbidden behaviors in an abstract manner.

Such a rule was instituted by a police ordinance of 19–22 July 1791, which we can take to be the predecessor of Article 330 of the Penal Code of 1810, even though the same text included certain forms of sexual violence against women, pornography and the incitation of minors to debauchery. According to Article 8 of this police ordinance, "[T]hose who are accused of having publicly offended the decency of women, through lewd acts or the exhibition or sale of obscene imagery, or by having promoted debauchery or corruption of youth of either sex, are liable to be arrested immediately [...]".

The precursor to Article 330 did not prohibit the violation of women's modesty, as has often been said. Instead, it forbade the act of publicly threatening morality with "indecent acts." Indeed, "indecent acts" committed in public violated public morality, whereas, within the framework of such a violation, the victims were women who were considered in their capacity as individuals. Publicity* in such cases constituted *the* offense not because public morality was upset but because the morality of a woman had been besmirched in public.[19]

This provision established—some years before the promulgation of Article 330 of the Penal Code of 1810—a conception of the public domain ("in public") as a uniform space in which a category of abstract acts ("indecent acts") was forbidden in order to protect morality.

These new rules, enacted by this police ordinance, and later by Article 330, were not satisfied with forbidding nude bathing, indecent costumes at the opera or people touching each other in ballrooms. They categorized an entire gamut of prohibited sexual behaviors into one abstract infraction. Thus, all "immoral" acts and all "indecent exposures" were included, and, as Monseignat observes so aptly in the report cited above, it would have been "superfluous to report these offenses in detail."

Previous judges had to settle for determining whether a person had complied, in a specific place, with a dress or behavioral rule laid down in advance. With these new provisions, judges were called to determine whether the facts submitted to them could first be held in "contempt" and then if the acts were committed in "public."

Thus, the invention of public modesty can be dated to this institutional act, which made *the entire public space* a domain from

* Translator's note: throughout this book, in keeping with the author's specific use of the term, *publicité* has been translated as *publicity*, to designate a term that, in the context of this legal discussion, refers to the nature of an act or a space that renders it "public" in the eyes of the law, often resulting in consequential interpretations of Article 330 of the Napoleonic Code, and its successors.

which *all behaviors seen to express sexuality* were banned. By contrast, it also allowed rendering private space a domain in which sexuality could be expressed without constraints. In this sense, public modesty was the offense that divided visible space into two spheres, each with conflicting rules in relation to the exhibition of sexuality.

III Indecent exposure and indecent assault

From its institution, Article 330 of the Penal Code was a rule that did not satisfy the spirit that animated other offenses against morality. It embodied a logic that was foreign to the system. While in the case deemed to be an affront to public decency the law differentiated sexual acts in terms of physical techniques employed, in the case of indecent exposure, *all sexual acts were given the same weight*. Moreover, Article 330 described as "sexual" many acts—for example, urination—that were far removed from our idea of sexuality.

In matters of crimes and offenses against morality, in order to distinguish prohibited relations from those that were permitted, partners' being married or not, or consenting or not, were determining criteria for a sexual relationship. In contrast, with Article 330, these distinctions were irrelevant. At every opportunity, jurists did not fail to make the following observation: even married couples with a normal sexual relationship, which constituted a conjugal duty, would be condemned if the act took place in public. This indifference affected both the partner with whom the perpetrator engaged sexually as well as the individuals in the presence of whom the act unfolded. The witnesses of such an act could be majors or minors, consenting or not, real or purely virtual, none of which had any bearing on the existence of the offense.

In addition, even when they had been truly shocked, witnesses of indecent exposure were not so much victims of this offense. The case law has always been very clear in this regard: "In contrast to indecent assault, the prevention of indecent exposure does not primarily target the repression of indecent acts committed in the case of a specific person. Rather it aims to repair the scandal caused by such acts because of their public nature."[20] Thus, for the prosecution to be admissible in court, it was not necessary to mention the name of or even refer to a specific victim.

The only relevant criterion to qualify a sexual behavior according to the logic of Article 330 was whether the act had taken place in public or in private. A legal category was needed to refer to the nature of spaces (streets, paths), or to the manner in which the witnesses of a scene had gathered in a certain place (the audience for a performance).

The public was thus a way to invoke the impersonal, the average individual, the random passerby on a street who becomes the witness of the indecent act in question. That individual who was supposed to be the victim of the offense was a pure abstraction who could be corrupted, shocked, excited or repulsed by a scene that the State did not want the individual to see.

Jurists sought to explain the functioning of this strange offense with a theory of sexual consent. An act committed in a public space—whether empty or populated with consenting individuals—could be seen by a passerby who could be shocked by the sight. But had it been intended to protect consent to viewing a sexual scene, then the law ought to have punished the same act committed in private in the presence of a nonconsenting witness. However, French law has never prohibited this type of behavior in private, even in the presence of a single witness. Even in the most difficult periods during which an extension of this offense to private spaces was attempted, imposing the sight of a sexual act on a single person in a private space was never enough to constitute indecent exposure.

Article 330 did not protect anyone in particular, because its function was to distribute sexuality in space. This new legal category forced society to relegate sexuality to confined spaces that were invisible from the outside. Thus, the interdiction did not target the nature of the act nor the way individuals engaged in it but it was aimed at forbidding the visibility of sexuality to the public.

As we shall see, to achieve these objectives, Article 330 turned the State into a kind of omniscient voyeur endowed with the power to claim to have seen acts that nobody had seen and to transform some scenes into obscene exhibitions produced by people who had, in reality, no intention of being (or becoming) exhibitionists.

IV Public modesty and affront to public decency

Article 330 was not the only criminal provision that organized the public visibility of sexuality. "Affront to public decency," the predecessor to the current crime of pornography, also encompassed pornography. Article 287 of the 1810 Code, which punished affronts to public decency caused by the publication of obscene material, handed out imprisonment from one month to a year and a fine of 16 to 500 francs for "any exhibition" or "distribution of songs, pamphlets, figures or images that troubled public decency." Following the law of 17 May 1819, this offense also included press laws.[21]

Yet, although they pursued very similar goals, affront to public decency and contempt of public decency did not penalize the same type of behavior. It was quite the contrary. For there to have been contempt of public decency, the perpetrator's behavior had to directly engage his or her body. In contrast, an affront to public decency punished acts of speech, images, drawings, engravings and writing. The body of the offender did not instigate the sexuality that was incriminated.

The law on affront to public decency punished the fact of being the author, distributor, propagator of signs, detached from their immediate context, that were meant to stimulate and awaken desire in others. So, unlike indecent exposure, in which perpetrators had to be present before the public, with an affront to public decency, it is precisely this presence that was lacking, which made the message identically reproducible in multiple contexts. Indecent exposure could be reproduced, but more akin to a concert or a performance, that is, the performance varies somewhat every time.

The distinction between the two offenses is very clear in the Arts. Only theater, dance and, in general, live performances were subject to indecent exposure, unlike literature, painting, prints, posters or songs. However, during the nineteenth century, the role of theatre was comparable to that of cinema in the twentieth century, and Article 330 was thus the main instrument used to combat pornography.

Hence, indecent exposure was more linked to sexual offenses committed against individuals than was the law on affront to decency. What mattered was the possibility of real contact between bodies. Article 330 regulated the comportments within a time and space shared between the offender and the public, whereas with affront to decency, the shared time and space were only imagined, making it impossible for the two worlds to enter into physical contact.[22]

One could of course argue that the theatre, dance, live performances also take place in a different level of reality than regular sexual exhibitionism. Nevertheless, the legal logic was only interested in the fact that one could touch the actress on stage, even if only to be rejected, and take her to be the character. In the case of theater and live performances, the confusion between the fictional and real worlds did not exclude the possibility of touching real flesh of a fictional character embodied by a real person. In contrast, with literature, painting or cinema, even if misfortune or folly led someone to confuse the two worlds, this individual would only have had in his hands a crumpled paper or damaged film.

However, when the content of a person's speech was sexually charged, there could have been co-presence and contemporaneity between the speaker and the public. Yet, the individual could be charged with affront to public decency rather than indecent exposure. For co-presence and contemporaneity to be relevant to indecent exposure, the offender had to express himself with his body and not with words. Thus, the offender needed to interpellate the public with corporal contact or acts, or gestures of a sexual nature.

The correlation between Article 330 and the possibility of real body contact explains the fact that it was placed in the same chapter in the code as rape, indecent assault and adultery, and that it has never been included in the section on violation of press laws. Even if the sexual rules that it imposed only applied to public space, it is the "corporal" aspect that made it closer to other offenses against public decency. Indecent exposure was designed as the minimal form of a sexual relationship between the exhibitionist and the voyeur, even if such a sexual relationship was not punished if it took place in private space. While obscenity depended on a sign to be read as sexual by the recipient and by the author, it did not institute a direct link between them. For, the barrier between the sender and receiver of the message was permanently, and by very definition, impassable.

V What deranged public modesty?

The abstract and indeterminate expression of indecent exposure, as contained in Article 330, delegated authority to the courts to designate the types of acts to be punished when they were committed in public—in other words, to determine the types of behavior that should be held as in contempt of "public decency."

In this regard, a famous ruling of the Court of Limoges in 1975 produced a synthesis of almost two centuries of jurisprudence. The case on which the magistrates had to deliberate was at once classic and curious. They had to consider whether the act of urinating in public towards police officers and then at a police station could be considered indecent exposure. The defendants denied the sexual nature of the act, which, at first glance, was not devoid of common sense. Recalling the facts clearly, the Court of Limoges decided the following:

> The fact that two defendants have, first, after unzipping themselves, released their genitals and urinated in the direction of the police officers, and then, urinated in front of the police station, establishes material evidence for the offense; regarding violation of public decency, if the legislature has not defined it and it is very difficult to do, one can nevertheless remark that a moral instinct forbids one to display in public certain body parts because they relate to the sexual act, or to make certain sexual gestures in front of others. Such exhibition has the effect either to arouse some desires in others or to cause repulsion due to its obscenity [...][23]

So, the problem with urinating in public was mostly that the defendants had displayed their genitals, as these organs are associated with the sexual act. In older cases, we can find a conviction handed down by the court of Poitiers in 1858, in which a person who had opened the window of an inn overlooking the street, and from this point of sight, had urinated onto said street showing his genitals.[24]

Legal scholars had developed a typology of behaviors that were classified as either direct (sexual acts themselves), by direct contiguity (exhibitions of the genitals) or even by indirect contiguity (sexual gestures without display) to the sexual act, all of which constituted the material evidence for the offense.

The first category comprises sexual acts themselves, which are, if we stick to the definition of the Court of Limoges, at the heart of what was qualified as obscene or offensive to modesty whether by direct or indirect contiguity. Jurisprudence included in this category a broad variety of sexual acts including heterosexual coitus, homosexual acts, masturbation, sex with multiple partners, all without making any distinction or hierarchy of the techniques employed. The first conviction for contempt of public decency—which we will analyze in detail—was made in 1813 and involved two lovers who engaged in a sexual act on a street at night.

Jurisprudence has included among the sexual acts forbidden in public certain assaults deemed not to be very severe, such that they be characterized as indecent exposure and not condemn the defendants with more severe criminal penalties. When perpetrated in public, these assaults were qualified by jurisprudence as offenses against public decency. Thus, for example, the verdict handed down was "indecent exposure" in a case in which a man was touching himself indecently on a highway, while talking lewdly about lustful women.[25] The Court of Cassation also decided that there was contempt of public decency in the act of placing a hand under the skirt of a girl over 13 years of age,[26] kissing a woman without her consent and touching her inappropriately,[27] grabbing a 15-year-old without her consent and kissing her for a long time.[28]

The second category comprised total or partial nudity, in which case law history became very active and controversial beginning in the late nineteenth century. Of course, before this period, convictions based on the exhibition of nudity were handed down (e.g., an 1859 decision that condemned an individual who was fishing in a river separated from a public road by a field. He was wearing a jacket over his shoulders, while the rest of his body and genitals were completely uncovered).[29] However, the Court of Cassation declined to convict a person who had been seen wearing just a shirt at the entrance of a mine gallery for indecent exposure. In the absence of positive evidence, truly offensive to public morals, it was not sufficient that he behaved suspiciously, even though it left one to fear that he might have given in to exhibitionism.[30] Solicitation also was sometimes considered an affront to public decency when accompanied by the exhibition of genitalia.

Finally, the third type of actions required for contempt of public decency consisted of obscene gestures and attitudes without exhibition of any indecent nudity. As such, in 1898, the courts convicted an individual for having put his hands close to his genitals and shouting at a woman: "Hey, this is for you."[31]

Among the actions taken to be obscene, one can cite the case of the Realist Theater—which we will analyze in detail—in which the director, a certain Mr. de Chirac, was sentenced in 1892 for having simulated an abortion, as well as a sexual act without any nudity on stage.[32] In contrast, attempting to watch individuals in intimate or inappropriate situations never constituted the offense of disrupting public decency. Article 330 only struck the exhibitionist and not the voyeur.

A famous 1911 decision of the Court of Cassation[33] had to examine this question in particular. The Criminal Court [tribunal correctionnel] of Marseille had deemed Charles Berti to be guilty of the offense of indecent exposure, having been found hidden in the water closet of a washroom in Château de Fleurs in Marseille, so that he could see the genitals of people who came to relieve themselves. The Court of Cassation held that the voyeur had himself shown nothing that could offend public modesty. This curious manner in which voyeurs were exonerated has not changed during the twentieth century, including during the explosion of provisions that aim to protect the intimacy of private life [vie privée].

Pursuant to a 1970 law, certain prohibitions against spying on the privacy of others were introduced into the Criminal Code. However, on considering these new offenses, one soon realizes that they are not intended to punish the voyeur but those who capture, store or transmit speech without the consent of the person who was heard, or those who take, store or transmit images of a person in a private space. Similarly, the Penal Code punishes manufacturing, importation, possession, exhibition or sale of equipment designed to perform these operations of espionage. Thus, this amounts to indirectly prohibiting the act of exhibiting the privacy of others—that is to say, controlling the act of showing and not watching—and leaves alone those who are content to spy on or watch such private acts.[34]

VI Shameless and negligent individuals

In order to be held in contempt of public decency, was it necessary for the perpetrator to act with the intent to expose himself or was it sufficient that he had just been negligent? Before understanding how the jurisprudence of the nineteenth century responded to such a question, we must clarify the significance of the distinction between will and intentionality on the part of the individual who commits prohibited acts in criminal law, that is, what is called the *moral element* of offenses.

Criminal law designates as "intent" or "willful misconduct" the "will of the agent to commit the crime as defined by law" and "the consciousness of the guilty that s/he broke the law."[35] The person who commits theft seeks to appropriate an object that s/he *knows* belongs to others. Thieving constitutes *wanting* to acquire property that does not belong to us. The intent is "the consciousness and the will" to commit the offense. It is therefore both a knowledge and a will. While intent is defined in an objective manner—the intent to commit a forbidden act—the motive is the particular sentiment that inspires the instigation of such an act. The reason that motivates the individual, could, for example, include greed, the desire to defy morality, hatred, vengeance, compassion or lust. One can steal because of greed, because of a desire to be rebellious or to take revenge on someone who has offended us.

Criminal lawyers also single out intention of fault. The latter is conceived of as noncompliance with respect to society and not as the result of a particular will, as is the case for intent. For example, the fact of not taking sufficient precaution to avoid an accident that injures others is not the same as having intentionally caused the injuries.

Criminal offense, or "ordinary fault," is not presumed of an action, which differentiates it from strict liability. For example, if I hurt a pedestrian while driving, my fault cannot necessarily be inferred from the outcome produced. It must be proven that I was negligent and that the pedestrian was not trying to commit suicide. With ordinary fault, the agent does not seek the outcome. Ordinary fault is a more or less conscious breach of a responsibility that results either from an action or abstention.[36] So when I hurt this pedestrian, I was driving too fast or I was not attentive to the fact that he was trying to cross the street.

Unlike criminal offenses, situations with strict liability are derived from fact. Let us take not wearing a seatbelt as an example. If a policeman finds me driving without having fastened my seatbelt, I will be punished without anyone wondering what I had in mind when I failed to do so.

Just as with the offense currently on the books, indecent exposure was constituted from two separate acts, which could be treated separately from the point of view of the intent. First, there was the act designated as obscene, followed by the one that made it public. Consider, for example, the fact of being naked in public. I could have chosen to be naked before showing myself in public. But nudity, just like publicity, need not be voluntary. It can be involuntary if a defect in my clothes makes them drop away or if I am undressed by force. In this case, even if I decided to walk on the street, I did not choose to be naked. It was the same with making a lewd act public. I could have decided to undress myself at home thinking that the windows were closed or I can do so knowing that they are open. Thus, there are two different components in indecent exposure, both of which can be the result of intent or fault.

Let us first consider what the court observed regarding the act of rendering a lewd act public. The Court of Cassation took a position on this issue in the famous Marie case of 28 April 1881, establishing a doctrine that has never been overturned to this day. The court decreed the following:

> [...] the aim of legislators in promulgating Article 330 would almost always be missed, if this provision were only to be applied when the perpetrator of the indecent act had intended to make the act public. Intent is not a prerequisite for the offense. In fact, in order to protect public decency and to prevent scandal, the law punishes the vice either because it is displayed with effrontery, or because it fails to conceal itself. Such negligence is sufficient to establish the guilt of the agent, because negligence in and of itself reveals the agent's contempt for public decency. The offense exists irrespective of the affront to publicity, simply because all necessary precautions to avoid it were not taken.[37]

The perpetrator of an indecent act could not escape punishment by proving that he did not think he was going to be seen. For the law to clearly attain its objective, the lawyer Émile Garçon thought it was necessary to punish the perpetrated act, that its public character be recognized whether or not it resulted from negligence, carelessness or a lack of foresight.

According to this famous jurist, this offense is not merely inferred from the facts of the case, as with violations. In addition, this unintentional offense required a fault, which consisted of committing an indecent act *in a place in which the perpetrator had to predict that he would be seen and yet not have taken the necessary precautions to avoid scandal.*[38] It was thus essential to acknowledge the existence of fault by negligence.[39]

If the offense was always constituted when an obscene act took place in a public space, it is because everyone is supposed to have the right to pass through that space at any given time and be able to witness the scene being enacted. The fault is inferred from this very fact: the person knew self-exposure to a passerby was a given in such a public space. In contrast, when the exhibition was set in a private space, the judge had to verify, according to the particular circumstances of each case, that the perpetrator had failed to take sufficient precautions not to be discovered.[40]

Thus conceived, the offense imposed on individuals *the responsibility of being constantly vigilant* when committing an act that could be qualified as sexual, even though they felt they were safe from prying eyes.

So this is what led public acts to being considered obscene. But did an obscene act itself have to be treated in this manner?

A clear jurisprudence allows us to show that, just like publicity, such acts were informed by a simple fault by negligence. The most interesting case in this regard was the conviction of a certain Father Bérard for contempt of public decency, on which the great criminologist Alexandre Lacassagne wrote a short book.[41] While giving confession to his congregation, in August of 1889, four young girls saw the Capuchin priest's penis through a hole in his cassock. Although the judges admitted that it was an accident because of the position he had taken (sitting, feet up on a chair), and that his penis was not erect but limp, simply spilling out through the opening in his cassock, he was condemned by the Appeals Court of Chambéry in 1889.[42] The same situation recurred in the 1930s with the loincloth of a dancer that likely moved by accident during a performance, revealing his private parts.[43] Thus, one could not only blame an individual for making public a sexual scene without meaning to do so but also for having become inadvertently the author of such a scene.

Clothes were just like doors and windows: they contained something sexual and therefore needed continuous monitoring. If a garment accidentally revealed nudity in public, the person could be sentenced for contempt of public decency.

This may be one of the reasons that pushed the female population to wear underpants beginning in the last quarter of the nineteenth century. This undergarment enabled women not only to be freer to move and to dance or ride a bicycle without the risk of being indecent but also not to be disturbed by the police if ever the wind were too strong and lifted their dresses.[44]

However, although fault by negligence applied equally to the obscene act and to the fact of making it public, it served mostly to render private spaces public. As we shall see, the fact of not having taken sufficient precautions not to be seen by the public was one of the main tools used by the courts to incessantly broaden the notion of publicity.

Notes

1 Collection Duverger, 1825, p. 150, and 1830, p. 278.

2 Until the law of 1891, in order to apply punishments for repeat offenses, it was necessary to have a first correctional sentence greater than a year of imprisonment, cf. Émile Garçon, *Code pénal annoté*, 2nd edition, updated by Marcel Rousselet, Maurice Patin, Marc Ancel, Paris, Sirey, 1956, art. 330, p. 173.

3 This relegation was begun first outside of metropolitan France, and then followed by time in penitentiary establishments in France, according to a variable duration. It was replaced in 1970 by penal supervision.

4 Louis-Michel Le Peletier de Saint-Fargeau, *Rapport sur le projet de Code pénal foit au nom des comités de constitution et de législation criminelle,* sessions of 22 March and 23 May 1791, in P. Lascoumes, P. Poncela, P. Lenoël, *Au nom de l'ordre, une histoire politique du Code pénal,* Paris, Hachette, 1983, appendices, p. 329.

5 See Pierre Darmon, *Le Tribunal de l'impuissance : virilités et défaillances conjusales dans l'Ancienne France,* Paris, Seuil, 1979, as well as «Le Marriage des impuissants», in Marcela Iacub, *Le Crime était presque sexuel,* Paris, Flammarion, 2002.

6 Decision of 6 April 1903, D. 1904. 1. 395; S. 1904. 1. 273.

7 For more, see Marcela Iacub, *L'Empire du ventre, pour une autre histoire de la maternité,* Paris, Fayard, 2004.

8 Cass. crim., 19 March 1910, Bull. crim. 1910, n° 265.

9 See Elizabeth M. Makowski, "The Conjugal Debt and Medieval Cannon Law," *Journal of Medieval History,* Amsterdam, vol. 3, no. 2, June 1977.

10 For a history of this issue in the nineteenth century, see Louis Poughon, *De la séduction envisagée au double point de vue civil et pénal,* Doctoral thesis, Paris, Librairie ancienne et moderne, 1911.

11 For more, see Iacub, *L'Empire du ventre.*

12 Crim. 25 June 1857, S. 1857. 1. 711.

13 *Gazette des tribunaux*, 10 August 1865 and 21 August 1878, quoted by Émile Garçon, *Code pénal annoté*, (art. 295–401), p. 196.

14 A 1863 law changed the minimum age to 13 years, which was further raised to 15 by an ordinance of 1945.

15 Monseignat, "Rapport au corps législatif," 17 February 1810, cited in the *Old Répertoire Dalloz*, Attentat aux mœurs. *Répertoire méthodique*

et alphabétique de Législation, de Doctrine et de Jurisprudence, 1846-1864, 41.

16 *Nouveau commentaire sur l'ordonnance criminelle du mois d'août 1670. Avec un abrégé de la justice criminelle*, Paris, Debure, 1763.

17 *Les Lois criminelles de France dans leur ordre naturel*, Paris, Merigot le jeune, 1780.

18 For a comprehensive set of police rulings, see Claude Laplatte, *L'Outrage public à la pudeur et la contravention d'affiches indécentes,* Troyes, Éditions de la Renaissance, 1967, et Jean-Claude Bologne, *Histoire de la pudeur*, Paris, Olivier Orban, 1986.

19 A majority of legal scholars thought that the origin of Article 330 lay in the rule contained in this police ordinance, which referred to "public indecency against women." However, this provision did not seek in any manner to protect public modesty but instead to punish sexual violence, other than rape, committed in public, and the victims of which were women. According to an old ruling by the Court of Cassation, these actions could consist of obscene acts or gestures addressed toward women. The Court of Cassation took pains to distinguish between types of behavior to which this infraction applied. Notably, it differentiated them from verbal abuse, a distinction that would be taken up once more in the Code of 1810. The Court judged "that this decision cannot be understood to be based on simple insults, however offensive, however uncouth they may be, but rather on actions or gestures that are detrimental to the modesty of women" (Decision of the Court of Cassation, 30 nivôse, year 11, *Journal du Palais*, 3rd edition, volume 3, p. 116). The presence of this provision, intended to protect the honor of women, can be explained by the gaps in the Penal Code of 1791, which did not punish any sexual violence against adult women besides rape, as the Code of 1810 would later do. It thus fell upon this police law to protect women by punishing indecent gestures and actions committed against them; the law applied, however, only when these acts took place in public.

20 Cass crim., 27 October 1932, Bull. crim. 1932, no. 220.

21 Following this tradition, the law of 29 July 1881 continued to criminalize any affront to public decency by making a distinction between those that were committed by drawings, engravings, paintings, emblems or images and those committed by other means of publication. The former were brought to criminal court [cour d'assises] and were governed by all the specific rules established by press laws. The latter were referred to the magistrates' court [tribunal correctionnel], for which *corpus delicti* had to be proven. A law of 2 August 1882 brought under common law affronts to public decency that were committed by any means of communication other than speech or writing.

22 The most eloquent reflection on this impossible encounter between image and life is no doubt to be found in the short story *L'Invention de Morel*, by Adolfo Bioy Casares, in which the very possibility of such an encounter constitutes an essential part of the plot.
23 Limoges, 13 June 1975 ; D. 1976, Somm. No. 17.
24 1. Poitiers, 18 February 1858, D. 1959. 5. 37.
25 Cass., 1 December 1848, S. 1849. 1. 543.
26 Cass., 8 February 1900, D. 1900. 1. 279.
27 Dijon, 20 April 1859, D. 1859. 5.37.
28 Aix, 22 November 1854, D. 1856. 5. 302.
29 Montpellier, 8 August 1859, S. 1859.2.490 and D. 1860.5.29.
30 Cass., 29 October 1926, cited by Garçon, *Code pénal annoté* .
31 Cass., 3 March, 1898, D. 1899. 1 . 59.
32 See Chapter 6, pp. 121–127.
33 Cass., 21 July 1911, Bull. crim. 1911, no. 372.
34 Articles 226-1 to 226-3 of the Penal Code.
35 Garçon, *Code pénal annoté,* art. 1, no. 77.
36 See Jean Pradel, *Droit pénal général*, Éditions Cujas, 2000–2001, p. 445 *sq*.
37 Cass., 28 April 1881, D. 1881. 1. 447. The doctrine laid out in this decision is reconfirmed by the verdict of 20 October 1955, D. 1956. 1. 117.
38 Garçon, *Code pénal annoté,* p. 187.
39 The theory according to which the fault punishable under Article 330 was purely a misdemeanor (petty offense)—that is to say, the most drastic and the most demanding possible option, while providing for severe penalties for offenses—was exposed and strongly criticized in the twentieth century by Roger Doublier. A legal scholar and nudist who devoted many interesting essays to Article 330, Doublier maintains that, "by repressing indecent exposure without requiring the existence of a victim, and thereby virtually removing by necessity the intention of guilt, the jurisprudence indeed treats this offense as a violation." But, he adds, "the violations sanction prohibitions precisely defined in their materiality, which suggests that the notion of modesty is clearly determined" of which "we are not convinced" (*Le Nu et la Loi,* Paris, Nature Éditions et LGDJ, 1976, pp. 32–33). In addition, this author observes that if indecency was an offense of clumsiness, negligence or inattention, it was necessary for the errors identified to have caused harm, that is to say that there be a victim. But this observation is no longer true following the reform of 1992, which establishes certain negligent faults as offenses, even in the absence of any victim (on this subject, see Pradel, *Droit pénal général*).
40 Admittedly, in this regard, the case law supported by the doctrine,

distinguished different acts that were committed in ways that the law did not allow it to do. For Chauveau and Helie, "the acts constituting the contempt of public decency are of two kinds: on account of their cynicism and immorality, the first type demonstrate—by the mere fact of their material existence—proof for the indecent intent that propelled agent to act. The second kind do not damage integrity or decency by themselves, and only become objectionable when the agent creates a scandal through the manner and circumstances in which they occurred and especially the intention that directs it. The intentional element, a necessary condition of the offense, is, in this case, the very immorality of the act, whether it is present in the action itself, or in the facts external to its perpetration" (Adolphe Chauveau and Faustin Helie, *Théorie du Code pénal*, Paris, Edward Legrand, 1843, vol. IV, no. 1514). Bathing naked in a river was not the same as engaging in sex with multiple partners in a hotel room, the interior of which could be seen from outside through the keyhole. This explains the famous Mercier case that is often cited when it comes to the history of this offense. Thus, an individual who had bathed in the Loire without underwear was acquitted because no evidence of his intention to defy and offend public decency was provided (see Cass., 6 October 1870, D. 1870. 1. 433). But we can clearly see that in this case, the Court of Cassation based its decision not on intent or fault but on the motive, which ought not to have any impact on determining the responsibility of the author. It was isolated as a subterfuge to acquit the perpetrator of an act that was not held to be serious.

41 Alexandre Lacassagne, *L'Affaire du père Bérard,* Bibliothèque d'anthropologie criminelle et des sciences pénales, Lyon, Storck éditeur, Paris, Steinheic, 1890.

42 This case reached the Court of Cassation, which overturned the previous ruling on flawed procedural grounds, and when it arrived at the Court of Appeals of Lyon in 1890, the priest was acquitted. The expert Alexandre Lacassagne had shown that it was not materially possible for the priest's penis to hang out through the hole in his cassock and the four young witnesses had experienced a sort of visual hallucination.

43 See pp. 96–100.

44 On this subject, see Pierre Dufay, *Le Pantalon féminin. Un chapitre inédit de l'histoire du costume*, Paris, Charles Carrington, 1906. The author reports the unpublished conviction of a woman who was said to have ridden a bicycle without wearing underwear. See also Paul Laure Flobert, *La Femme et le costume masculin*, a talk given at the Archaeological, Historical and Artistic Society, 28 March 1911, Lille, Lefevre-Ducrocq Printing Press, 1911; and John Grand-Carteret, *La Femme en culotte*, Paris Flammarion, 1909.

2

The conquest of private space by public space

Article 330 prohibited violating "public" modesty. Publicity was therefore the central element of the offense, which gave the crime its specificity within the penal framework to punish crimes and offenses against morality.

Publicity was constituted either by space—in this connotation, juxtaposing public with private spaces—or by (institutional) structures that helped congregate a group of individuals in a certain space. A *public* space was, just like *the public*, a type of meeting of individuals in which the impersonal could emerge. A public space was one to which anyone had access. For there to be a public, the persons present must not have been convened individually, and their right to be present for reasons other than those envisaged by the organizers of the meeting had to be respected. For example, everyone has the right to be on the street whether by day or by night. In a public theater, spectators only have to pay an entry fee in order to enjoy the show.

The two sources of publicity had a common root, since in both cases one alluded to an assembly—actual or potential—of individuals who were not otherwise related to the exhibitionists in question through family ties, friendships, professional connections or as neighbors, etc. While publicity based on the nature of spaces radically changed between the beginning and the end of the nineteenth century, publicity that is founded on ways in which a group of people is convened has remained intact until today.

I Public spaces

In public spaces, any sexual exhibitionism was prohibited, even if there was no witness, and even if it took place in the most absolute darkness, such that an eventual passerby would have been able to see the indecent act only by casting light on the scene with a lamp.[1]

The first ruling of the Court of Cassation dedicated to this subject dates from 26 March 1813 and is particularly clear.[2] During his nightly patrol, a police officer found Corneil Smit and Bernardine de Haan "in carnal copulation" on the street. It was not as if the lovers sought to be on display. Quite the contrary, they believed they had sheltered themselves from all public gaze at the crossroad where there was no light to reveal their embrace in the middle of night.

Pursuant to the police officer's report, they were prosecuted by the criminal court for indecent exposure, but they were first acquitted by the trial judges of Arnheim for the following reasons: "The act in question is not punishable by law, and because it was committed at night, modesty was not violated."

The court thus advanced two arguments for acquittal. First, the woman was a consenting partner. The judges thereby revealed that they did not fully understand the meaning of Article 330, which did not require consent to be violated by others. Second, and this was the main argument, the court thought that the concept of publicity could not be sustained when the act took place in the dark. In their view, the scene had to be visible and to have been enacted in a specific place.

Seeking therefore to correct this misinterpretation of the criminal law, the Court of Cassation overturned the ruling in a decision that was truly instructive. The high court maintained:

> the provisions for indecent exposure punishable under Article 330 are those non-violent or non-coercive acts that need not offend the modesty of the person on whom the indecent act could have been performed. These acts need only offend morality, and due to their licentious nature and the publicity involved, *become the occasion for public scandal by violating the decency and modesty of those who were incidental witnesses.*

The court continued:

> this type of offense, less based on wickedness than forgetfulness or self-contempt, as the speaker of the Assembly has said, is punishable by Article 330 only with correctional penalties—whereas indecent exposure, exercised without consent and involving violence, is punished with harsher penalties under Section 331 and subsequent arti-

> cles, which qualify such an act as indecent assault. Even if Bernardine de Haan might have given consent to Corneil Smit, given that they were found violating public modesty and integrity on a street, they cannot escape the application of Article 330 and the penalties that it prescribes; the fact that their shameless and licentious act took place at night does not invalidate publicity, *since passage and circulation on the streets are rights, and the space is often in use at night as during the day* (my emphasis).

In the following years, the court reiterated these principles with even greater clarity: "[w]ith the matter of indecent exposure, publicity is constituted [...] by the nature of the space in which the act was committed, due to the fact *that the act was offered to the public gaze, and that it could be seen even accidentally*" (my emphasis).[3] Or further, "with the matter of indecent exposure, publicity may result in a clear manner by the nature of the places in which the act is performed; [even] when, for example, it is perpetrated on streets, squares or other public thoroughfares, even at night, and out of sight of any witnesses."[4]

It was sufficient for the *possibility* of *someone witnessing the scene* to exist for publicity to be constituted, even if it had been purely *virtual*. It could be argued that publicity was not so virtual, because a police officer had indeed seen the two Belgian lovers mentioned above. But in subsequent cases, the courts handed down sentences not just based on a police complaint but based on simple statements made by the accused. Such was the case for a couple on a street. The woman had accused the man of rape. Nobody had seen the act, the court observed that the woman was consenting and condemned the pair for contempt of public decency, and the Court of Cassation upheld the decision.[5]

The scandal that the law sought to avoid needed only to be virtual: the act *could have been seen* or *even noticed* by the virtual co-presence of the accused and any potential passerby in the same space for it to be sufficient for the offense to be constituted. What mattered was the fact that the first passerby could have found himself *in the same place* in which the prohibited act was taking place, even if it were not visible. Public space was therefore one in which one posited the *possibility of co-presence* of the entire community, every time a sexual deed was committed.

The public nature of a place did not depend on its legal status. For example, a path established by agreement on private property could fall into this category with respect to Article 330. The main criterion to qualify public space was that it had, *de facto*, freedom of circulation such that an innocent passerby could be confronted with an erotic scene without seeking it.

Legal scholars classified these very special spaces into two different categories. Either they were public *by nature*, such as roads, streets, promenades, because public passage was possible at any time. Or, they were public *by destination*. This latter category included places such as schools, shops, presbyteries, or public transport, which, rather than being open to the public all day or at all times of the year, restricted access to certain times and periods.

In 1864, the Supreme Court decided that "one can rightfully consider that publicity does not exist with regard to indecent acts committed by a primary school teacher on one of his communal school students, if the event took place after class hours in the absence of any witness, and precautions had been taken to prevent anyone from seeing the act." For, "although modesty can result in an absolute manner from the nature of the place where the act was committed, and where it was encountered, for example, when the offense is committed on a public road, even at night and in the absence of any witness, it cannot however be the same with respect to certain public places that are only public at specific times, such as a classroom or the theater."[6]

But, during opening hors, these spaces were similar to spaces public by nature, that is to say, it was not necessary that any individual actually witness the sexual act. It was sufficient that anyone might have been able to see it and that it was *offered* to the public gaze.

The courts soon considered a space to be public not just if the general public had access to it, but also such spaces to which only one category of people could enter, such as apartment buildings, businesses, associations, clubs. Publicity could exist as clearly in the streets as in a police station when it was open to the public, but also when a specified number of people could have access to it. In such cases as well, publicity could be just virtual.

II The first extensions of publicity: private spaces visible or accessible from a public place

Soon, the concept of publicity was extended to the fact that the exhibition could be both visible and/or accessible from a public place. Thus, public space began to extend its reach, thanks to the fact that it could be a *point of focus* or *access*. With regard to *visibility*, spaces open around the public spaces in question were considered public if, due to their physical layout, nothing obstructed the view of passersby. Thus it was with open windows overlooking the street, cracks in the walls or even keyholes that allowed the private space to be seen from the street.

It was held that Article 330 was applicable to an individual who had undressed in front of three young girls in a garden adjacent to a public road and exposed to passersby.[7] In this case, the court decided that publicity existed not because of the children's presence but due to the nature of the site. Similarly, in another case, an act that was perpetrated on the ground floor of a dwelling in an open courtyard, crossed by a village trail, was deemed indecent exposure because the door remained fully open, allowing one to see what was happening inside.[8]

These private places visible from the outside became public in the moment of a sexual act, even though nobody had witnessed it, that is to say, they gained or suffered from a purely virtual publicity. But the publicity of these places only concerned spaces visible from the outside. It is this potential visibility that delimited within these private spaces the demarcation between the public and the private.

With regard to *accessibility*, jurisprudence rendered a private space public because a number of people had the possibility of entering it. It was held that a sexual act in a corridor two meters from an open door was public according to Article 330 because the passageway led to a cul-de-sac where some houses were located and accessible to the public without hindrance, even if traffic was restricted.[9]

More delicate was the question of whether an unlocked door could constitute an access point liable to turn a location not visible from the outside into a public space. A distinction was established according to whether or not the space in question was the home of the person who engaged in such acts. In the first case, it was sufficient that the door was simply pushed shut. If it was not his home, the door had to be locked shut.

A very special case occurred when a man entered the room in which he lived with his grandmother and caught her engaged in sex with a man. The Court of Appeals in Limoges sentenced the grandmother, who ought to have locked the door because she shared her home with her grandson.[10] Much later, in 1938, an individual was sentenced for engaging in lewd acts in the bedroom of an association without locking its door.[11]

Henceforth, *to be in a space*, *to be visible* or *to be accessible from such a space* became equivalent in terms of publicity. This extension of the concept of publicity to private spaces had a very important impact in the status of spaces. A space such as a house that was private, lost its strength and importance as a private space due to the issue of visibility and accessibility. It was less important to know whether a space was private than if it was open or closed, visible or invisible from the outside.

Yet more than accessibility, it was visibility that allowed publicity as defined by Article 330 to expand considerably, due to the scope that the *field of vision* can take when it comes to spaces that are far removed from each other.

The case of the young Aristide Briand reveals the type of exercise in which judges could engage to measure the visual field of neighbors and passersby when a sexual act took place in a particular place.

During the months of June, July, August and September 1890, Aristide Briand and Lady G. regularly walked together in the environs of the village of Toutesaides, and would meet in an orchard belonging to Mr. Porcher. The couple arrived separately by different routes to this place of rendezvous, and they exchanged handshakes and kisses when meeting or parting. These meetings triggered emotions among people who had started to think that these two young individuals were engaging in extramarital relations. Guillou, the witness, said he saw the defendants kissing half-lying down near each other and saw Briand put his hand on Lady G's thigh over her dress. But the Court of Appeals of Poitiers said "[…] at the distance where he was situated (73 meters) the witness could have been mistaken about the nature of this act, which, as Briand alleged, could only be the result of a mechanical movement and not a lewd caress." The court further specified that "besides, what Guillou could see exactly is in doubt, for honorable witnesses who, having conducted experiments at the scene, have sworn before the court that from the point of view of Guillou's position, the line of sight passed forty-one centimeters above where the defendants were situated."

With regard to the witness Geffroy "who claims to have seen Lady G. lie down, raise her skirts and Briand lie on her," the court clarifies that "from point B on the [provided] plan, where Geffroy was placed, and according to the above-cited witnesses, the line of sight goes forty-four centimeters above where he states that the defendants were"; "from the observation made, it follows [...] from Geffroy's position, one can see the upper body but not the legs."[12]

This decision shows us that an entire action could not be inferred from a single constitutive element, given that the scene is not likely to be reconstructed from any of its visible parts because they were not acts that were illegal in and of themselves, but only became so for having been performed in public. It was not the morality of human behavior but its visibility that Article 330 attempted to probe.

Such were the first rulings by which judges extended publicity to a large number of private spaces. But beginning in the mid-nineteenth century, the first stage of jurisprudence was radicalized.

The Court of Cassation thus posed a crucial question. Could a private space be declared public if it was only visible or accessible from another private space rather than a public space? In other words, should the point from which one viewed a private space—or the point of access—be mandatorily in a public place for the former to become a public space? The Court of Cassation replied in the negative to this question on 7 April 1859.[13]

The Court of Bordeaux refused to consider a violation as indecent exposure because it was committed in a private space, which could be seen only from another private space without the intermediary of a public space. But the Court of Cassation held that the existence of this intermediate public space was not essential.

From a decision of 1859, a space was considered public under Article 330 if it could be seen from another space, whatever the space. The notion of "the exterior," which was in the beginning synonymous with "a public space," now covered a much broader exteriority because, henceforth, it meant "another space." Sometimes this new concept of exteriority was applied to a same dwelling unit, just as long as one could distinguish between different spaces due to a particular configuration.

Thus, the Court of Cassation decided on 28 April 1881[14] that Article 330 was applicable to an individual who had committed indecent exposure in a bakery adjacent to the house of a farmer, when the room in question was lit by a window that overlooked a pasture, which was itself a private space not accessible to nonresidents of the house.

This jurisprudence, which was uncontested, reached a peak in a case that the Court of Cassation heard on 7 December 1960. It sentenced an individual for obscene acts aimed at a young woman in his barn, which had a small hole in the wall leading to another stable belonging to the same owner, which allowed his son to watch the act.[15]

Even if one could *see* these spaces from a public or another private space, even if it could be *accessed* by opening a door, one could indulge in sexual acts without fear of being condemned if some precautions so as not to be seen or overheard were taken. But in each case, judges had to study with great care the type of actions that people had taken so as not to be seen or chanced upon. And, as we shall see, they proved themselves to be particularly exacting during these challenging examinations.

Despite everything, the possibility of taking precautions to limit visibility and accessibility of the private spaces differentiated them from public space by nature, such as streets. In the latter, the courts only needed to be assured that the act had been committed—accessibility and visibility being presumed. Whereas, if the obscene act had taken place in private, how the scene had become visible or accessible had to be indicated; if not, their decisions could be overturned.

III Insufficient precaution and morbid curiosity

What kinds of precautions had to be taken so that a sex scene enacted in a private space would not be deemed to have been in public? To answer this question, we must consider the conditions used by the courts to hold someone guilty of having committed indecent exposure.

To be condemned, it was enough, as I have pointed out, that the defendants were merely negligent—it was not required to prove their intention to render public a sexual act. In this light, the theory of adequate precautions could be rearticulated to ask the following: had the defendants been seen from another public or private space because they had been negligent?

If the answer was positive, the sex scene was treated as having taken place in a public space and the defendants were guilty. Otherwise, if they had taken adequate precautions, the act was deemed to have occurred in a private space. Thus, the publicity of a scene enacted in a private location was related to precautions taken by the perpetrators of that act. Consequently, liability and publicity were two elements that overlapped when it came to private spaces.

But, from the second half of the nineteenth century on, the courts began to require unprecedented conditions in order to consider precautions as sufficient. This helped to greatly expand the conditions for the emergence of publicity in private spaces to such an extent that jurisprudence always held that precautions taken by the defendants were insufficient, barring exceptional circumstances.

This was the case when the witness of a scene had trespassed, for example, on private property, or when s/he changed the layout of the space, or even when the individual had gone to great lengths to see or to enter into the space in which the sexual scene was being enacted. Judges named this type of behavior, which killed publicity, "morbid curiosity." This way of looking undermined the witness in his or her representative status as the eyes of the State, and thus, the witness no longer exercised a public function, even if, as we have seen, s/he did not necessarily commit the offense of indecent exposure, or any other criminal offense.[16]

A relatively large number of cases provide some examples of exceptional circumstances that prohibited a private space from being considered public. For instance, on 30 July 1863, the Supreme Court decided that, "for the defendant to have committed an immoral act in a field belonging to him in broad daylight, which, by coincidence, had a third witness, does not constitute contempt of public decency, if the field's setup was such that it was enclosed on all sides and sloped and away from all homes and was far from any public road, to preclude others from seeing the act, and if the immoral act was only seen because the witness trespassed on private space in which the act was being committed."[17]

With regard to the change observed in layouts by witnesses, the most famous case took place in the French Caribbean and was the subject of two cases of the Criminal Division of the Court of Cassation.

After having dined, some young men had locked themselves in a room in the company of several women on the ground floor of a hotel to engage in "acts of debauchery." But some people, approaching either the keyhole or the gaps between the lowered shutters, were able to see these acts.

The Court of Pointe-à-Pitre, charged with the matter, said there was indecent exposure, that the conditions for publicity were sufficient because one could see from the outside what had happened. The Court of Guadeloupe reversed this ruling on the ground that the defendants, having lowered the shutters and locked the door, had taken all necessary precautions not to be seen. But the Court of Cassation was not of this opinion, and on 18 March 1858,[18] it decided that all precautions had not been taken since one could see from the outside without having to change the state of the premises, without any witness having to change the layout of the place. The court thus deemed that publicity as required by Article 330 had been clearly established and sent the case back to the Court of Martinique. So, to be seen through the keyhole or through the interstices left by lowered shutters was considered to be an act of negligence with regard to public decency and therefore constituted a voluntary exhibition.

But the young "profligates" were lucky, because new facts were presented before the Court of Martinique. The defense showed that in fact the witnesses of the obscene acts had pushed a piece of paper blocking the keyhole, and had also lifted the slats of blinds. This discovery led to the acquittal of the defendants. The Court of Cassation,[19] which had the last word, sided with the reasoning proffered by the Court of Martinique, as it had been shown that, contrary to the facts first presented in the case, the witnesses had changed the physical layout.

However, the limitation of publicity in these specific cases was applied sparingly. If the witnesses did not directly intervene with the physical configuration of the premises, even if they took a lot of trouble to watch, it was thought that they had transgressed no limit and that it was thus the man or woman who was observed that had not taken adequate precautions to avoid being seen.

In this respect, a famous case that came before the Court of Cassation in 1881 is very enlightening. An employee had locked himself in one of the rooms of the house in which he worked in order to engage in sexual behavior. The exterior window panes were so dirty that one could not see outside, unless one completely stuck one's eyes against the glass. The court held that the fact of having to come so close to the window pane did not constitute a change in the layout and punished the poor employee.[20]

The fate of Sacareau and Nougarolès, two men who were denounced for indecent exposure by Mr. Roux in 1874, was very different. The defendants were in a sharecropping farmhouse looked after by Nougarolès, a kind of rural house located thirty-five meters from the public road. The bedroom in which the two men were located had only one entry, closed by two doors opening in opposite directions, one full and the other with a glass window in the upper part. Both were half closed.

The Court of Cassation specified that, from the public road, or even when passing in front of the house, it was absolutely impossible to see inside the room and especially the bed on which the two defendants were lying. Despite the layout and the precautions taken by the defendants, Mr. Roux saw the obscene act they committed by "introducing his head, and part of his body, between the two half-closed doors inside the house." According to the court, "consequently, the fact that the defendants could not foresee this circumstance is not due to their negligence and is not likely to meet the publicity requirement of the offense as stipulated in Article 330 of the Penal Code."[21]

By applying the same principles, in cases where witnesses force their way into an enclosed space in which obscene acts are being committed, such acts do not necessarily satisfy the criteria for indecent exposure. The Court of Orleans ruled as such in the case of friends who, knowing that their acquaintances were engaging in a sexual act, had entered by force into the room in question.[22]

The courts had held that publicity did not exist when witnesses hoisted themselves over each other to reach the first floor or when they climbed onto an enclosing wall. Similarly, it did not exist when an individual, realizing that another had locked himself in toilet facilities with a child in order to commit lewd acts, hoisted himself up in order to reach a transom located above the door and was thus witness to the scene.[23]

Notes

1 Abel Maillefaud, *De l'outrage public à la pudeur,* Doctoral Dissertation, Lyon, Imprimerie des Facultés, 1896, p. 45.
2 Bull. crim. 1813 no. 58, p. 144.
3 Cass., 23 December 1858, Bull. crim. 1858 no. 317.
4 Cass., 1 May 1863.
5 Cass. crim. 19 April 1939 as well as Cass. Crim. 18 July 1930; GP, 1939, 855 and DH, 1930. 462.
6 The Lacombe Decision, Cass., 1 May 1863, D. 1864. 1. 147.
7 Cass., 5 February 1863. D. 1864. 1. 324.

8 Cass., 28 November 1861 cited by Garçon, *Code pénal annoté.*
9 Court of Appeals, Aix, 22 November 1854, D. 1856. 2. 302.
10 Limoges, 1 April 1887, D. 1890. 2. 24.
11 Cass. crim., 18 February 1938, DH, 1838. 293.
12 Unpublished Decision of the Court of Appeals, Poitiers, 27 July 1892, cited by Laplatte, pp. 208–209.
13 Cass. crim., 7 April 1859, D. 1859. 1. 239.
14 Cass. crim., 28 April 1881, S. 1881. 1. 389.
15 Bull. crim., 1960, no. 573; For a more detailed analysis of this case, see pp. 130–131.
16 See the 1911 decision the Court of Cassation cited on p. 31.
17 D. 1864. 1. 147.
18 Cass., 18 March 1858, D. 1958. 1. 561.
19 Cass., 11 March 1859, D. 1959. 1. 626.
20 Cass., 28 April 1881. *Journal du Ministère public,* 1882, p. 49.
21 Cass., 5 June 1874, Bull. crim. 1874, no. 158, p. 293.
22 Orléans, 11 November 1861. D. 1862. 2. 9.
23 Court of Lyon, 2 March 1896, as cited by Maillefaud, *De l'outrage public à la pudeur,* p. 119.

3

The invention of interior publicity

The major crusade by the courts of the second half of the nineteenth century to annex an ever-increasing number of private spaces to the public world left no choice for the population than to hide systematically in the only places where they could indulge in sexual behavior without fear of being condemned. These places were private spaces where the public could not penetrate because they were both *inaccessible* and *invisible* from the outside. There, those who indulged in sexual activities in the presence of others did not risk being disturbed.

With regard to public decency, an apartment or a house was not divided into several units. They constituted a single unit of space within which there was neither outside nor inside. For example, with respect to sexuality, the bedroom did not have a specific status compared to the living room or the kitchen. Thus, they were not required to be locked. Even if (key)holes permitted one to observe one room from another, one could not consider that the scenes took place in separate spaces.

These spatial units were protected from the gaze of the State, which usually had no right to interfere with them, other than in violent situations, for which proof had to be provided. For this reason, these spaces were thought to be the last haunts of vice by many judges, just like those heretical lands that had received neither the benefits of the good word, nor, more importantly, the light of the State.

As the cases we have examined thus far demonstrate, from the second half of the nineteenth century on these spaces were subject to intense assault. How else could one interpret the tenacity with which judges encouraged the curious to look through the slightest opening to watch the sex scene hiding within? How could one understand otherwise the intense interest in windows, doors and keyholes or other such passages that were seen to link the private side and the public side of the wall of shame? Was it not a slow but inescapable way to ensure that the omniscient eyes of the State finally penetrated these closed houses, conquering them less by force than by shrewdness, annexing them with skill and patience, so as to have them finally pass over to the public side of the wall of shame?

Yet, there was a real danger in trying to conquer these fortresses within which a little private world survived. If they fell, all of visual space would potentially become public. The very rationality of political morality based on the distribution of sexuality in the two visual spaces with conflicting rules would be destroyed. Was not the pact that the Napoleonic order had sealed with the populace contained in this border that separated the dark and lawless private space from a public space in which sexuality was to be absent?

Resistance that opposed the Court of Cassation to defend the last strongholds of private space was robust, but it finally relented. This legal battle led to *interior publicity*, that is to say, the conditions needed to characterize as contempt of public decency a sexual act that took place in a private space, invisible and inaccessible from the outside. Thus the wall of shame could be finally demolished and the population fully exposed to the blinding light of public decency.

I The precedents

The legal canon traced the nagging question of interior publicity back to the Baylar case, an old case of the Court of Cassation from 22 February 1828, which was the subject of much comment throughout the nineteenth century.

In this case, the court quashed a ruling of the Criminal Court of Carcassonne which did not hold Martin Baylar in contempt of public decency on the grounds that the indecent act he had committed had taken place in a private space, namely in an unharvested field, although these actions had actually been seen by several people.

The court clarified on this occasion that "the provision of this article, on the nature of the publicity of the violation, states in a general and all encompassing manner, that it refers consequently to all kinds of publicity that indecent exposure may have, either by the place where it was committed, or by other circumstances which accompany it."[1] The court took care to specify that it is because this scene had a real and effective public that there had been publicity in the sense provided for by Article 330. Why was this case so important in the eyes of the supporters who fought for interior publicity for the Court of Cassation to change its doctrine in this domain?

The jurisprudence that I have parsed so far focused on the publicity attached to the nature of the space. That is why the actual presence of the witnesses was not necessary for it to be recognized. We know that this form of publicity could be purely virtual. It was the nature of the premises, their configuration—that is to say, that they were visible or not from the outside, accessible or inaccessible—that produced publicity.

But the fact that, in this 1828 case, the court effectively evoked the presence of a public as a condition of publicity changes the stakes. One could consider as public a scene that took place in private, invisible and inaccessible from the outside, by the mere presence of some *actual* witnesses ... Would publicity be the result of other criteria than the nature and layout of the site? It would then be possible to decide that a sexual act staged in the living room of a house in front of a few neighbors was public, even if the space by nature or configuration was not considered to be public.

What seems certain is that, in the 1828 case, the Court of Cassation privileged the actual presence of witnesses because it could not yet link the publicity of a space to its nature. Until the mid-nineteenth century, publicity was not constituted when private space could be seen from another private space. However, those who saw Baylar had to have done so from another private space. Otherwise the court would not have highlighted the presence of several witnesses; publicity could have been, in that case, purely virtual.

Referring to the presence of an actual public, the court evokes the other form of constitution of publicity that I have mentioned before, that which pre-existed and was not bound to the nature of the space. It had to do with the way in which the spectators of a scene had been recruited. The question was no longer whether the space was visible or accessible from the outside but how the people who were there had gathered. For example, anyone can enter a theater by paying its entrance fee. Participants form a public because, under the law, they have not been invited in an individualized manner. The theater is a private space in which a public can be found. However, if in the same theater a performance is restricted to a few individually invited guests, they would not constitute a public within the parameters set by Article 330. The establishment of a public could result from circumstances of its recruitment, and not just the space in which it gathered.

Let us leave the performance halls for the moment to return to the Baylar case. Imagine that an individual invites everyone at random to see a sexual act in his or her home, and to do so he or she beats the drum on the street. Those who do enter will be in a private and even closed space, but they do not form a public, at least according to Article 330. For, by public, this article of the Penal Code meant, as we have seen, a group of impersonal, undifferentiated beings who were not individualized.

This category of the public can be constituted not only by voluntary recruitment—for example, by publicizing on the street—but also by happenstance.

In the Baylar case, even if the decision of the court was too terse for us to know the precise circumstances, witnesses of the scene had to find a space that was itself private, nearby, where they had the right to be for whatever reason. We can imagine that these people had been invited by his neighbor for any reason. It was by chance that they witnessed the scene that Martin Baylar enacted. In other words, it is the fact of having viewed the scene that constituted them, in a legal sense, into a public.

For there to be indecent exposure, the actual presence of these witnesses was essential. In other words, all the individuals that the neighbor invited would have constituted the public with regard to Baylar's act to the extent they would have actually been witnesses to the act. The courts could condemn Baylar by claiming that the individuals who had seen the act had constituted a public in the same way as they would have for certain types of performances at the theater.

But if the Court of Cassation never allowed itself to be moved by the reminder of this 1828 ruling, it knew that this situation had nothing in common with other everyday life situations to which they wanted to apply the notion of publicity in Article 330. It considered that the homes that were closed and invisible from the exterior were not public spaces within the meaning of Article 330, despite the presence of actual witnesses, e.g., when children viewed the sexual activities of their parents, the servants saw their masters walk naked, or friends saw one of their own engaging in sexual relations in a corner of the room in which they had congregated. To the Supreme Court, the Baylar decision was only a solution for the case at hand to resolve the question of the visibility of a private space from another private space. To this end, the court used the tools it had at its disposal to define the public from performances to which a generic audience had access.

In any case, the court's position did not change until 1877, and appellate courts that chose to rule otherwise were systematically censured. However, the decisions handed down by courts of appeal, which did not rule like the Court of Cassation in the application of Article 330 in these circumstances, did not seem to follow the logic of the arguments the higher court advanced for its refusal on a systematic basis. For example, in 1855, the Court of Grenoble ruled that an orgy organized at the home of a widow named Tardy with five other young individuals did not constitute contempt of public decency. According to the Court of Grenoble, "the law is not meant to aid those who, having renounced any modesty, would have participated in the debauchery of which the defendant is accused."[2] The Grenoble Court based its decision on the fact that the participants had consented to sex and not on the manner in which they had been invited.

Yet, this reasoning was meaningless if one considers that in the case of public performances, consent or nonconsent of the spectators did not change anything in defining indecent exposure. Moreover, in the case of performance in private, not consenting to the scene that was witnessed did not make it public. The notion of consent had no influence on the publicity resulting from the nature of the space, nor on the one that depended on the manner in which the audience had been brought together.

In the case of the widow Tardy, even if the young individuals had not consented to seeing the lady do a striptease or engage in sex with one of them under the outraged gaze of others, there would have been no indecent exposure, for two reasons: the scene was neither visible from the outside nor had the young men entered the lady's residence as a result of a public announcement.

This is how the court interpreted it until 1877: it never ceased to repeat that in a private space, enclosed and invisible from the outside, where people had gathered on an individual basis, contempt of public decency could not occur, even if those individuals had been shocked by the sexual act that they had seen. In this case, the court could not conceive of publicity as a phenomenon that was linked to the nature of the space. Thus, only architectural configurations were capable of transforming a private space into a public one.

But this became a nagging issue from the 1860s on, when appellate courts began frankly manifesting their discontent with regard to the perceived laxism, and began to pressure the Court of Cassation in a more sustained manner. On two occasions, in 1869 and 1872, the higher court resisted. But, like all besieged fortresses, before too long, it eventually surrendered in 1877, with the famous Ponce case.

The Armand case (1869)

The old legal annals report quite laconically that on Christmas Eve 1868, a certain Mr. Armand and Miss Lombard met in a bedsit (*un garni*), along with another couple. They charged a young 14-year-old apprentice, who worked at the same place as Armand, with getting provisions, then upon his return, they invited him to supper. But, just after dinner, the young woman offered herself to Armand in the presence of the young apprentice.

Brought before the correctional Court of Orleans, Armand and Lombard were declared guilty of indecent exposure by a ruling on 14 January 1869, and the former was sentenced to three months imprisonment and a fine of 50 francs, while the latter received 15 days in jail and a fine of 16 francs. They appealed this decision on the grounds that the publicity was lacking for there to be contempt of public decency. The Advocate General requested that the imperial Court of Orleans uphold the conviction on the following grounds:

> In my view, it does not matter that no one can see from the outside what is happening in the room, if a third party unwittingly became witness to this supposedly secret theater. I set aside of course all those who had come to participate in the act. But I maintain that when jurisprudence, interpreting the law, says that it is sufficient for the immodest act to be seen from the outside, to be punished, it is unacceptable that one is free of guilt, even though one has only consulted oneself to have spectators, without regard to the offense felt by those viewing the act. The private house to which one brings an outsider who is not aware of the cynical display that is reserved for him ceases to be a respectable home, as should be any type of intimate home. If you knowingly bring someone into your home, it does not matter if you close your doors, you are no longer in an exclusive tete-a-tete;

> you have spectators, brought by you and whose modesty you should care about, to be in keeping with the law. You have rendered public that which was only permitted out of sight [...]. This is indecent exposure, whatever the nature of the space, as soon as one has acted in a way that reveals a contempt of public decency. The space in which one sets a bad example to others is no longer a domestic space; one is no longer in the private sphere as, by not being embarrassed by such an act in front of a third party, one transforms him into an involuntary witness.[3]

This moving defense recalls yet another that the Advocate General Greffier made in the same imperial Court of Orleans a few years earlier in 1862,[4] and deserves to be cited for us to understand the institutional tensions that had begun to attack the wall of privacy, as protected by the Napoleonic Code. In order to reverse the ruling of the trial court, which the imperial court had to consider in a very similar case, he observed:

> [...] "They had shut the door and we saw nothing from the outside; thus the act lacked publicity." My human reasoning revolts against such an interpretation of the term publicity! [...] I do not hesitate to say it, there is another kind of publicity, which applies to the offense which we are trying, and which we could call publicity under *ratione facti* or *personae* [...]. An act that offends modesty is in contempt of public decency when it is committed outside of the secret and intimate private life of the perpetrator, in the presence of those who did not seek the spectacle ... I firmly believe that publicity in matters of indecent exposure results from when the perpetrator of indecent acts does not contain them within the secrecy of his private life. On the contrary, he offered voluntarily—or even involuntarily—and in any place whatsoever, such acts to the people, who despite themselves, were the witnesses. These individuals form the public, in opposition to the private nature of the perpetrator's interior life [...]. There exists a strange confusion when it comes to the protection due to the secrecy of private life. Yes, the privacy of the offender must be contained, as we used to say; but does it not stop being private if the evil actions, which one can find even deep within a domestic household, are produced for the stranger's gaze?[5]

In the case of Armand, the imperial Court of Orleans followed the Advocate General and upheld the decision of the trial court in the following terms:

> Whereas in the matter of indecent exposure, publicity is characterized either by the nature of the space or the circumstances accompanying the material fact; whereas in the present case, publicity results from the acts of debauchery which were perpetrated by Armand and the Miss Lombard on the night of 24–25 December, though in a closed room, in the presence of young Grison, aged 14, the child who was apprenticed to the same master as Armand—who was called by the latter only to run errands and render service to the four defendants—who could not foresee that the scene of debauchery that Armand and Miss Lombard were not afraid to perform for several hours in his presence would make him an involuntary witness. Given that the elements of the trial reveal so clearly the defendants' contempt for public decency which violated an eminently respectable person—a child and a subordinate no less—there is good reasoning in the decision of the trial judges who declared them guilty of the offense provided for and punished by Article 330 of the Penal Code.

But the Supreme Court was not at all sensitive to these arguments; it upheld the classic principles with regard to publicity in enclosed spaces with a very terse decision handed down on 23 April 1869.

The court stated: "Whereas the acts of debauchery as recorded by the contested decision took place in the room of one of the defendants, this room was closed, and no one saw nor could see from the exterior that which transpired within; whereas the sole witness to the scene had come into the room with a particular reason, called upon by one of the defendants to run their errands, and whereas the modesty of the young apprentice was offended, it nevertheless does not follow that the modesty of the public was also compromised."[6]

With this decision, the court here used two classic criteria: the existence of a closed space, without opening to the outside, and the fact that the witness was not on site by chance, as would have been a passerby, as in the Baylar case. Rather, it was because those who occupied the premises had called him for a particular reason, in this case to run errands. What mattered to the court was not having been either a voluntary or involuntary witness but rather the nonrandom nature of his presence. The court went on to consider whether this witness could embody the figure of the passerby who could have seen the scene and thus have effectively constituted a public. We should also acknowledge that the court gave no weight to the fact that there was just one witness to the indecent act.

The Salmon case[7] *(1872)*

The famous Salmon case was the second important case heard by the Court of Cassation, in which it refused to take a scene produced in a closed private space as public. Mr. Salmon paid a visit to the home of Madame Delannois, who lived with her young daughter, Miss Daguet.

Mr. Salmon and Mme Delannois settled into the bedroom, leaving the door open, and engaged in sex. The daughter entered the room and found them in the act. Salmon was not only not embarrassed at having been caught in an intimate act but he began to fondle the young girl, seemingly with her consent.[8]

A ruling of the Criminal Court of Fontainebleau of 23 August 1872 had held "that results from the preliminary investigation and deliberations prove that Salmon and Mme Delannois touched each other in an obscene fashion, in the presence of Miss Daguet. Furthermore, these events took place in the bedroom of Mme Delannois, and the defendants voluntarily made their act public by performing it in front of this girl. Thus, they have committed the offense of contempt of public decency."

On Salmon's appeal, the Criminal Division of the Paris Court could not agree that these acts constituted the elements of the offense provided for by Article 330, and reversed the ruling which had condemned the accused, by pronouncing his acquittal on 25 September, on the grounds that "the acts in which Salmon engaged were enacted in a private space, without witnesses other than the woman and the girl who were the objects of his attention."

The public prosecutor appealed to the Supreme Court. In his memorandum, he presented the following argument:

> [...] The home consists of two parts. None of the interior or exterior doors were closed. Salmon and Delannois went through to the bedroom, according to Salmon's testimony, and engaged in acts of debauchery. The young child, who remained in the kitchen, entered of her own will to witness acts of lust, to which she then fell victim. In such circumstances, given that free access was voluntarily given by the accused, anyone could have entered, and, in fact, the child did enter. Publicity provided for by Article 330 is general and encompasses all circumstances of time and space; publicity may even just be coincidental.

Thus, to attack the classical theory of publicity in enclosed spaces, the criminal court [of Fontainebleau] and the prosecutor put forward two arguments. The first is the same as that of the Court of Orleans. The sexual scene that should have been kept hidden took place before an unwitting witness, thus becoming public within the meaning provided for by Article 330. The second, proffered by the prosecutor, seems more daring, because he considers the closed housing as divided into an "outside" and an "inside" by the door separating the bedroom from the kitchen. As if somehow, with respect to Article 330, the dwelling was the bedroom, while the rest of the apartment was its outside.

But none of these arguments managed to convince the Court of Cassation. On 8 November 1872, it upheld the acquittal of the Court of Paris, for "the contempt of public decency of which Salmon was accused did not present sufficient character of the publicity necessary to constitute the offense provided for and punished by Article 330."

The author of this quite concise decision articulates what seems quite clear in the Supreme Court's theories of publicity. He writes:

> The fact that the space was private, and the fact that the victims were the only witnesses, do not in and of themselves exclude publicity, because the private space in which the act was committed could have been disposed in such a way as to allow for the scene to be seen from the outside. But although, in the present case, the physical disposition was neither indicated nor cited by the previous ruling, it is clear that, for the Court of Cassation, the possibility that the indecent act could be seen from outside was implicitly denied by the fact of the judge's assertion that there had been no publicity.[9]

It was not until the Ponce Case that the Supreme Court finally abandoned this restrictive doctrine.

II The Ponce case[10] (1877)

On the night of 18 March 1877, Rosalie Ratel, aged 46, widow of Gros, and her daughter Melanie Marie, 14, had slept in their stables to watch over a sick cow.

Around midnight, while they lay close to one another on a heap of straw in the most complete darkness, Eugene Ponce entered the stable. Without uttering a word or making any sound, he approached Mme Gros, brought his hands under her clothes and started touching her "indecently." Convinced he could not overcome the resistance of this woman, he threw himself on the girl, took her hand to his virile member, and then, lifting the clothes of the girl, tried to "satisfy his passion."

Aided by her mother, the girl managed to disengage herself from Ponce, who, furious, violently struck both women and only left when they shouted for help.

On 10 May 1877, the criminal Court of Saint-Jean-de-Maurienne found Ponce guilty of contempt of public decency on the grounds that,

> with regard to indecent exposure, it is not necessary that the space in which the immoral act has been committed be considered public by nature in order for the element of publicity to be recognized, and that the essential character of contempt of public decency was to injure the integrity of those who are witnesses. Consequently, regardless of the space in which it was committed, the act shall be considered indecent exposure, if it had as witness an individual whose modesty had been offended, while the perpetrator of the indecency had taken no precaution to escape the gaze, knowing that there were witnesses to the scene. Whereas, according to the circumstances described by the mother and daughter Gros, Ponce's alleged acts took place publicly, because the latter, by engaging with each of these women in indecent acts, made them alternately witnesses of the indecent acts he committed knowingly on one to the distress of another; for these reasons the court finds Ponce guilty, [...]

On 22 June 1877, the Court of Chambéry confirmed the decision of the trial court and the reasoning on which the ruling was based.

By relying on theories about traditional publicity, the Advocate General Lacointa asked the court to overturn the conviction handed down to Ponce. The learned lawyer stated:

> Given that Article 330 is only applicable to offenses committed in a public space by nature or destination, or in a private space exposed to public view, I argue that in this case, the offense does not stand legal muster.
>
> The space was absolutely private: a stable attached to an inhabited house. Nobody was outside to witness what transpired, and even during the day it would not have been possible. Moreover, at the time when the incident occurred around midnight, the stable was not lit, and the widow Gros and her daughter were not able to see the acts with their eyes, but had felt them, having undergone Ponce's odious advances. Hence, there was neither a public space, nor a

> visual regard, either from the outside or from the interior, only the perception of the contact with the perpetrator, in a private space by its inhabitants.

According to the Advocate General:

> under similar circumstances, the criminal court has never found the elements of the offense of contempt of public decency. As for acts performed in a private residence, the character of publicity is only found if it is proved they could have been seen from the outside, either because of the physical layout of the space itself, or for the lack of proper precautions being taken. An offense has been committed when the acts are—or could have been—seen even accidentally from the outside, without prying efforts. There is no other precedent; publicity, the essential element, must result at least from this circumstance.

After recalling previous cases in which the court had decided to follow the classical theory of publicity, the Advocate General adds that, "after the findings of the ruling of Chambery, proceedings could be initiated against Ponce, either for assault or for indecent assault with violence, but the act ought not to be classified as contempt of public decency. Is it not in fact the case to say, following the 1869 decision, that although the modesty of the widow Gros and her daughter 'had been offended, it does not follow that modesty of the public has also been compromised'?"

But the Court of Cassation refused to follow the Advocate General:

> Whereas according to precedent, a violation of modesty becomes contempt of public decency by the very fact of the inherent publicity of the space in which it was committed, even when the act was not witnessed by an individual; it is generally accepted that the act takes on this character when enacted in a private space, if it could be seen by others, or in the absence of adequate precautions taken by its perpetrators to keep secret. Whereas, in this case, Gros and her daughter, who were unexpectedly assaulted in their home, were by turns both victims of and witnesses to a violation inflicted by the accused on the modesty of each woman; whereas the mother, having barely escaped the accused's lustful touching distinctly perceived the shameful practices exercised on her daughter, just as the latter too had found herself witness to the lewd acts performed on her mother; thus, the modesty of each individual was successively violated by the spectacle that the accused imposed on them. It does not matter

> that this spectacle took place inside the locale in which they were found together, *no difference can be rationally established between this case and one in which one of the two, upon entering from the outside, would have unexpectedly witnessed the immoral acts being committed inside on the other*; under these circumstances, far from incorrectly applying Article 330 of the Penal Code, in classifying the odiously immoral acts of the accused perpetrated on the mother and daughter as contempt of public decency, the contested decision is based on sound interpretation.[11]

The *interior publicity* that the Court of Cassation thus invented in this ruling still exists as such in French law, even after the last reform of the Penal Code of 1992. Only one of the conditions for it to be constituted—the number of nonconsenting individuals that need to witness the act—has changed following a subsequent decision of the court in 1954.[12] In order to measure the scope of this legal revolution and analyze the techniques that the court has used, it is essential to consider the Ponce case with the others that have followed, and which can be held to shed light on the resulting doctrine.

The Ponce Decision, or how judges opened an entirely enclosed space without the use of a hammer

For a sexual act to be held as having taken place in public inside a closed space, the court demanded the presence of witnesses. In the Ponce case, these witnesses were mother and daughter, both nonconsenting to the spectacle to which they were, despite themselves, the spectators. Subsequently, the courts always required the need for the presence of two witnesses. In opposition to some lower courts, the Court of Cassation never found that a single witness was sufficient for this form of publicity. Some subsequent important cases leave us no doubt in this regard.

Thus, on 16 June 1906, the Court of Cassation said that even in a space not visibly accessible to the public, publicity can be constituted in cases with multiple victims of obscene acts, when each is unintentionally by turn victim or witness. The same cannot be true when, under the same conditions, an offense targets the modesty of a single person, without any offense to the modesty of the public, when that person is at once victim and thereby witness to these acts. The court stated that, in contrast to indecent assault, "the prevention of contempt of public decency does not aim primarily to condemn indecent acts committed with respect to a particular individual. Rather, its special purpose is to provide reparation for the scandal caused by such acts and to afford protection to third parties who may be witnesses to such acts; it is this scandal that makes a crime of the act, and not the violation of modesty of the individual subjected to the act."[13]

We find the same doctrine in a case heard on 15 June 1911, in which an individual exhibited his genitalia in a locked bedroom in the presence of a woman who had simultaneously been both an involuntary witness and the victim.[14]

Soon after, however, the court found that it was not indispensable for the two individuals whose presence allowed for the emergence of publicity to be nonconsenting and very quickly, it merely required only one of them to be nonconsenting. Thus, barely two years after the Ponce case, in the Darnal case,[15] the Court of Cassation ruled that two men who were hiding in a bedroom behind a partition to engage in sexual relations were in contempt of public decency due to the fact that a nonconsenting third person had heard them. Publicity was constituted because their sex act had been heard by a single witness and because the perpetrators of "obscene acts" were aware of this presence.

This ruling introduces an important clarification to the Ponce case. One of the two witnesses that the law requires for interior publicity can also be someone who took part in the obscene act. In this case, there was a witness whose modesty was violated and another witness who could be either one or the other of the two men who were hiding and knew that someone heard or could hear them. So, in the Ponce case, even if either the mother or the daughter had consented to the sexual acts, the interior publicity would have still been constituted. What mattered the most was that the witnesses were two in number, and one of them had not consented to witness the act. Thus, in 1932, an individual who photographed a young woman's genitals in the presence of another who protested strongly was held to have committed the offense of contempt of public decency.[16]

Moreover, for the witness to be held to be nonconsenting, according to the court's jurisprudence, it was not necessary that the individual be shocked by or opposed to what s/he saw. In order for there to be publicity, it was sufficient that the witness did not consent in a manifest and conscious manner due to various circumstances such as his or her age, lapse in concentration, or because s/he was asleep.

On 4 March 1880, an individual named Marbier was convicted for having indecently caressed a girl, before daybreak, in a room where her father, mother, brother and a neighbor were present. Even though nobody had seen anything, given that they all were in the same room, they *could have witnessed* the act, because the individual in question had not taken any precaution to hide it.[17] Following the same logic, on 21 January 1944, the Court of Cassation sentenced a couple for contempt of public decency for having engaged in sex in the presence of three sleeping children, aged 2, 7 and 9 years, because had the children awakened, they could have witnessed the act.[18] The consent that the court required of the witness was formal and active, like the one a woman was meant to give for a sexual act, for it not to be classified as rape.[19]

In the Ponce and Darnal decisions, the two witnesses had not seen the act, but just *felt* the presence of a third, by touch in the former, and by hearing in the latter.[20] It was the same with the Court of Cassation case of 7 May 1897, in which publicity could be established in the case of an individual who, several times during the night, joined a bed occupied by two sisters and had sex with the elder. Even though the younger, aged 12, had not distinctly perceived the indecent acts in which her sister had been involved, she was at least aware that the culprit repeatedly crept into their bed, which was deemed to be sufficient to offend her modesty.[21]

It was therefore not necessary to have seen anything to become a witness to contempt of public decency when committed in an enclosed space. This is because interior publicity was a special case of publicity constituted by accessibility, so sight was not considered a required criterion to constitute contempt. Indeed, in the Ponce case, when the Court of Cassation justified the way it was able to establish the equivalence between a private space that became public because of accessibility and a private space that was completely enclosed, it stated [as cited before]: "no difference can be rationally established between this case and one in which one of the two [women] would have unexpectedly witnessed from the outside the immoral acts being committed inside on the other."

Thus, the court not only created a new form of publicity specific to enclosed spaces, it broadened the notion of public space to include these spaces, by creating a kind of fiction in which one of the witnesses would not be present at the beginning of the act, but discovers it by opening a door that linked the interior to the outside.

It is as if, in substance, the presence of two witnesses besides the perpetrator in this room, which was neither visible to nor accessible from the outside, would have produced an effect similar to opening an unlocked door.

Therefore, these enclosed spaces in which an individual exposed himself had to be considered as if they were unlocked spaces, such as a club, a store, an inn's kitchen or an office in a business, into which outsiders had the right to enter without permission. The court extended the notion of public space defined by accessibility to enclosed spaces with certain social configurations, most clearly when there was the presence of three persons of whom at least one was not a consenting witness to the scene at hand. The role of the two witnesses was to transform the nature of the space. Thus they filled a spatial function: their very presence, along with the disagreement of one of them, simple nonconsent, transformed the private space into a public one.

Presumably the courts put in place this curious operation because they could not find that contempt of public decency had been committed in a private, invisible and inaccessible space. For that to be possible, it was necessary for this space to become public.

But did the court have access to other tools to bring about this metamorphosis? What were the benefits as well as the costs of this conversion? In order to apply Article 330 to spaces that were inaccessible and invisible from the exterior, the court could have just sought recourse in a purely social notion of the public, which already existed for performances. But, as we shall see, this notion did not allow for the spectators' consent to have any influence on the public character of the performance. Thus, if the law had applied this notion of the public to enclosed spaces, it would have prohibited sexual scenes enacted even in the presence of a consenting individual.

And if, to avoid excessive strictness, the court had required consent, it would have taken the risk of being obliged to apply this criterion to performances, and thus would have liberalized them in a radical way. The Court would have made theaters venues of debauchery, as an unfortunate consequence of its attempt to bring enclosed (private) spaces under the purview of the State.

It is for this reason that the court sought recourse in the spatial criterion. It needed to create a situation equivalent to the one found in a space rendered public by accessibility, in a space that was enclosed and invisible from outside. However, with respect to Article 330, a public space is both a spatial and social reality. It is a physical space that can be crossed by the public, that is to say, by a passerby.

To transform a confined space into a public space by access, the court demanded the presence of an exhibitionist in front of two individuals, one of whom had not consented to witness the act. By so doing, the court substituted public space with the presence of two people who became, in its view, the functional equivalents thereof. However, since this legal maneuver was based on the co-presence of two individuals embodying the two dimensions of public spaces, it is impossible to say much about who held the social role and which of the two played the spatial role.

III Living at home after the Ponce case

The Ponce case and its prolific descendants had a very noticeable impact with regard to sex and nudity on the status of private spaces, especially within homes. Following the Ponce case, living spaces became possible theaters not only for public sexual exhibition but also for the more mundane kinds of nudity.

As we have seen, all private space, even if invisible and not accessible from the outside, could also become as public as a street provided that at least three individuals were present. If one shared housing with someone other than one's sexual partner, that party could arrive on the scene at any moment and transform the dwelling into a public space. It was sufficient for one of these three people to declare not to have consented to witness the act of a sexual nature for there to be publicity.

If a private residence had only one room, it was almost impossible to protect one's sexual relations from the possible gaze of other inhabitants. And, once closed off, they had to take place behind a locked door to avoid any breach. If all parts of a house were potentially public, one could suspend this publicity by locking oneself in a bedroom in the same way that one could lock oneself in the bathroom of a train station.

A room in which a sexual scene was enacted could therefore be differentiated in the same house as if it were a separate unit from the rest of the home. Everything that was not this room was its outside. Thus, in view of the visibility of sexuality, private homes were intermittently segmented, and sexuality as performance could put an end to the unity of lived space. The Ponce case became the matrix of production of new spaces that architects had to take into account to consider the internal distribution of space in apartments, including the separation of bedrooms from other spaces. Thus, contempt of public decency was a great tool for the creation of new rules for the visibility of sexuality in the context of family life.

Yet, we must not think of this multiplication of internal residential units as the juxtaposition of several units of the home. The home was more protected than a bedroom, because one could not enter it without first gaining permission. Such was not at all the case for bedrooms, according to the courts. Any individual who lived in or found herself in a house for some reason had the right, at least for the purposes of Article 330, to enter a bedroom without knocking.

Thus, in a 1943 decision, the court held a man in contempt of public decency because a woman who entered into an apartment discovered him caressing her daughter in the bedroom. More recently still, in 1971, the Court of Cassation upheld the conviction of a man for contempt of public decency because he had been caught in his own room, with a closed but unlocked door, by the children of the woman with whom he was found and who had been told to go outside and play.

Thus, interior publicity indirectly created new rules for sex, the effects of which are still detectable throughout the law. Henceforth, private spaces, in which one could hide one's sexuality because of the nature of the spatial configuration, would no longer exist; it was up to sexuality to give itself spaces, that is to say, the extent of the spaces in which it could be enacted.

Notes

1 Bull. crim. 1828, no. 48. This phrase was often cited in other succeeding cases. For example, see the case of 7 April 1859, D. 59. 1. 239.
2 Cited by Garçon, *Code pénal annoté*, p. 182.
3 D. 1869. 1. 305.
4 D.P. 1862. II. 9.
5 Claude Laplatte, who commented on this case a century later, couldn't capture better what was at play in these debates. He writes that there were two walls in the confined and enclosed space of the home. The first, "the famous wall of privacy, which surrounds the home in which mem-

bers of the family live; secrets of private life are shared and defended by them—in principle—against outsiders ('one washes one's dirty linen within the family'), but, inside the home, there is the holy of holies, or if you prefer, the alcove: the small circle of sexual life, that is to say privacy to the power of two. The family members who are not included in this small circle are, in this respect, outsiders, compared to those who are included. [...]. From the moment it is agreed that the terms public and private have a different meaning in the sexual sense, or rather, a different scope from their connotation in common language, everything becomes clear." (Laplatte, *L'Outrage public à la pudeur*, pp. 83–84).

6 D. 1869. 1. 305.
7 D. 1873. 1. 176.
8 Maillefaud, *De l'outrage public à la pudeur*, p. 105.
9 D. 1873. 1. 176
10 D. 1877. 1. 287.
11 D. 1877. 1. 288.
12 See Chapter 6.
13 Cited by Garçon, *Code pénal annoté*.
14 G. P. 1911. 2. 259.
15 Cass., 15 May 1879, D. 1879. 5. 30.
16 D. 1933. 1. 133 and footnote Vandamne.
17 Cass., 4 March 1880, S. 1881. 1 44.
18 Cited by Garçon, *Code pénal annoté*, p. 190.
19 See p. 21.
20 The court explained "this witness was fully aware of the profoundly immoral acts being committed in his presence by the words [the accused] spoke, the inarticulate sounds that escaped their mouths [...] in such a way to have shocked his sentiment of modesty." Cf. the prior cited *Affaire Darnal*.
21 Bull. 1897, no. 158, Pandectes 1898. 1. 453.

4

The demolition of the wall of modesty and the new fate of Article 330

The new political spaces opened by the Ponce decision sparked off many thoughts and concerns. Legal scholars protested, and even playwrights attempted to unravel the mysteries of the (in)famous Article 330 of the Penal Code, which had, much like a burglar, broken into every home. Indeed, the way the courts made use of Article 330 in the last quarter of the nineteenth century implied the abolition of the wall of shame as it had been constructed by the legislation of the Second Empire (1852–1870).

The wall of shame was a technique destined to protect both sexual freedom and public morality, and it was based on the status of spaces. This order ensured such freedom to the extent that the community did not see sexual acts—so that individuals could avoid becoming agents of society's corruption by the way in which they were seen. This approach explains why almost total liberty was afforded in confined spaces while it was so severely restricted in public spaces.

The wall of shame could be held as a kind of puritan-liberal covenant that the State had made with the People. With this quite singular pact, the population could enjoy an unprecedented freedom of morals, unmatched in the future, during the first half of the nineteenth century. This "pact" nevertheless presumed that everything that was sexual was immoral and licentious, whether it was a speech, an act or a performance that came under scrutiny.

But when, following the Ponce decision, the wall of shame was finally demolished, this order was reversed. If the State was only liberal because it did not see inside people's homes, then—and only on that condition—the act of expanding its field of vision meant exposing its own restrictive ideas of sexuality. Now unable to have the same status, sexuality would no longer be just one element of private life, among others. It now came under a special regime, becoming a constant source of anxiety and self-monitoring in private spaces in which people were supposed to be at home.

However, we cannot take away from this process only the repressive moralizing aspect, because, at the same time, Article 330 contained new functions within the framework of attacks against morality and sexual politics of public spaces. But before analyzing the strange and unexpected fate of Article 330 after the Ponce decision, it is important to reflect briefly on how this rule was enacted on stage by Georges Courteline and Georges Feydeau.

I Article 330 at the theater

Between the late nineteenth and early twentieth centuries, Article 330 was the bane of artists, entertainers and libertarian intellectuals alike. In effect, this offense resulted in condemning the performing arts such as dance, theater or popular music at the music hall.

However, two important plays of that time devoted directly or indirectly to Article 330 consider it not as a tool for artistic, but rather private, censorship. It is not trials against nude dancers or directors of nudist scenes that these plays target and parody. Rather, it is the more ordinary effects of Article 330 on everyday life. The two plays—*Article 330* by Georges Courteline[1] and *Mais n'te promène donc pas toute nue* [So, don't walk around naked] by Georges Feydeau—may be read as great studies on the functioning of this criminal offense.

Georges Courteline and Article 330

Article 330 by Georges Courteline was first performed at the Antoine Theater on 12 December 1900. The idea for this play came from a lawsuit against the Electric Transport Company [Société des transports électriques] initiated some time before by Mr. Poussin, a watchmaker. The reason for this trial was the World's Fair, held in Paris to celebrate the turn of the century. Eighty thousand exhibitors were dispersed throughout Paris, and to help move the uninterrupted flow of visitors, a moving walkway was laid from the Champ de Mars to the Invalides. This sidewalk on stilts was, apparently, one of the most sought-after attractions of the Exposition.

Unfortunately, the walkway did not bring happiness to all, as many Parisians had to resign themselves to a steady crowd walking past their windows. It is for this reason that Mr. Poussin, whose studio was located at 34 Avenue de La Motte-Picquet, sued and won a lawsuit against the Electric Transport Company.

This story amused Courteline, who had the idea of transforming the watchmaker into the character La Brigue, who describes himself as a "defensive philosopher," and who attempts to gain justice in a way perfectly contrary to Mr. Poussin. Rather than being the plaintiff, he becomes the defendant, who above all seeks to compel judges to judge the law instead of applying it. Of course, unlike the watchmaker, La Brigue loses his case because, even in theater, laws are not made to be on the docket.

This one-act play takes place entirely in court. La Brigue is accused of having shown his bottom from the window of his apartment to a crowd of exactly 13,687 people, and therefore of having violated Article 330 of the Penal Code. He nevertheless presents himself as a victim and takes his time to tell the courts about the tragic events that led him to commit this illegal act.

La Brigue had rented an apartment at 5 bis, Avenue de La Motte-Picquet and, like Poussin, became a victim of harassment by visitors to the Universal Expo:

> I heard the moving walkway from eight o'clock in the morning to eleven o'clock in the evening, which disturbed my sleep at night if I wanted to go to bed early, and woke me up in the morning even if I wanted to sleep late!! Before my windows streams of people: men, women, children's maids, and good soldiers, all people in good spirits, in a jovial mood, who spoilt my furniture, by spitting at my house moving from the right to left, singing: "oh là là, c'te gueule, c'te binette!" And cherry pits, alternating with peanuts, olives and pumpkin seeds, rained down into my bedroom from their joyously indifferent fingers.

Outraged by such violence, La Brigue decided to lodge a complaint against the various people who could be responsible for his fate, but, disoriented in the bureaucratic maze, he lost time and money. Frustrated and desperate with such impunity, he decided to take the law into his own hands.

He explained to the court: "plunging myself into wrongdoing up to my neck in an effort to turn it into the truth since nine times out of ten, the law—the good girl that she is—smiles at whoever violates her." Thus he made the decision that led him to court.

The bailiff who recorded the case reports the following facts: "We clearly distinguished at the end of an apartment, revealed for everyone to see through a large flat open window, a kind of imperfect sphere split in the vertical direction, with almost exactly the appearance of a two-leaf clover, which we recognized to be the lower limbs and posterior of a person bent over to kiss the ground."

"I was not kissing the ground," says La Brigue. "I was looking for a penny."

But, far from advocating for the defensive value of his gesture, he takes on Article 330 of the Penal Code directly, which, much like the walkway of the Electric Transport Company, did not allow him to live in peace in his own home. The speech La Brigue gives the court shows the absurdity of the notion of publicity in this offense.

The first of these arguments addresses the confusion that Article 330 creates between the acts of showing and seeing. He denounces the feature of Article 330 that consists of giving the power to the viewer of transforming the act of the man or woman he sees into an intentionally exhibited act for the benefit of the viewer. Thus, he targets the very heart of the State's all-seeing gaze postulated by the offense.

"Do you know of what you are accused?" the presiding judge asks La Brigue. "Of having shown your behind," he adds. To which La Brigue replies: "I invoke the notorious purity of my morals. Show my ass! Why would I do that? I agree that these people saw it, but I formally deny having shown it to them."

The second argument is that the concept of publicity of the infraction is contrary to other criminal laws that protect the home against any intrusion. Indeed, Article 330 calls a space public if an individual undresses without regard to windows or other openings that allow the person to be seen from the outside, but in doing so he or she violates the respect that the law imposes on those spaces and indirectly affects the right to private property. It is as if there were a contradiction between the right to see, which the State accords everyone under Article 330, and the right to private property.

"Did I put my behind against the window … exposed to the sun like an unripe melon?" La Brigue asks.

"We have identified," replies the Bailiff Legruyère, "'AT THE BACK OF AN APARTMENT...' What is too convenient, sir, is to seize the property of others and use it as if it were one's own. It is to acquire their money under the false pretext of ensuring their right to sleep, to privacy, rest, under the authority of inaccessible power, an offense under Article 405."

The third complaint La Brigue lodges against Article 330 is that it creates permanent instability in the status of different spaces. In this case, Article 330 confers on La Brigue's home, like all other homes, an *intermittent status* that is sometimes public and sometimes private, according to whether what we see from the outside is qualified as sexual or not. Why, he wonders, would sexuality have the exorbitant power to transform spaces? Why would it enjoy a special status in relation to other acts of life?

La Brigue asks the following: "For me, having paid taxes, thus having paid my money for the right to breathe—that God gave me for nothing—could I keep my windows open, if I am too hot? Yes or no?"

"Yes," the judge replies.

"In a home that is mine, since I pay what is due, can I, if I lose a penny, bend down to pick it up? Yes or no?"

"Yes," the judge replies once more.

La Brigue continues, "In the same house, can I, if it takes my fancy, dress up as Mexican?"

"Yes," the judge acquiesces.

"As a Turk?"

"Yes."

"And as a Scotsman."

"NO!" The deputy responds with brio.

"This is new," says La Brigue, "and it is a strange justice that, pushed against the wall, forced by logic, comes to choose between Turkey and Scotland, at the risk of bringing complications and disturbing the foundations of European order."

But all of La Brigue's criticisms of the inconsistency in the law do not prevent him from being sentenced to thirteen months imprisonment, a fine of 25 francs and payment for the costs of the trial. For as the president explains: "If judges begin to accede to all those who are right, we will no longer know where we're headed, if not to the disintegration of a society that has become accustomed to being so upstanding."

Mais n'te promène donc pas toute nue

Georges Feydeau's play[2] was first performed in 1911 at the Femina Theater. It does not directly attack Article 330, and in fact never cites it. However, this comedy is a sort of caricature of the effects that the jurisprudence surrounding Article 330 had on minds and spaces, making the character of the Député [member of parliament/congressman] Ventroux the incarnation of the new legal rationality that it brought about. As he tries to convey to his wife, Ventroux knows that domestic space *is* a public space when it comes to sexuality, that is to say, almost all the time.

The entire play is set in the living room belonging to the Député and his wife Clarisse, with a large window at the far end upstage. There are three doors from the room, which lead to Clarisse's bedroom, Ventroux's study, and finally to the exit. The importance acquired by enclosed spaces and other structures that permitted or interrupted visibility had become central in life, as in the plot.

The plot structure presents itself like a series of domestic scenes, the focus of which is the negligence displayed by Clarisse with regard to her own nakedness and the disproportionate anger that it provokes in her husband. Ventroux constantly calls on his wife to become aware that she is being watched, that she is never alone, that she is never completely covered up, that people see her all the time, that even in her bedroom she is not in her home, and that even when dressed, one can see through.

His reproaches begin while Clarisse is in her room and wants to change in front of their 13-year-old child. She says, "He is my son, my flesh! My blood! Eh! So … let the flesh of my flesh see my flesh. There is nothing improper in that, except prejudice! Hasn't he watched me wash myself twenty-five thousand times since he was very little? And you never said anything!" Ventroux replies, "These things must stop one day," to which Clarisse asks, "When? At what time?"

"But, really," asks Ventroux, "why is it that you have this habit of walking around always naked?"

"Naked?" Clarisse responds. "I had my singlet on."

"Which is even more indecent!" replies the husband. "They can see through you like tracing paper."

And the discussion continues about the servants. "Sure, wash yourself!" says Ventroux! "But stay in your room to do it! … and close the door! It is always open at those moments! Very convenient for the servants."

"What? They do not come in," says Clarisse.

"They do not need to come in to see you, they just have to look," replies the husband.

"If you think servants look!" retorts his wife.

"Yes, oh yes, aren't they men like other men?" Ventroux interrupts.

And he continues to blame her again for her ablutions, "You turn on the lights in your dressing room and you do not close the curtains. Since you cannot see outside, you're like an ostrich: you imagine that we do not see you from out there."

Clarisse replies, "Oh! Who do you think will look?"

Ventroux continues, "Who?"—gesticulating at the window—"But Clemenceau, my dear! ... Clemenceau who lives opposite us! ... He's at the window all the time!"

Here is the most important element of the story: the window through which Clemenceau supposedly spends his time observing the Ventrouxs' living room, much like the law itself, faces the audience. The scene that takes place in the living room has two sides, one facing the audience and the other toward Clemenceau.

Feydeau uses this dual stage to make Clarisse eventually do, through a series of errors, what Ventroux fears the most: showing her behind to Clemenceau without revealing herself to her audience.

But if this scene is almost a quote from Courteline's play, in which the exhibition is recounted, not shown, it is also a veritable *staging* of the functioning of Article 330. Indeed, one might suspect that Feydeau sought to oppose Clemenceau with the audience, while putting them in a position close to one another, as if one was the obverse of the other. They are face to face, without nevertheless seeing the same things or, especially, being spectators in the same way.

Clemenceau thus transforms a private scene from which he is excluded into a theatrical scene because the law gives him the power to watch as if people were trying to show off voluntarily, to any passerby or to the whole community, even if nobody ever consciously tried to show him anything. All of this plays out while the spectators are allowed to watch because they have come to the theater and paid their entry for the performers to act and show themselves to them.

But the most clever part is that, while Clemenceau has the power to watch the scene because Clarisse's nudity is visible from behind the window, the audience from Feydeau's time did not have such a right. We know that the famous war that artists had lost a few years previously banned nudity in the theater.[3]

This face-to-face between Clemenceau and the spectators at the moment when Clarisse bends down and shows her behind through the window would not have been possible in the opposite direction. In such a scenario, Clemenceau's gaze would have had no relevance because a scene viewed through a window only becomes public when it is sexual. The spectators themselves would not have been there because the room would have been found in violation of Article 330. If the artists did not commit any offense, it is because Clemenceau, unlike the spectators, was pure fiction.

II Crisis in the politics of spatialization of sexuality

Some legal scholars found the new jurisprudence of Article 330 very dangerous and invasive. Abel Maillefaud, who dedicated his 1896 doctoral dissertation[4] to the study of contempt of public decency, thought that if this jurisprudence continued to spread to include confined spaces, "one [would] no longer punish public indecent exposure, but indecency in general, devoid of any aspect of publicity."[5] Of "publicity," one might add, in the sense that we give to the word in today's language. For, in truth, the whole point of this jurisprudence is that it proceeded by extending publicity to private spaces and there was never any question of its disappearance during this process. It is because any space could potentially become public that the offense was being transformed, not because publicity no longer had any relevance. After having criticized this trend in jurisprudence, Maillefaud adds:

> [...] it is nevertheless easy to understand what feelings have guided the courts and tribunals. In our repressive law, the offense of Article 330 is, so to speak, a *subsidiary* offense, or at the most, almost a marginal offense. Given the principles that led to the writing of our penal law, the facts of a revolting immorality are ignored and unpunished. When the courts have found themselves face-to-face with such scandals, it is understood that they have expanded so slightly in their assessment of the principles of the contempt of public decency under the influence of some ideas of moral philosophy they tried to strike these scandals in an effort to make them fit into the framework of crime.[6]

This theory according to which Article 330 was a way to catch up with the more liberal laws on sexual matters met with some success in the second half of the nineteenth century. And many authors claimed that the form of publicity of this offense depended on the type of act that was committed. Thus, doctrinal authorities such as Chauveau and Helie make this distinction, which, a century later, was almost enshrined in a 1960 decree that created a specific aggravating circumstance when the scene in question was enacted with a person of the same sex.

However, the abolition of boundaries between the public and the private cannot be explained only by the willingness of judges to introduce a little virtue into domestic spaces. When considering this process more closely, we understand that this is, indeed, a turning point in the politics of spatialization of sexuality from their conception in the early nineteenth century. These changes did not only have repressive effects—quite the contrary.

When one examines the jurisprudential development of Article 330 in light of changes in the whole system which punished indecent assault, one realizes that the progression to confined spaces and the willingness of the State to open its control went quite well together (initially at least) with the overall severity of prosecutions and convictions regarding moral matters.

Court statistics show that since the 1840s there was an exponential increase in the number of persons convicted of sexual crime[7] to the point that it could be compared to the increase that France has known since the 1980s. To a very large extent, this is due to a change in age of sexual majority (which passed from eleven years in 1832 to thirteen in 1863), with a strong will to persecute the *scourges* that these crimes entailed, that is, the corruption of youth and women, and to a lesser extent, the appearance of more extensive criteria for sexual violence.[8]

But if, at first, the extension of the concept of publicity in Article 330 coincides with the increase in the overall severity in sentencing for crimes, beginning in 1870 these reports take a new turn. Indeed, from this decade, prosecutions and convictions for crime (rape and indecent assault with violence) start to diminish for the first time since 1840 for Article 330 was now being used as a tool to bring crimes to trial. From the 1870s on, according to M. R. Santucci, 50 percent of the cases of indecent exposure tried in court, that is to say, for the offense of Article 330 of the Penal Code, were in reality sexual assaults or rape.[9]

If Article 330 created offenses that the Code did not punish, it also served to soften the harsh sentencing judges sought not to apply for sex crimes. The increase in the severity of penalties for the offense, first in 1863, then in 1885, gave broader reach to the functions that Article 330 would fulfill up until the moral revolution [of 1992].

Thus, Article 330 fulfilled a double and almost contradictory function: it allowed, on the one hand, for the moralizing of people's peaceful sexual lives and, on the other hand, for bringing to trial the most serious crimes. If it had a distinctly repressive function in confined spaces, it was exactly the opposite on crime. It was as if the logic of Article 330 had approached the structure of indecent assault. Thus, it became the ultimate tool for repression of all "bad sex" qualified as such just by being visible. Consent or lack of consent, which was characteristic of other moral offenses, had been set aside in favour of the purely spatial logic of Article 330. When the visible world as a whole was considered potentially public, any consensual (or nonconsensual) sexual conduct could become the subject of a conviction for contempt of public decency.

But, just as unexpectedly, the extension of Article 330 to private spaces had another consequence. Since any space potentially became public, it was no longer constructed in opposition to the regime of formerly private spaces. So how could the old rigors governing the public world continue to be justified?

Indeed, a few years after the Ponce decision, a process of liberalization of the visibility of sexuality in the public sphere began. There was a veritable explosion of nudity and eroticism, which invaded theaters and instigated the strongest legal disputes. It also manifested itself in a massive way, from the 1900s on, in the world of fashion.

Thereby, the conviction of the malicious Eugene Ponce, who wanted to abuse two poor women who were watching over a sick cow, was not to hand a final victory to the champions of virtue and order.

Notes

1 Georges Courteline, "L'Article 330," *Théâtre, contes, romans et nouvelles, philosophie. Écrits divers et fragments retrouvés,* Paris, Robert Laffont, 1990, pp. 169–181.

2 Georges Feydeau, *Mais n'te promène donc pas toute nue*, Play in One Act, Paris, Librairie théâtrale, 1911.
3 See Chapter 5.
4 Maillefaud, *De l'outrage public à la pudeur*.
5 *Ibid.*, p. 112.
6 *Ibid.*, pp. 112–113.
7 For a comparative study of these data, see Georges Vigarello, *Histoire du viol*, Paris, Seuil, 1998.
8 For more on this subject, see *Le Crime était présque sexuel*, *Le Sexe des imbéciles* and *Histoire juridique du viol*, in which I analyze the transformation of the criteria for consent to sex and the new importance given to concepts such as "surprise," which equated physical violence to having sex with a person sleeping, hypnotized, or in an inebriated or mentally disabled state.
9 Cited by Vigarello, *Histoire du viol*, p. 188.

Part II

The visual liberation of public spaces

In 1900, the liberation of sexuality came in the guise of public visibility. Instead of demanding, as Feydeau did, that people be allowed to walk around nude in their homes, the movements that fought against Article 330 claimed the right to reveal themselves and to be seen in public places. It was as if that which was to be repressed "even at home" sought to be expressed outside the home.

Even though it was sufficient to be seen in one's bedroom through a hole in the wall to be punished for indecent exposure, theaters were filled with nude female dancers, models from art studios exposed their breasts at parties, directors staged imitations of sexual scenes, nudists undressed in the great outdoors. Certainly, these daring dancers, models, and directors were well and truly worried about the court and, if the nudists were not, it was because they set up their spaces such that they could not be seen from the outside. Nevertheless each of these contemporaneous movements constituted a true force of resistance against Article 330. And they ended by winning, at least in part, in the 1930s, although up into the 1970s, society continued to punish persons caught in their bedrooms because they had not locked their doors.

This seeming peculiarity can only be explained by the crisis in the politics of space initiated by the Ponce decision. In the public world, insomuch as it was instituted by the 1810 Code, individuals were required to hide everything *because* people could see everything and show everything in private spaces. It was therefore logical that Article 330's invasion of private spaces produced a certain loosening of the grip that it held on public spaces.

Two methods were used to liberalize visibility in public spaces. The first was that of the chaste nudes. Courthouses became the theater for struggles aimed at admitting that nudity could be no more obscene than the wings of angels. A naked person was chaste, even more chaste than a clothed body as long as it was "veiled" by artistic, hygienic, athletic or philosophical goals. In substance, nudity could dress itself in chaste motives to divest itself of all obscenity. This battle was first won in theaters, before being waged on the beaches and in other open public spaces during the 1960s and 1970s.

The second method was much more radical than the first, for it sought to attack publicity rather than the meaning that judges were required to attribute to nudity. This could allow people to witness sexual scenes that were much cruder than the chaste nudes. The goal of these theories was to permit people to see in public spaces the same things that they saw in private spaces.

In order to do this, society sought first by means of deceptive measures to pass off public performances as private. Then, the beginning of the 1950s saw the development of certain theories, the goal of which was to convince people that the consent of participants could transform public spectacles into private spectacles. The new, more liberal case law of the Court of Cassation in regard to publicity gave these theories a more solid foundation. Indeed, for the first time since the Ponce decision, the Court of Cassation conferred on consent not only the power of extending publicity but also of imposing limits upon it.

During the 1960s, the tolerance of the office of the public prosecutor and successive administrations strengthened these novel theories. Thus, in theaters one could see plays with lots of "sexual" content without giving rise to any convictions for indecent exposure.

But this sort of "enthusiasm" for public exhibition of sexuality was curbed near the end of the 1970s when it became clear, through a series of decisions handed down by trial judges followed by the Court of Cassation, that the old doctrines were still alive: *the consent of spectators was not always sufficient to consider a public spectacle to be a private spectacle.* It was therefore necessary for the law to change so that these new practices could be situated on a more solid foundation.

In any event, French society was in the midst of a slow but inexorable bleeding of the public world into the private: a process of homogenization, of which no one was yet aware, had already been set in motion. In an experimental and halting manner, this period—still haunted by the past while being drawn towards the future—saw the beginning of the decline of spatial techniques as hegemonic structures that governed sexuality.

5

The wars of the chaste nude

From the final decade of the nineteenth century, a social movement at once powerful and multi-faceted, spontaneous and rational, disorganized and logical, tried to convince society to accept nudity in performances and fought against the traditional interpretation of Article 330 of the Penal Code, which understood nudity as a punishable act when committed in a public space.

Indeed, the groups that comprised this movement did not share the same values, and they sometimes did not show solidarity with one another. Those who considered themselves true artists did not want to be put in the same category as those who sought to partake in the business of eroticism. In this demand, liberals perceived a willingness to separate the law from a religion-inspired morality, while others denounced the lascivious and pornographic character not of the act of being nude but rather the act of dressing oneself.

The argument that brought these philosophically divergent groups together was that nudity did not have to be understood as a signifier to be associated with a fixed signified: obscenity. Rather, society and its judges were meant to understand that nudity could be dressed in the veil of art, hygiene and sport, thus neutralizing all its sexual or pornographic connotations. The defenders of the nude lost their struggle at the beginning of the twentieth century despite the outrage of artists and intellectuals. But the argumentation that they had advanced to distinguish between chaste and obscene nudes would triumph some decades later, until nudity was finally admitted in public space. And, henceforth, the entire culture of the body and appearance would come to be split in two.

I Precedents

The event considered to be the trigger of the "war of the nude" was the decision made by the Parliament to end theatrical censorship. The National Assembly withdrew authorization granted to inspectors who were responsible for censorship on 17 November 1904, and the Senate confirmed this measure on 8 April 1905.[1]

However, this war had already broken out a dozen or so years before, at the Bal des Quat'z'Arts, organized by several students at the Moulin-Rouge on 8 February 1893. The first Bal des Quat'z'Arts had taken place on 23 April 1892 in the most peaceful and suitable manner possible in the ballroom of the Élysée Montmartre. Henri Guillaume, an architectural student, supervised its organization with the studios of the École des Beaux-Arts. This celebration was so successful that they decided to hold it again the following year in the Moulin-Rouge Theater, but they added one detail that would turn it into a true affront to Article 330.

The students envisioned a procession in which four young women, all models at the artists' studios, would march, "dressed" as if for a sitting—that is, almost nude. The question that this "performance" posed to public opinion was more or less as follows: why can a woman be nude when she is posing for artists and students at the Beaux-Arts but be in contempt of public decency outside of this setting? This question became the most important weapon in the battle for nudity. No doubt, less for its *logic*—we know well that in the domain of customs, rules that societies make for themselves do not respond to constraints of ordinary rationality, but to other rules for which anthropologists, sociologists and jurists try to discover secret patterns—than for its *tactical* power.

Indeed, this question made it possible to point out the privilege of painting and sculpture schools over other arts, such as theater and dance, in the exploration and utilization of nudity. In so doing, it became possible to outline a general theory of artistic nudity, free of all obscene or pornographic content. In any case, the question raised by the students of the École des Beaux-Arts was so important that even twelve years later Pierre Louÿs used it to protest against the suits filed against dance and theater in the name of equality in art with respect to nudity. He wrote:

> Why don't you conduct police raids in all rooms where women undress in public? It is not in the theater that you must begin your inquiry; it is at school—On Rue Bonaparte, the State runs the largest school of higher learning in the world [...], where the fine arts are taught. Each of our artists is obligated to go through this establishment [...]. And when a young man enrolls [...], he is made to draw nude women. These women are not presented as they are in the theater, from a particular perspective, with lighting tricks that turn their bodies into virtual apparitions [...]; they are exposed in plain daylight, three paces away from schoolboys, who are ordered to copy all the lines of this nudity that you declare shameful in other settings—a spectacle that you refuse 50-year-old men in a theater, but impose upon minors in your classrooms [...]. And the State that pays these models to undress in front of these young pupils is the same State that says to artists currently being prosecuted: Have you played Galatea, mademoiselle? I will send you to Saint-Lazare [...]. I will give you a criminal record that will shut you out of the Odéon. I will end your career in formal art.[2]

But nobody judged the performance of the Bal des Quat'z'Arts in that same way. Some days later, following commentaries and drawings appearing in the newspapers, Senator Béranger, the president of the League Against Licentiousness in the Streets, protested, and an investigation was opened. A union of models joined the League together, declaring themselves scandalized that the "models" were used for exhibitionism at a "pornographic ball."

The director of the École des Beaux-Arts handed a petition over to the Minister of Justice, signed by several hundred students who claimed not to have been instigated by any pornographic motives. However, the investigation followed its course, and Henri Guillaume and the four models were summoned to the 11th Criminal Tribunal of Paris.

During the case, the rowdy audience took the side of the accused, and *Le Courrier français* produced with delight a report as a sort of continuation of the trial of the Bal des Quat'z'Arts. Even a police superintendent made a deposition that nothing that he had seen had shocked him. He stated: "there were models in academic or artistic poses that could not offend anyone. I had been a peace officer for seven years when I was tasked with overseeing the Bal de l'Opéra. There I witnessed many more obscenities than at the Bal de Quat'z'Arts. With the procession finished, all the models retired to their lodgings."[3]

The Public Minister showed himself to be very merciful and each person found guilty was punished with a fine of 100 francs. The defenders of nudity took this sentence as a veritable success.[4] One journalist from *Le Courrier français* allowed himself even to end the judicial episode with this line: "Eh, time for Modesty to make an exit." But this somewhat premature joy would cost a great deal.

On 1 July 1893, in the Latin Quarter, students organized a "joyous procession" to "shout down" Senator Béranger. The Chief of Police Lozé brought in the Central brigade to intervene with such brutality that an employee of a café was killed by a police officer. The student demonstration then turned into a riot. On 4 July, the dragoons and armored regiments set up camp in the Luxembourg gardens. The Central brigade and Republican Guard occupied Boulevard Saint-Michel and adjacent roads. Under the pretext of tracking down the demonstrators, the police invaded the Charité and Hôtel-Dieu hospitals, brutally attacking interns and penetrating as far as the sick wards. During this time, students were arraigned in the Criminal Tribunal, where they received sentences of unusual harshness.[5] But, at the turn of the century, neither tanks nor violence nor arbitrary sentences would stop public nudity.

With the music halls, there were other legal problems.[6] The police were required to intervene several times to prevent performances that were liable to cause disorder. In 1897, Clara Ward, Princess of Chimay, was forbidden from exhibiting herself in a singlet at the Scala. A performance at the Moulin-Rouge, of an erotic scene played by Colette and the Marquise of Belbeuf, was also shut down.

However, at the same time, stripteases that lacked any great improprieties began to gain tolerance, which would give rise to the idea of the chaste nude in contrast with the obscene nudes of censored performances.

In 1897, Henriette de Serris, assisted by her husband the painter Jean Marcel, had the idea of reproducing on stage, using live models wearing singlets, the most well-known monuments and bas-reliefs from the ancient and modern statuary. Thus, to have the same privileges enjoyed by painters and sculptors on the subject of nudity, these spectacles tried not to push models out of the studios, as during the Bal des Quat'z'Arts, but to imitate the very works for which they had posed. The bodies were motionless and the mise en scène made them appear to be "hidden" by the gaze of the painters and sculptors.

While these living statues began to occupy the stage, the end of theatrical censorship triggered the multiplication of the quantity and types of nudity. In 1907, the same Madame de Serris produced a "genuinely nude" girl at the Alhambra, covered with great care in white [makeup] and pearls. This spectacle, "one of the most beautiful and chaste in the world," created no scandal. Some said, "these are statues themselves, which we believe we see in bronze or marble, and even with opera glasses the illusion does not erase itself."[7] On 12 February 1907, the League Against Licentiousness in the Streets intervened for the first time in order to put an end to such "immodesties,"[8] but without success. People claimed that the "reports" and the way in which newspapers had represented them had been greatly exaggerated.

It took another member of the League to send an officer the next year, in April of 1908, to make a first assessment at the Little-Palace. Thereafter, other official reports were drawn up by the police chiefs and given to the Olympia, the Folies-Royales, and the Folies-Pigalle.

The court cases and the fines began to multiply when a memo from Clemenceau, then the Interior Minister, prohibited the booking of café-concerts outside Paris [en province], "in order to protect these artists' too-revealing charms from any audacious touching by audience members."[9]

But the legal battle would take another, this time cultural, turn and artists, art historians, politicians, moralists and philosophers all took sides for or against nudity. So, apart from the League Against Licentiousness in the Streets, Robert Guillou created l'Action théâtrale [Theatrical Action], which claimed "to keep the French from throwing themselves into modern dramatic depravation, which would end by wiping them out like opium did the Chinese in the past."[10] In the other camp, the defenders of chaste and less chaste nudity protested with a surge of comparable passion.[11]

II The first judges of chaste nudity

On 27 July 1908, the 9th Division of the Criminal Tribunal of the Seine had to decide three cases[12] concerning women who had shown their breasts during performances in Paris in 1908.[13] After numerous debates in the newspapers, magazines and books, both intellectuals and artists—but also all those who fought against the perversion of tradition—waited anxiously for the judges to say what one could show and see in theaters.

For the first time, the judges of the 9th Division made the distinction between chaste nudes that could be shown without risking punishment provided for by Article 330 of the Penal Code, and obscene nudes that had to remain hidden. But this first victory for chaste nudity was, unfortunately, very short-lived.

Motionless nudities in the Théâtre des Folies-Royales

The first case that the judges had to examine concerned nudities produced in the middle of a performance that had taken place at the Théâtre des Folies-Royales on 5 April 1908. One of the actors had announced to 200 audience members that the presentation would conclude with the appearance of naked women. Upon this announcement, the curtains rose, revealing at the back of the stage a frame in which well-known paintings were reproduced in succession—*L'Amour et Psyché*, *La Femme au masque*, *Les Trois Grâces*—whose characters were acted out by Mlles Laisney, Thierry and Dauhault, all professional models.

In these "tableaux," the Tribunal said, "the aforementioned appeared completely nude, and keeping absolutely still, so as to give the illusion of groups in painting and sculpture." The Tribunal also took care to point out that "the sexual parts, as well as all that which could allow them to be seen, were concealed by a piece of flesh-colored fabric, tied by invisible thread; that the characters' hands were placed in order to conceal the middle of the body, covered by a scarf of light gauze."

And here is what came to divide the heated debates that had invaded the books and newspapers: "if, given our current customs and theater, the tangible act of which the defendants are accused can appear to be suggestive and risqué, it would be prudent in assessing the act not to visualize it as isolated but to take into account the space in which it was enacted, under which circumstances and the goals it pursued." And yet, according to the Tribunal:

> the distance of the characters placed in the frame at the back of the theater's stage, the makeup with which they were covered, their purely plastic poses devoid of any detail of lascivious inspiration, their motionlessness for the duration of the performance, and the care taken to efface anything that could give the tableaux an obscene and licentious allure in order to give the audience only the impression

> of art coming from natural and plastic beauty, all made it permissible to think that Cohen, in presenting these tableaux publicly, and Mlles Aisne, Thierry and Dauhault, in lending their support to this presentation, committed no immoral or licentious act of a nature that could lead to scandal or harm the modesty of those who witnessed it.

The living statues of the Théâtre de la Folie-Pigalle

The second case related to a performance that had taken place on 5 April 1908 at the Théâtre de la Folie-Pigalle before around 400 persons. It contained a pantomime entitled "In a dream" [Dans un rêve], and performed by Mlle Aymos. In the course of this act, "the young lady Aymos, having to serve as a model for a sculptor infatuated with beauty, appears at the back of the stage in a frame separated from the audience by a screen adorning the bay window; first she is draped in light cloth. Little by little, in plastic poses, she removes the cloth so as to reveal herself at the end of the piece, and at the moment when the curtains drop, she is completely nude, with only a necklace and a belt of glass jewels."

However, the Tribunal continued:

> in addition to the screen placed in front of the bay window, where the artist moved about amid electric projections of varied tones shading the body and its contours, the model's sexual parts were concealed by a piece of pink taffeta silk; whereas, it is true, as the chief of police mentioned in his report that he had been able to observe that the young lady Aymos had 'shaved her armpits and pubis'; inasmuch as the precision is noted by this magistrate, far from lending the nudity an element of obscenity, it served on the contrary to diminish its licentious nature.

Thus, "this detail, which did not at all escape the visual perception of the chief of police, worried about faithfully fulfilling the mission that had been given to him, must have escaped the notice of spectators more perceptive than he in art impressions, and whose own concerns were not the same as his."

By returning to the distinctions established in the previous case, the Tribunal articulated clearly "that it would be excessive to isolate the material act for which the defendants Aymos and Parcelier are blamed, to consider the act separately from the circumstances under which it was committed and the pursuit of artistic interest that it could represent." Thus, the Tribunal stated:

> the young lady Aymos, passing for an artist of talent, seems to have been, in her performance, in her gestures, and in her plastic poses, inspired only by an aesthetic sentiment devoid of all obscene or licentious intentions. Given the precautions taken, combined with the lighting effects and artistically prepared and deployed gauzes,—along with the distancing of the artist changing positions at the back of the stage, behind a gossamer curtain, the artistic charm that emanated from the grace of her movements, the elegance of her postures, and the makeup in which she was covered—all worked together to remove any immodesty from the spectacle by giving the impression that the audience found itself in the presence of a statue that had truly come to life.

In support of its theories of chaste nudity, the Tribunal cited the letter of an academician named Jules Claretie, who had rushed to Mlle Aymos's aid. The judges said: "the artistic effect provided by this spectacle is attested by a letter appearing in the case file and written by a member of the Académie Française, whose authority and sincerity in matters of theater cannot be placed in doubt." "In this letter, after having professed his respect for the president of the League of Licentiousness in the Streets [sic], the author notably said 'that in M. Parcelier's play at the Folies-Pigalle, there was nothing that could awaken unhealthy thoughts, that the appearance of the dancer contained nothing that could resemble a corrupt exhibition ... Finally, the spectacle left no impression but that of art.' This assessment, so valuable to the Tribunal on account of the uncontested artistic competence of this leading figure as well as the circumstances outlined above, do not allow us to consider the act of which Aymos and Parcelier have been accused as *constituting indecent exposure.*" This was how the Tribunal justified its second and resounding acquittal.

The less chaste and less motionless nudities of the Little Palace

The individuals charged in the third case did not meet with the same fate, for they were far from resembling statues. On 12 May 1908, at the Little Palace Theater, directed by M. Chatillon, a pantomime titled "Intoxication of Ether" [Griserie d'éther] was performed in front of numerous persons at the end of the spectacle:

> During this pantomime, the young ladies Bouzon and Lepelley interpreted a scene of inebriation and lesbian passion. Lepelley bent backward over an armchair, revealing her torso and breasts, while Bouzon

> sat near her and also uncovered her own torso and breasts, pressed against her partner, throwing herself into her arms putting her mouth on hers, caressing her breasts with the hand that she also let go lower down. The hugging only stopped to allow Lepelley to express erotic arousal through her facial expressions and the quivering of her body that was provoked by the caresses ministered upon her. By the end of this scene and after this caressing, Bouzon was standing upright, her shirt fallen beneath her knees, and was holding a bouquet of roses that she placed in front of her genitals. Such an exhibition of nudity accompanied by these poses, hugging, caresses, kisses or their simulacra, and solely intended to display perverse passions, could only be considered as a call to the crudest, most unsettling and dangerous lechery, and could not be judged and denounced too severely.

According to the Tribunal, since M. Chatillon's spectacle did not have an artistic mission, it could only have aimed to make money with an eye to awakening unhealthy curiosities in its audience. But the actresses were considered to be "influenced" by M. Chatillon, the theater's director, and thus, not completely free to escape from such obscenities. Thus, they were only sentenced to fifteen days in prison—which was suspended—and a fine of 50 francs. M. Chatillon himself was sentenced to three months in prison without remission, and a fine of 50 francs.

How the Criminal Tribunal of the Seine stopped believing in the existence of chaste nudity

Some months later, on 1 December 1908, the same Tribunal entirely changed its first doctrine[14] that allowed it to distinguish between chaste and obscene nudities. The case that it had to judge concerned a group of seven artists who had presented themselves nude, that is, showing their breasts, in the Pigall's restaurant, in 1908. These women, according to the Tribunal, wore only "a belt of glass jewelry, 5 to 10 centimeters in thickness, and a G-string; that Ms. B.'s upper body was fully nude but was covered below the hips by a skirt."

Even if, according to the court, the defendants

> only confessed to artistic dances that were not obscene in character—neither in the pose taken nor in the gestures accompanying them—and it is also quite clear that, given the distance between them and the public, they were unable to communicate with the audience; they were separated from it—whether by transparent curtains or by gauze

> veils. So, given that no obscene or pornographic character could be discerned, the only question that is posed is whether the living nude can by itself be considered to be liable to cause scandal, wound the modesty of those who can witness it, and thus fall under the heel of Article 330 of the Penal Code.

Evidently in discomfort, the Tribunal makes clear "that it is not at all about demarcating where a neckline must stop. Such a definition would be impossible to formulate since it necessarily varies with customs, climates and countries."

To justify this turnaround in doctrine, the court added that:

> each case submitted to the Tribunal must be specifically examined and can lead to a different decision; to provide for a healthy and just application of the law, it comes down to judging with reason, good sense, and taking account of the place where we find ourselves, and of the state of civilization and the progress of the habits and customs of the country where we live, regardless of all other thought. Thus posed, the question could not create any doubt, and the act of showing oneself in public, whether completely nude with a simple belt of glass jewelry and a G-string, or with the upper body nude down to the hips, is incontestably liable to cause scandal and wound the modesty of those who have this spectacle in front of their eyes.

This is why the actresses were sentenced to a fine of 50 francs, and the director of the spectacle to a month in prison without remission and a fine of 200 francs.

Chaste nudity and the Court of Appeals of Paris

Meanwhile, on 27 July 1908, the acquittals of the Criminal Tribunal, made on the grounds that nudity in these cases was motivated by artistic intent, came under scrutiny when the public prosecutor filed an appeal.

The Court of Appeals of Paris confirmed the reversal in doctrine of the Tribunal of the Seine on 1 December 1908, which could no longer conceive of the existence of the category of the chaste nude in regard to Article 330 of the Penal Code. Contradicting the 27 July 1908 decision of the district court [*première instance*] that had acquitted the "statue dancers," the Court of Appeals decided as follows on 16 December 1908:

> The law, not having defined indecent exposure, this qualification must be applied to the public display of nudities to such an extent

> that exceeds established customs. Specifically, the act by a woman of exhibiting herself in the nude on a theater's stage, having only a light G-string around the waist, constitutes indecent exposure; the more or less artistic frame given to this exhibition does not remove its immoral character.[15]

The theories of the League Against Licentiousness in the Streets had triumphed. But, as numerous commentators noted, the actresses' costumes were from then on kept to the bare minimum. Thus, to the small piece of fabric that hid shaved genitals, there came to be added two other small triangles of cloth that served to hide the nipples. It was the symbol more than the part of the body itself that one attempted to hide.

Nudity was ready to lead all of the fights to come, for it was already at that point where none of these minuscule triangles could henceforth ignore or stop it. It took until the 1930s for the doctrine that had emerged from the legal decisions to be transformed and for society to return to what the Criminal Tribunal of the Seine had established on 27 July 1908.

III The implicit triumph of the nearly-nude: the Joan Warner case[16]

In January 1935, the beautiful Joan Warner was dancing at The Bagdad, a tea shop in Paris, when a witness, M. Boverat, the vice president of the Superior Committee on Birthrates and the national secretary of the National Alliance for the Growth of the French Population, shocked by the spectacle, denounced it in a letter addressed to the police chief on 7 January, accusing Warner of indecent exposure. M. Boverat declared in front of the Criminal Tribunal of the Seine "to have seen a part of what the G-string was supposed to cover up."

On 9 January, the police commissioner reported that Joan Warner took her clothes off successively and began to appear nude, when she performed her last steps, which lasted around fifteen seconds, at the end of which, covered in an overcoat, she disappeared. However, according to the commissioner, "the brevity of this exhibition, the half-darkness in which she was presented, the purity of the choreographic expressions [...] allow us to attach to this spectacle an artistic character." And, thinking he was contributing by his support to not punishing the dancer, he believed it good to add that the artistic character of her nudity came from the care that she had taken "to powder her body so that the flesh tones and brown spots of hair were covered up by a whitish tint reminiscent of statues."

But this bothered the dancer, who affirmed that she was wearing a G-string and that the makeup was only supposed to hide the small piece of fabric and not her pubic hair. Rather belatedly, her lawyer submitted the supposed G-string to the Tribunal, but, unfortunately for the dancer, presented on its own, it proved nothing. The question thus remained intact: Was she or was she not wearing this face-saving piece of fabric?

However, the Criminal Tribunal of the Seine found the question too difficult to answer and declared "that it is enough to affirm that makeup and such a minuscule and invisible G-string cannot make the character of nudity disappear; furthermore, that the advertisement announced the performance to include full nudity, and all the arrangements were made to give a complete impression of it."

The most important thing was not, therefore, to know whether the dancer was wearing a G-string. Only the visual illusion of nudity that came from the entire mise en scène counted. But, given "the real character of art without any ambiguous detail of the spectacle," the Tribunal only imposed a symbolic sentence of a fine of 50 francs. And if it applied this fine in spite of the artistic character of the performance, the truth is that the act served a similar function in the eyes of the judges as did the small G-string. Indeed, according to the Tribunal, "given that the impossibility of defining with precision the extent to which the domain of art extends and where lechery begins, an attitude, a gesture, a look that is able to pass instantaneously from one to another, we are led to conclude that full live nudity is not acceptable in public."

The Court of Appeals of Paris judged the position of the Tribunal to be frivolous. To the higher court, it seemed evident that one could not remain only on the level of illusion and that one had to know *truly* whether or not the dancer was wearing a G-string. From the resolution of this delicate enigma there had to come a decision of acquittal or punishment.

The commissioner of police had believed that Joan Warner was fully nude, but what he had really seen was only white powder and so the question of knowing if the makeup was placed on the skin or on a piece of fabric could not be solved based on his testimony. Thus, although the court only had the statements of the witness

Boverat at its disposal, it found it suitable to interpret them despite their flagrant contradictions.

Indeed, this individual had first written to the chief of police that the dancer was totally nude, then stated to the examining magistrate that it was not impossible that she was wearing a G-string "but that he had the impression of noticing the top of the female sex." Then he had affirmed at the hearing "that he had seen that she did not have a G-string and that the top of her genitals was visible."

The conclusions that the Tribunal derived from this were thus inevitable. If the witness has seen the top of the defendant's genitals, the truth of the matter is that the dancer did have on a G-string, but which did not fulfill its task, or by some accident it had failed to do so. Thus her responsibility came from the fact of not having taken sufficient precautions to protect public modesty in procuring herself a G-string effective enough to accomplish its functions in an adequate manner. In a way, this brings to mind the case that I discussed briefly in Part I, which was brought against Father Bérard for not having taken care of a hole in his cassock.[17]

But the decision of the court finally concurred with that of the Tribunal. Additionally—and this is without doubt the most extraordinary part—the question of Joan Warner's G-string made them forget another that was almost as important. For, by dint of discussing the dancer's genitals, everybody admitted tacitly that the fact that she showed her breasts did not entail any harm to public modesty, which contradicted case law from 1908.

Thus, those who were interested in these debates understood immediately that the question of bared breasts had been resolved thanks to Joan Warner's G-string. And they had a resounding confirmation of this sometime later with the so-called "case of the Pezon menagerie."

During a performance in Clermont-Ferrand, a female tamer had entered, undressed, into the lions' cage. The Criminal Tribunal had acquitted her and, on the appeal of the public prosecutor's office, the Court of Appeals of Riom decided on 16 November 1937 that there had been no indecent exposure when a bare-breasted woman showed herself in the cage of a menagerie among wild animals. This ruling was derived from the fact that the "spectacle of the nudity of the human body—frequent in our era for reasons of hygiene and aesthetics—has nothing in itself that can offend a normal, even delicate modesty, if it is not accompanied by the exhibition of sexual parts or by lascivious or obscene attitudes or gestures."[18]

This rule would be applied for nearly forty years in Parisian music halls. The public powers remained impassive in front of performances of live nudity when a minuscule opaque triangle covered just the genital split, without showing any more, the pubis itself being shaved and made up—without a doubt, in Roger Doublier's words: "to give to this part of the body the 'pallor of statues' that the police commissioner so appreciated on 9 January 1935."[19] The decision handed down by the judges of Riom not only invoked art but also hygiene as being a good reason to be naked. The judges doubtlessly were alluding to French nudist practices, which were beginning to be seen with a great deal of benevolence by the authorities. But what seems the most groundbreaking in this decision is that it was no longer a question of motion or motionlessness, of art or the absence thereof to make it such that nudities were not obscene. On the contrary, for there to be obscenity, it was necessary for the exhibition of genitals, or breasts for that matter, to be accompanied by lascivious attitudes. Obscenity was like a piece of clothing that made nudity unacceptable. This implied a radical change in relation to the theories in force at the turn of the century.

However, some years later, on 8 November 1950, the Tribunal of Saint-Lô punished a stallholder at a fair who had been presenting inside his stall, in a glass box, one naked woman with only a G-string, on the grounds that this spectacle could not have presented any artistic character.[20] For this tribunal, as opposed to that of Riom, the veil of art was indispensable to protect the spectacle of all obscenity.

This debate was to become central during the period when the new fashion of the monokini would be judged, for the fact of knowing if, to be legal, bare breasts must be covered or not would determine the fate of this new bathing suit in communal spaces such as beaches, streets and in open public. This question would also be decisive in making fashion compatible with law.

Indeed, historians of fashion and culture have not stopped foregrounding the indisputable fact of the progressive baring of women, but also of men, in communal public spaces since the beginning of the twentieth century. Female dancers, actors, nudists, and even beast tamers were not the only protagonists of this central event in the history of customs that constituted the rendering visible [*mise en visibilité*] of nudity in public spaces.

The French fashion designer Paul Poiret made the corset disappear around 1900, and since then the “true” body has been put on stage, skirts have shrunk, swimsuits have been reduced, and trousers have been made more formfitting.[21]

The case of the monokini constituted a turning point in this story, for it would oblige the Court of Cassation to say whether the judges of Riom or those from Saint-Lô were correct. And we will see that, following the court’s decision, fashion—which as we know, sets forth constraints occasionally much stronger than those set by the sword of judges—was placed in a state of contradiction with law. But not for long.

IV The monokini affair, or the last war of the nearly-nude

Some years before its decision regarding the monokini, the Court of Cassation had come to a decision on the exhibition of bare breasts in public space other than beaches or theaters.

One individual, A., had invited a young lady, P., with whom he had maintained friendly relations, to take a seat in his automobile for a ride in the surrounding area. A. had stopped his car on the road’s shoulder, so he could photograph his friend in the middle of the countryside after helping her to take off her sweater and getting her to take off her bra in order to exhibit her breasts. The case came to court, which did not find this behavior acceptable. This is how, on 4 May 1961, the Court of Appeals of Nîmes decided that “for a girl, the act of exposing one’s breasts in a deserted place in and of itself constituted indecent exposure […] and the proposer’s act of suggesting to said person that she be photographed in this manner characterized an act of complicity in said crime.” This decision signaled the triumph of the old theories, for it did not even make reference to the absence of the veil of art to hide obscenity but rather directly to the restrictive doctrines of the 1908 Court of Appeals of Paris.

The mysterious Mr. A. appealed this decision. He claimed that “even though in many public spaces the sparse nature of a woman’s clothing allows one to see and imagine much more than a woman’s chest, the police do not intervene” and “that in any case, indecent exposure consists of an act that is obscene, immoral, or against modesty, that does not include the fact of uncovering her breasts when there is no one around." But on 9 May 1962,[22] the Court of Cassation rejected this appeal and confirmed the decision of the Court of Nîmes, thus confirming the most restrictive doctrines with regard to nudity.

The case of the monokini blew up two years after this first decision.

But, before analyzing the case, let us take a moment to review the arrival of the item of clothing itself. The monokini was invented in 1964 by the Austrian fashion designer Gudi Gernreich (1922–1985), considered to be the creator of the clothing of the sexual revolution. He baptized it the "monokini" as if it derived from its ancestor the "bikini," suggesting implicitly that it resulted from a nearly biological evolution, going from "bi" to "mono" by the elimination of the superfluous. However, the "bi" of the bikini had nothing to do with the two pieces of this other bathing suit invented twenty years earlier by the French fashion designer Louis Réard. "Bikini" designated an archipelago in the Pacific where the Americans had conducted failed nuclear tests on 1 July 1946. Thinking that his creation was going to have the same impact as an atomic bomb, Réard chose this name for the item of clothing that Micheline Bernardini wore on 5 July 1946 during the election of the most beautiful swimmer of the Piscine Molitor.[23]*

But, if the bikini led to a certain scandal, it was not because it offended public modesty but rather because the suit respected it in a disconcerting manner. As small as the bikini was, it covered the parts that the case law had mandated be hidden, as if it wanted to highlight, through its economy of means, the absurdity of the conventions that territorialized the body into so-called authorized and forbidden parts for the public gaze. The monokini, on the other hand, for the first time came to break this tacit agreement between fashion and the rules protecting public modesty.

As soon as they began to hear of this new item of clothing, the mayors of seaside cities immediately took their stand, either forbidding or authorizing it. Upset by these initiatives, the Interior Minister issued a memorandum instructing the courts to punish women dressed in this manner for indecent exposure. Certain

* Translator's note: The Piscine Molitor was part of a now-defunct swimming pool complex at Porte Molitor in the 16th arrondissement of Paris.

somewhat zealous magistrates proposed the creation of a special offense of "indecent accoutrement," which would be applied both to those who wore the monokini as well as its manufacturers.[24]

Perfectly indifferent to these governmental tensions, in the month of July 1964, M. Milanini, the director of the "Hawai [sic] Beach," situated on the Promenade de la Croisette in Cannes, asked 21-year-old Claudine Durand to play ping-pong dressed in a monokini, in return for payment of 35 francs. He had not sought to gather the fifty or so gawkers crowded on the sidewalk above the beach but rather to photograph this young lady in order to promote his establishment. The two accomplices were punished by the trial court of Grasse on 22 September 1964.[25]

However, the monokini was not the principal defendant. Other external elements intervened to perturb the logic of this legal decision. Indeed, according to the trial court, the accused woman had exhibited herself "in return for payment, at the instigation of an individual pursuing an advertisement campaign, in the middle of a veritable theatrical set, on a cloudy day, on a deserted beach, with a scandalous advertisement for background." The wise commentators maliciously concluded that, "if the weather had not been cloudy, if the beach had not been deserted …" then the girl in the monokini would have been acquitted by the trial court of Grasse.

In any case, in January 1965, the Court of Appeals of Aix acquitted the accused individuals on the grounds that the performance of nudity had nothing in it that could outrage the modesty of a normal, even sensitive person, given that the act had not been accompanied by the exhibition of sexual parts, or by lascivious or obscene attitudes or gestures.[26] The Court of Appeals of Aix thus applied to this beach case the same reasoning that the judges of the Court of Appeals of Riom had used in 1937, involving the exhibition of a woman's breasts in a menagerie.[27] This was a victory for the more liberal theories that did not require any artistic veil to hide the obscenity of bare breasts.

The decision was extensively covered both in legal reviews as well as in the daily papers. *France-Soir* published a photo of the young lady "in work uniform," to use the expression employed by the defenders of modesty. The jurist Hugueney, who did not condemn this decision, nevertheless hoped that "the two pieces minus one does not abuse its victory, that it remains on the beach and does not embark on a conquest of the city."[28] It is as if the beach were not a communal public space, such as a street, but sort of compartmentalized, separated from other public spaces.

But the wishes of this benevolent jurist were quickly crushed, for on 29 May 1965, the criminal trial court of Grasse punished another young woman who, this time, had "shown herself in a monokini, with her breasts bared, on the Boulevard de la Croisette in Cannes, in front of at least 150 persons."[29] The trial court pointed out that, "in France, following our present customs, the sight of a woman exhibiting her entire naked breasts on the streets of a city, even in the proximity of a beach, is liable to provoke scandal and offend the modesty of the greatest number of people."[30]

This decision added to the prevailing confusion, because the expression "even in the proximity of a beach" removed from this space its status as a communal and open public space, and aligned with Louis Hugueney's implicit theories of compartmentalization of public spaces.

Sometime later, the public prosecutor at the Court of Cassation, following the orders of the Minister of Justice, appealed the decision of the Aix Court on 20 January 1965, which had acquitted the two accused individuals for the wearing of a monokini on the beach. However, this decision was struck down by an appeal in the Court of Cassation only "in the interest of the law," that is, the charged persons were still exonerated.

Following the government's position, the Court of Cassation decided on 22 December 1965 that the acts prosecuted were "a provocative exhibition liable to offend public modesty and hurt the moral feelings of those who have borne witness to it."[31]

The Court of Cassation [la Cour Suprême] maintained its position in 1972 in a case in which two women had been fined 200 francs for indecent exposure on the grounds that, "they had only worn thongs, leaving their breasts bare on a beach that was not private and was accessible to the public."[32]

From these decisions, we could thus conclude that, according to the Court of Cassation, bare breasts were only authorized in theaters because they were cloaked by artistic goals. Fashion could not take on the status of a veil in the same way as was afforded to art. Or, in any case, breasts were required to be covered by something, and that the absence of obscene gestures or exhibition of genitals alone was not enough not to offend modesty.

But these frameworks did not prevent either the increasing popularity of the monokini, or the fact that certain mayors, such as the mayor of Nice, since 1975, authorized it expressly, even though these authorizations had no legal basis.[33]

Furthermore, bare breasts were visible from 1975 onwards, even on streets, and in cities such as Juan-les-Pins, where women clothed in this manner exhibited themselves in bathhouses. The same year, a survey published in *L'Express* revealed that 76 percent of French persons were not shocked by the monokini.

To be sure, no official act legalized the fact of exhibiting one's breasts on the beach, but prosecutions ceased. This tolerance marked the implicit triumph of the judges of Riom, just as the decision of the Court of Appeals of Aix had anticipated.

The fact remains that wearing the monokini to this day seems to be tinged with this past of the chaste nude. In this way, the rule set forth by the case law of the 1930s, according to which bared breasts did not constitute indecent exposure as long as they were not accompanied with obscene or provocative attitudes, seems still to haunt the users of the monokini like those who look at them.

Some recent studies conducted by sociologists on naked breasts on the beach show us to what extent these constraints are respected.[34] In this way, women who reveal their breasts have a non-provocative attitude; they justify their choice by claiming the natural character of the nudity of their chests, the pleasurable contact with the water, as well as the advantages of tanning without lines. The aesthetic criterion works since those who deem their breasts to be ugly do not uncover them.[35] These constraints concern men equally. It would seem that they do not approach women with bare breasts on beaches in the same manner as they do those who have them covered—that a restraint takes hold of them, as if the fear of desire provoked by these bare chests imposes an indispensible repression. What's more, the monokini seems to transform the politics of the gaze, by inverting the asymmetrical logic that existed formerly between those who exposed themselves as always guilty, and the onlooker as always innocent. People do not look at a woman in a monokini in the same way as one whose clothes cover her more. It is as if the monokini had only been able to impose itself to the extent that its sexual charge had been erased.

With the monokini, the theory of the "scandal," for inciting unlawful assembly or an unbridled arousal resulting from certain public performances of a sexual nature, can no longer be effectively argued. It is those who look and not those who expose themselves who will have to control themselves. The appearance of the monokini is thus the foundational moment of a new kind of legality concerning nudities and eroticisms in open public spaces. Beaches are no longer the only spaces to enjoy the privilege of chaste bare breasts. Bare breasts will no longer constitute an offense in all public spaces, as long as the "genitals" remain covered and women who expose their breasts do not take on obscene attitudes. The beach is not an enclosed space such as an auditorium, and people can show the same things there as in other public places.

Thus, from now on, nudities will have to be "covered" by nonprovocative attitudes in open public places, while clothes can permit behaviors with a stronger erotic charge. And if, after the mid-1970s, women have not exhibited their breasts anywhere else besides beaches, it is not due to the constraints posed by Article 330 but because it is only when we are dressed in an open public space that we can adopt more erotic behaviors.

This rupture between nudity as the signified and the obscene—if not the sexual—as the signifier was radicalized after the 1992 moral revolution, and came to impact, as we will see, the genitals themselves.[36]

But French society has not yet acknowledged what it owes to nudists in the creation of this new legality of nudes in open spaces. This is why it would behoove us to focus on the group of individuals that deeply reflected on the theories of the chaste nude, well before the monokini fashion trend was imposed on the beaches.

V Naturistic nudities

Originally, naturism[37] was a philosophy of care, a neo-Hippocratic medicine that sought to utilize natural elements toward therapeutic ends. Clothing appeared to be an obstacle to this medical use of nature, especially to the exposition of the entire body to sunrays.

But, for that matter, for naturists, nudity had—and has always had—another political and ethical meaning. Clothes were conceived of as being unnatural to man, artifices that served to disguise oneself and prevent the individual from finding his or her *true being*. According to this doctrine, clothes were the vehicle for lies, sickness and falsity. Moreover, they were thought to have brought pornography and obscenity into being.[38]

The expression *Nacktkultur*, or "culture of the nude," appeared for the first time in Germany in 1906, coined by Heinrich Pudor, who was the first to claim a "right to nudism." The expression "nudism" was conceived to fight against the possible confusion between pornography and this *chaste* form of baring oneself.

In Germany, naturism was perceived as a new political philosophy of life, free for good from the grip of medicine. Nudity was inscribed in a program to reform lifestyle, and which radically critiqued industrial society, and contested bourgeois values. To bare oneself, according to this philosophy, was a necessary step for both individual and social regeneration. Naturism saw great success in Germany. At the outbreak of World War I, more than 300 nudist associations could be counted.

In France, naturism took more time to emancipate itself from its purely medical dimension, and certain doctors rebelled against full nudity, which they considered immoral. It took until 1927 for Marcel Kienné de Mongeot to create the first nudist organization in France. From then on, nudity became an imperative for life in the open air. His concept of "gymnosophy," or wisdom of the nude, quickly constituted a central element of naturism.

For Kienné de Mongeot, current morals lead us to look at flesh as an impure object, and reveal themselves to be impotent in fighting against the perversion of morals. The obligation to hide one's genitals, far from guaranteeing the purity of human behaviors was seen, on the contrary, to allow a "vagrancy of the imagination" to develop, leading to vice and debauchery. Conversely, frank, full and non-erotic nudity was seen to be a powerful factor for the collective strengthening of morals. The nudity of the nudists, unlike the clothes of a hypocritical society, was supposed to lead to a chaste and virtuous existence. However, according to them, one ought not to join a nudist center in order to become chaste by shedding one's clothes. Rather, one had to be chaste *before* deciding to go there.

Thus, to join a nudist center, candidates were required to present a medical certificate and a certificate of good conduct from their municipality's city hall. The rules, under pain of exclusion, forbade smoking, drinking alcohol, putting on makeup, and wearing jewelry. Married and non-married couples were forbidden from showing any sign of affection, and holding hands was barely tolerable. The behavior of each member had to be irreproachable and unambiguous.

The nearly monastic purity of the nudists quickly won them the sympathy of the authorities. So, on 23 June 1933, the commune of Hyères passed a decree, still in effect today for the Île du Levant (which falls under its jurisdiction), which assessed a fine only for those who were completely nude in the village of Héliopolis and on the roads. The required outfit is the small triangle of fabric that only hides the genitals, for both women and men, which has given the Île du Levant the name "the island of bare breasts."[39]

In February 1950, the French Federation of Naturism was formally founded and its statutes were registered. On 26 November 1950, the FFN counted twenty-six associations comprising 1,630 members, that is, people who were granted *naturist permits* to access these centers.[40]

As Francine Barthe-Deloizy rightly noted, the naturist circles are utopias in the proper sense of the term, for they did not have a space where they could come into being.[41] They had to create new spaces to protect themselves from the surrounding society, which has understood nudity as a crime.

In France, naturists have had to find a way to be able to undress in the open air without violating Article 330 of the Penal Code. Therefore, since the 1930s, they have developed specific architectural forms in order to shelter themselves from complaints and convictions.

As astute observers of the existing case law in regard to spaces that are open but invisible from the outside, such as private fields distant from the view of passersby, naturists have constructed their centers according to the principle of *double enclosure*, that of *access* and that of *visibility*. The first enclosure is constituted by barbed wire and mesh fencing that forbid entry to the property. When the site is situated close to a public road, it is lined with fences and walls, in order to prohibit seeing in from the outside.

Non-visibility and inaccessibility of the exterior assured them the absence of real and virtual publicity. But, because, since the Ponce decision, publicity had also been able to exist in spaces that were nonvisible and inaccessible to the exterior, the fact that persons were required to be nude—that is, that they could not say they were outraged by what they saw—assured them further protection.

From the legal point of view, naturism is practiced between consenting persons, in spaces that are closed and exclusive to publicity much in the same way as it is expressed in theaters. Persons who were admitted into naturist centers were not just anyone who desired to be there, or some random passersby. They were carefully sorted and hand-picked, and even given a membership card: a naturist permit. They all indulged in exhibitionism that, in other contexts, would have been punishable. Indeed, the members of a naturist center formed a set of individuals who not only consented to see, as in performances, but also to *participate* in these performances. As such, it was like a theater only meant for naked actors and actresses without an audience.[42]

However, these persons did not constitute a "nonpublic" either, in the sense of performances, for they had not gathered in a personal and identifiable manner. This was not a group of friends or a network of acquaintances but a group of individuals, strangers to each other, brought together by a common philosophy. Yet, they formed a public in the legal sense.

Despite his extremism in matters of sexual morality and his aversion toward nudism, the magistrate Laplatte wrote: "If the denizens of a thoroughly enclosed naturist camp are truly associates—linked by *vinculum societatis* [the bonds of good company] and hand-picked like sectarians of a Masonic lodge or members of the Rotary—then we must put the sword of the law back into its sheath."[43]

But there is no doubt that the benevolence of the authorities in regard to the naturists came from their conception of chaste nudes. In each naturist center inspectors were charged with ensuring that everyone was completely naked, and that the nudity had no sexual content. Wrongdoers were immediately expelled. Their names were brought to the attention of the French Federation of Naturism, which would no longer renew their naturist permit and, for more security, wrote them down on a "green list" sent to all other centers from which they would be refused access thereafter.

This philosophy of nudity seems to have immediately influenced the case law concerning Article 330 of the Penal Code. Thus, in the decision that I cited regarding the "Pezon menagerie," the judges had included hygiene and sport in addition to art, among the "motives" that could serve to "veil" or redeem nudity.

The most interesting legal questions were posed with the practice of naturism in spaces that were not enclosed, especially since sea-bathing while completely naked was considered to be one of its principal therapeutic elements. Given that, in France, the maritime domain (which has a width of 10 meters from the water)—that is, beaches—is designated as public space where free circulation of individuals is the law, how was one supposed to avoid infringing Article 330?

As Albert Lecocq, the founder of social naturism in the postwar years, puts it:

> In 1950, [...] we started to practice full gymnity with around ten members on the isolated beach adjacent to the new center of Montalivet. This entailed some risks, reactions from the population and summer vacationers, and criminal prosecutions. There were reactions and complaints for years. More and more numerous, the naturists did not give in, or even compromise principles by wearing a minimum amount of clothing. [...] It is true that such experiments have been conducted in a serious manner, in a familial setting and under the vigilant control of naturists themselves.[44]

On 21 July 1967, the mayor of Vendays-Montalivet signed a decree, endorsed by the deputy police chief of Lesparre, authorizing the practice of naturism within a vast portion of the beach of Montalivet (more than 2 kilometers along the coastline, with a width of several hundred meters on average between the ocean and the naturists' domain, where the shops and bungalows, etc., could be found) on the condition that signs be planted at 100 meters from either side of the designated area of the beach, stating the following: "Naturist center in 100 meters. Free passage through beach on the waterfront. Remaining in this zone forbidden without a card from the Naturist Federation of France" (Article 5 of the order of 21 July 1967).

Article 7 states that people not in the Federation were forbidden to remain on this portion of the beach, free access being reserved to a 10-meter-wide band, starting at the water, parallel to the sea, thus making the surface reserved to naturism vary in accordance with the tides, in a manner so as to ensure respect of free public access to the maritime domain.

It is thus evident that persons who crossed this band would see naturists who could be found there as well, and that they could feel like victims of indecent exposure. The fact that they had been warned by the signs is irrelevant. Article 330 had to be applied nonetheless, for we know that municipal decrees cannot override the laws.

According to Roger Doublier, the government had spoken of a "tolerance of an act without legal basis but established by a municipal decree." However, since 1967, not only has no one annulled the decree, rather, on the contrary, other mayors have followed the example of the mayor of Montalivet, especially for the beaches of Jonquet, Sérignan in 1972, and Grau-du-Roi in 1973, etc. On the other hand, at the beaches where this practice is not authorized, for example, at Èze, enforcement of Article 330 remains very active.[45]

Thus, thanks to their theories and practices of the chaste nude, naturists have contributed to the detachment of nudity from obscenity in communal public space, to the extent that the "monokini-wearers," if we believe the sociological studies, have adopted the same irreproachable appearances as them.

But the nudists have gone much further in their process, for they tried by means of one of their members, the excellent jurist Roger Doublier, to create a true theory of alternative spaces of the public visibility of sexuality—the theory of semi-public spaces.[46] This theory conceived of public space as being compartmentalized by the many statutes of visibility and nudity, as a function of the collective consent of individuals who populated it: theaters, normal and nudist beaches, etc. It attempted to construct a politico-legal theory likely to account for what was being produced in the 1960s and 1970s in all spaces, starting from the tolerance—with no legal basis—of some mayors. But this theory, at once ingenious and partisan, did not survive. For, it must be said right away, it was *too chaste* to permit libertines as well to find a place for themselves in the new order born of the moral revolution.

Notes

1 But censorship has remained in place for cinema up to the present day.
2 *Le Journal*, 25 April 1908.
3 *Le Courrier français*, 25 June 1893.
4 During the 23 June hearing, in which the accused from this ball were heard, two other cases of public nudity were also judged. There was also the case of a ball organized by the newspaper *Fin de siècle* on 1 March 1893—with the same models who undressed in the same way—

to which 2,000 persons were invited. At the "supper for 200 women," in a restaurant, one woman undressed in front of all the invitees. Cf. *La Gazette des tribunaux* of 24 June 1893.

5 This turmoil resulted in the election to the National Assembly of a young lawyer named Viviani, who was a true symbol of the indignation that had been stirred up within the populace because of the extreme police brutality against the students. These events were reported by Maurice Garçon, *Histoire de la justice sous la Troisième République*, Vol. II, "Les grandes affaires," Paris, Fayard, 1957, pp. 294–295.

6 With regard to shutting down performances that can lead to public disorder, see Chapter 6, note 9, in which the authority of the administration of live performances is clarified.

7 Fantasio, II, 1907, p. 82, cited by Bologne, *Histoire de la pudeur*, p. 238.

8 This started with a letter that Béranger addressed to the public prosecutor in which he said the following: "Until now, in our opinion, the various nudities too widely allowed in theatrical performances have had to at least be covered with a singlet. At this time it appears that the small stages of the Alhambra and the Olympia offer the public such performances without even this insufficient attenuation. On the stage of the music hall on the Rue de Malte, a woman who, according to one newspaper, appears '*completely nude* and gives the illusion of marble [...]. One of the artists agreed to represent this statue *without even a singlet.*'"

Another paper stated that "at the Olympia, three shapely, *completely nude* young women, *covered only in a thin layer of gold*, appeared as living statues of the precious metal."

Our society does not hold itself responsible for such news; it even likes to hope that they are only deceitful claims, meant to draw in the public like bait to an audacious and unprecedented spectacle. But you will no doubt consider that it is up to the justice system, the only guardian of decency at the theater today, to inquire into this subject, and I have no doubt that, if the published claims are true, you would consider them as grave as the shortfalls as highlighted in my speech until now, and would prosecute them as constituting the crime of indecent exposure" (cited by Maurice Garçon, *Histoire de la justice sous la Troisième République* , p. 287).

9 Fantasio III, 1908, I, p. 360, cited by Bologne, *Histoire de la pudeur*, p. 240.

10 Fantasio II, 1907, 3, p. 809, cited by Bologne, *Histoire de la pudeur*.

11 Pierre Louÿs wrote: "The public has very quickly understood that the question of nudity was only concerned with religious law, not civil law, and that, even if admiring a naked woman were a sin, it was certainly

not a crime [...]. No article of our laws is applicable under these circumstances, since it cannot be seriously argued that a naked woman offends the modesty of citizens who pay one hundred pennies to see her. The theater is a closed hall. People who are shocked by nudity are free not to enter. What are they complaining about? No one is bringing dancers into their homes. No one is walking them about on the streets. No one is violating their gaze. Thus, given that individual sentiments have no pretext of calling themselves harmed, the public prosecutor's office does not pursue a legitimate complaint. Rather, it prosecutes in the name of a principle, according to which nudity is a shameful spectacle—an essentially religious principle [...]," *Le Journal*, 25 April 1908.

See also the speeches in defense of the nude by Georges Normandy, *Le Nu à l'église, au théâtre et dans la rue*, preface by Gustave Kahn, Paris, 1909, as well as those of Drs. G.J. Witkowski and L. Nass; *Le Nu au théâtre depuis l'Antiquité jusqu'à nos jours*, Paris, Daragon, 1909; and the short chapter by Jean-Claude Bologne dedicated to the war of nudity in his work, *Histoire de la pudeur*, pp. 238–244.

12 In the first two cases, four female artists—Laisney, Thierry, Dauhault, and Aymos—were accused of being in contempt of public decency. M. Cohen and M. Parceller were accused of being accomplices, the first crime committed by Mlle Laisney, Mlle Thierry and Mlle Dauhault, and the second committed by Mlle Aymos, by aiding and knowingly attending to the culprits in the acts that they prepared, facilitated or perpetrated. (The third case will be discussed further below.)

13 *Gazette des tribunaux*, 20 and 27 July 1908.

14 *Gazette des tribunaux*, 2 December 1908.

15 D. 1909.5. 18. 3 March 1909; the same court had confirmed the punishment of the lesbian scene of 27 July 1908.

16 Court of Appeals of Paris, 13th division, 26 February 1936, S. 1936. 2. 137.

17 See p. 34.

18 DH, 1938. 109 and RSC, 1938. 301.

19 Roger Doublier, *Le Nu et la Loi*, p. 65.

20 Tribunal of Saint-Lô, 8 November 1950. D. 1951 Somm. 21 and RSC, 1951. 273 obs. Hugueney.

21 See especially James Laver, *Costume and Fashion: A Concise History*, Thames & Hudson, 2003, as well as Valérie Mendes and Amy de La Haye, *Fashion since the 19th century*, Paris, Thames & Hudson, 2000. (French original cites both these titles in their French translations.)

22 *Journal des tribunaux*, January 15, 1966. This decision was not published in the *Bulletin des arrêts de la Cour de cassation* for unknown reasons, and it was thus only published four years later, in the *Journal*

des tribunaux. However, in the decision of 22 December 1965, which ruled on the monokini, this 1962 decision is cited in a footnote as being unprecedented. Cf. Laplatte, *L'Outrage public à la pudeur*, p. 210.

23 Patrick Alac, *La Grande Histoire du bikini*, New York, Parkstone Press, 2002.

24 Thus, for example, Laplatte, *L'Outrage public à la pudeur*.

25 Criminal trial court of Grasse, 23 September 1964, JCP, 1954. II. 13. 1974, note to Rieg.

26 Aix, 20 January 1965. JCP, 1965. II. 14. 143 bis.

27 Court of Appeals of Riom, 16 November 1937, DH, 1938. 109.

28 RSC, 1965. 422.

29 RSC, 1965. 422, Hugueney's commentary.

30 JCP 1965. II. 1423, note A. R.

31 Crim., 22 December 1965. JCP, 1966. II. 14. 509 and Bull. Crim. No. 289, p. 651.

32 Cited by Doublier, *Le Nu et la Loi* .

33 On this subject, see Doublier, *Le Nu et la Loi* .

34 In particular, see the very interesting work of Jean-Claude Kaufmann, *Corps de femmes, regards d'hommes, Sociologie des seins nus*, Paris, Pocket, 2006.

35 Thus taking us back to the idea of modesty according to Montesquieu, which would be "the shame of our imperfections," *De l'esprit des lois*, Book XVI, Chapter XI.

36 See Chapter 8.

37 The term "naturism" is a neologism that made its appearance in 1768, in a work by Dr. Théophile de Bordeu, *Recherches sur l'histoire de la médicine*, cf. Arnaud Baubérot, *Le Naturisme et la société française, histoire sociale et culturelle d'un mythe (fin du XIXe siècle–années 1930)*, doctoral thesis in history, University of Paris XII, Créteil, 2002.

38 In this sense, this philosophy can be conceived of as a crucial phase in the political history of clothing. It contests an older function of clothing as a statutory sign both from a social as well as sexual point of view, a function that came truly into crisis near the end of the nineteenth century. In particular, see Philippe Perrot, *Les Dessus et les Dessous de la bourgeoisie*, Bruxelles, Complexe, 1984, as well as, for the period preceding the French Revloution, Sylvie Steinberg, *Le Travestissement de la Renaissance à la Révolution*, Paris, Fayard, 2001, Daniel Roche, *La Culture des apparances* and *Une histoire du vêtement XVII–XVIII siècle*, Paris, Fayard, 2006. For the strictly legal aspect of this history of clothing, see Pierre Daubert, *Du port illégal de costume et de décoration*, thesis in law, Paris, Arthur Rousseau, 1904.

39 Doublier, *Le Nu et la Loi* , p. 43. Thus, rather than complete nudity, it

is the semi-nudity extolled by certain naturist doctors from the 1930s that seems to be promoted in the name of "tolerance" on this island.

40 This number rose to fifty-one associations that counted 2,259 members on 1 October 1951, a number which then further rose to 6,672 in 1956 and 8,903 in 1960; the naturist permit was granted for more than fifteen years (cf. Doublier, *Le Nu et la Loi*, p. 85).

41 Francine Barthe-Deloizy, *Géographie de la nudité: Être nu quelque part,* Paris, Bréal, 2003, pp. 142–143.

42 Thus the changing rooms where men and women undress are separated because, according to André Santerre, "As much as it is simple and beautiful to find oneself suddenly naked, in a group of nudists, it is downright unpleasant to go together through the stage of boxer shorts, etc.," cited by Doublier, *Le Nu et la Loi*, p. 79.

43 Laplatte, *L'Outrage public à la pudeur*, p. 85.

44 *Bulletin intérieur* of the *Club du Soleil*, cited by Doublier, *Le Nu et la Loi*, p. 93.

45 Barthe-Deloizy, *Géographie de la nudité*, p. 115.

46 When Roger Doublier, a jurist and nudist, published his work *Le Nu et la Loi* in 1976, he tried to develop a theory of spaces that attempts to take into account the transformations that had occurred in the preceding decades. He proposed a true theory of compartmentalization of public spaces, which meant, in substance, that these spaces would be numerous as far as the regime of the visibility of sexuality is concerned. Next to communal public space, such as streets and parks, there would be others—such as theaters, painting academies, nudist beaches or those that aren't nudist but are frequented by women in monokinis—in which the rules of the visibility of sexuality would not be the same as in the former.

Doublier named these partial spaces, which thus constituted a sort of small island within communal public space, "semi-public." If everybody could go there, one could be exempt from the regime of the visibility of sexuality and enjoy the space as a private one. But, according to Doublier, this marriage between the public and the private did not stop there. For, in these semi-public spaces, one could have more freedom than in communal public spaces, but not to the same extent as private spaces. The crucial point of this theory is that these exceptional spaces could not be counterparts to private places, as far as the visibility of sexuality was concerned. He placed them in an intermediate "almost private" world, which was fundamentally based on the chaste nude and not its obscene or "debauched" varieties.

What, according to Doublier, justified this exceptional status of semi-public spaces? Nothing other than the consent of the people who had congregated in them. Not a private, individual consent, but a sort of collective consent that was legitimate because it was given in the past, in the present, and for the future.

This odd kind of consent prevented someone, upon entering the space, from feeling outraged and being able to enforce Article 330. Such a person had to be informed in advance of what s/he was going to see. These spaces, therefore, could not be detached from the consent of those who had made them possible. Consent, according to Doublier's theory, was something other than an act of individual will for a precise situation. It was a question of an act of collective nature that *founded* a space.

But, such as I just highlighted, what characterizes this theory, whose name carries its philosophy, is that these spaces of exception, these semi-public spaces, could never be comparable to private and enclosed spaces. Indeed, since everyone could enter these spaces, people could not do whatever they wanted there. Collective consent thus had limits that individual consent did not have.

Rather than treat these spaces as being semi-public, thanks to the consent of those present, it would have been very different to treat them as public spaces transformed into private spaces. For, in so doing, the freedom that could be enjoyed in these spaces would have been the same as in private spaces, enclosed and invisible from the outside.

In reality, Doublier's theory was almost conceived just for nudist beaches and, as it was formulated, it was already not in a position to be applied to such enclosed spaces as theaters and clubs in which what one could see no longer had any limits. The theory of semi-public places is, in this sense, a theory of the limits of what can be done in collective spaces, by establishing nudism as the only alternative theory to the dominant visual-sexual legality. It is as if, in substance, the only alternative sexual visibility that could have been invented is chaste nudity.

But History was not going to prove Roger Doublier correct, for French law was well and truly in the middle of preparing within public space, places for "libertines," and not just chaste nudes—public spaces in which one could enjoy the same liberties as exist in private places.

6

The publicity of unchaste sexuality

In the early twentieth century, the questioning of the classical theories of publicity in theater served the cause of both chaste and obscene nudity. In the war of the chaste nudes, enterprising individuals used both the purity of immobile artists and the lack of publicity in performances to avoid the threats from Article 330 of the Penal Code. During this period the first challenges to publicity developed from new theories of consent at performances. Their arguments laboriously sought to legitimize a specific form of consent from spectators of public performances so as not to fall under the purview of Article 330.

From the 1950s on, the challenge to classical theories of publicity of performances became more radical when the Court of Cassation began conceding that witnesses' consent had the power to mitigate publicity in certain public spaces. With regard to performances on stage, these new rulings were seen as the beginning of a new era. Based on these new court decisions, some legal scholars believed that such performances could appeal to a similar treatment of publicity. Under this new doctrine, the consent of participants was sufficient to make a public performance private. The explosion of eroticism in theaters experienced in France from the mid-1960s onward was made possible largely by such theories of privatization of performances by consent.

I The classical theory of publicity in theater and its first challenges

According to conventional theories, Article 330 of the Penal Code could not be applied to private performances despite their obscenity. During a private performance in a space as public as a theater, you could see the same acts as those that could have taken place during an intimate encounter in a private individual's home. But exactly what performances or encounters between individuals did the law deem to be private? The answer that legal scholars gave to this question was very clear:

> Whatever the purpose of these encounters (political, entertainment, fun, social parties), the meeting will not cease to be private due to the number of attendees or the nature of the meeting place, provided that its mode of organization does not open the space to the public.[1]

But how can one completely exclude the public?

Scholars thought that it depended on how people were made aware of the meeting or performance. Thus, they wrote: "posters, inserts in newspapers, even oral proclamations usually announce a public meeting. And this can be for a political meeting, a formal banquet or a theatrical performance. In contrast, organizers of a private meeting use a completely different process. They can send letters of invitation or entry cards to specific persons named on a list, drawn up carefully; and finally they let their invitees know in some way that a meeting will take place on such a day and in such a place."[2]

"To admit them, the organizer of the private meeting considers the character of the invitees, while the one who organizes a public meeting is indifferent to such qualities; the former knows his guests, or at least broadly applies the saying that the friends of our friends are our friends, while the latter may know those who frequent the theater, but when one of them leaves, that individual will be replaced by the first stranger who asks for the vacant seat."[3]

A performance could become private, even though it was announced in the press, even if one had to pay to enter, even if the space in which it could take place was capable of accommodating a large number of persons, provided that "the organizers ruthlessly refuse entry to all those who cannot claim to know one of them or someone known to one of them."[4]

Thus, consent to the performance had no relevance in the consideration of whether the spectators constituted a "public." To avoid such a characterization, it was less important to determine whether the persons who attended had consented to what they would see than to verify that they were not passersby, that is to say, they had attended the event in response to an impersonal advertisement. In such a scenario, the theater or the performance hall also became as public as a street or a park open to everyone. Even if no one was offended, even if the audience was delighted, given that what they had seen was of a sexual nature, the performance fell into the clutches of Article 330.

The public space established by Article 330 had to be held as indivisible with regard to the regime of visibility of sexuality. The pluralism of norms in this domain could only exist in the private world, that is to say one in which sociability was organized through networks of acquaintances and to the extent that the spaces in which such encounters took place were not visible or accessible from the outside.

Certainly, since the 1877 Ponce decision, spectators were required to consent to what they would see. If ever they did not, were they personally invited but did not know the content of the show and were shocked, then Article 330 would apply. In such a case, even if I had not brought my guests together to constitute a public in my home, the absence of consent from one of them would transform my home into a public space, as if I had invited my friends to watch an obscene spectacle in the middle of the Place de la Concorde.

In 1892,[5] the Court of Cassation had occasion to state in a clear and distinct manner that spectators' consent to a public performance was not sufficient to give organizers shelter from Article 330. The facts that motivated the decision of the court were not really a stage performance, but the show that a prostitute put on in her enclosed room in the presence of an audience solicited and brought in from the street by her pimp and her landlord. The defendants argued that the act did not constitute a crime because the solicited witnesses were perfectly aware of the lewd nature of the acts that they had agreed to watch. However, the appeal was rejected on grounds that it resulted from statements made by the judge of the lower court that individuals solicited at random on the street had witnessed lewd acts.

However, for some legal scholars this was more a solution to a specific case than any clarification of principle. They believed that, in reality, the court had made a wrong decision about a fact arising from interior publicity. For, if the people who had congregated had not constituted a public as the court said—if they had been friends or known to the organizers in one way or another—Article 330 would not have been applicable if one of them had not expressed outrage at the show. But in this case, as they had been forewarned of what they would see, any complaint post factum could be rejected because it could be viewed as arising from what the law called "morbid curiosity."[6]

However, the court was not wrong in its judgment, for, in fact, it applied another notion of publicity, which found its definition in the way the audience was constituted. In this case, their consent was in no way a criterion to escape from applying Article 330. Rather, what mattered more was that they were indiscriminately solicited on the street. The distinction between "the public" and "a group of acquaintances" could, however, give rise to ambiguities. Thus some show producers tried to use audaciously fraudulent schemes to act as if their "public" was in reality a group of people known to them.

II Putting an end to the publicity of performance by fraud

In 1908, to take shelter from Article 330 of the Penal Code, a show producer imagined a novel procedure to transform an "audience" into a "group of acquaintances." The show was divided into two parts: the evening began with the performance of a play, no more daring than the usual repertoire seen in some small theaters. Then the curtain fell, the stage manager announced that the spectacle was over, requested the public evacuate the room and announced that a performance by invitation only was about to take place. The guests of this alleged private performance were none other than the audience of the first performance, who were given, at the same time as the ticket for the first part, an invitation card for the second. Once the auditorium had been cleared, they were admitted to the party dubbed private by presenting their previously received cards and occupied the same seats as before. Nobody was forced to attend the second show, but everyone could.

Nevertheless, the 9th Division of the Tribunal of the Seine thought that publicity was proved and therefore the director and actresses fell within the scope of Article 330. The judges explained as follows:

> Although they claim in vain that the performance was private, it is nevertheless determined that any person who presented himself at the theater box office received the invitation without asking for it, along with the ticket, allowing him to attend the pantomime, which was basically a continuation of the performance previously paid for; that

> the audience was asked by the manager to leave the theater at the end of the first part of the program and reenter immediately thereafter with the invitation ticket distributed at the beginning, stating that the representation would be private, became a purely illusory precaution to erase the obviously public nature of the performance [...][7]

A few months later, the same division of the Seine Tribunal had to decide on a new case of the same type. This time, the performance took place in a restaurant during dinner on certain fixed days. The director of the establishment claimed, too, that the character of publicity was entirely lacking in these performances and Article 330 could not apply. He stated that only guests attended these dinners, so the restaurant should be considered a private space. But the Deputy Public Prosecutor Granié, providing some insights revealed by an investigation on how the invitations were handed out, rightly pointed out in his report to the court that this restaurant was a public space.

He stated: "In the current circumstances, the host did not know the guests. The following question then arose: who are the people—by profession or reputation—who are capable of spending 50 francs, and can come well-dressed? Publicity remains clear in this case for it suffices to ask for a ticket to be allowed in, and many who had received tickets had not requested them." The court accepted these conclusions and ruled against the defendant.[8]

Since the classical theory of the public was intractable and fraud was almost impossible, intellectuals and legal scholars tried for decades to soften its rigors. Thus they developed new theories to bring the rules of visibility of sexuality in public performances closer in line with those that existed for private shows. They proposed, unsuccessfully, that the consent of the public be acknowledged in order to prevent Article 330 from being applicable.

III Theory of the audience's double consent at public performances: the case of realist theater

Early theories of spectators' consent at public performances appeared at the same time as the chaste nude as a framework to avoid the application of Article 330, but were, quite simply, rather poor and far-fetched.

So, a theory of dual consent of spectators emerged in an effort to liberalize performances by focusing less on what should be permitted than on what Article 330 should always punish. According to its authors, this rule was designed to protect not an abstract notion but a concrete manifestation of modesty. If a performance evoked known disgust, anger or hatred in an audience that had nevertheless given its consent, it should be regarded as contrary to Article 330 of the Criminal Code. In essence, this amounted to saying that the public could not have actually consented to witness what they had found so offensive, even if they had ostensibly been informed of the content of the show and had agreed to attend it. Indeed, the public embodied this irruption of the impersonal, of the indeterminate person X into the social world, and therefore "consent" could not be the same thing in its case as that given by a particular individual. Consent for the public meant that they were not actually outraged by what they saw, even if each person who composed the public had knowingly attended the performance.

This convoluted and frivolous theory was born—and nurtured for over fifty years—after the 9th Division of the Criminal Tribunal of Paris convicted Frédéric de Chirac, the creator of the ephemeral and pitiful "Realist Theater," on 14 January 1892.

The trial of Frédéric de Chirac

The young Frédéric de Chirac, 22 years old at the time of his trial, had been an employee of a railway company for several years. According to Maurice Garçon, who commented on this and several other cases with great irony and contempt, this young man "was an enthusiast of naturalist literature and free theater." But "incapable of understanding the true scope of the efforts of men of letters, Chirac only saw some crude examples and thought he could outdo them. As an amateur playwright, he feverishly sought the singularity that could give him the same success as achieved by an entire young generation with a vision for great art, which unfortunately Chirac could not even conceive."

He produced his first play, "*Prostitute!*," directed by Paul Fort at the Art Theater. In the play, a man goes up to the house of a "girl," who disappears behind a screen to appear again after a few minutes, pretending to touch up her makeup, and deposits a coin on the fireplace before leaving. The reception of this first play was unanimously negative and the theater's director broke with de Chirac because he thought that their collaboration could be compromising.

So, thereafter, to put on his plays, M. de Chirac founded his own theater in the Galerie Vivienne, and whether it was due to a lack of means or true calling (we don't know), Maurice Garçon wrote, "he added to his talents the roles of director and actor." The "Realist Theater" thus came into being and the sad fate of Mr. de Chirac was set in motion.

His first show was composed of three works with the eloquent titles: *Symbolists and Realists* [*Symbolistes et Réalistes*], *Death violated* [*La mort violée*], a study in two tableaux, and *Paternity* [*Paternité*], a comedy in three acts. The show was private and thus was not supposed to be the object of the prerequisite censorship[9] or prosecution under Article 330, for the audience had been informed before entering what they would see. Even if viewers found the plays atrocious, nobody protested openly, but the poor young man was fired from his job with the railways. A second performance took place on 16 October 1891, and did not provoke any more reaction from the guests.

On 22 December, he staged five new plays of his own, including *The Beggar* [*Le Gueux*] and *The Abortion* [*L'Avortement*], in the Fantasias-Parisiennes Theater. The day before, he asked permission from the Chief of Police to keep his show private and sent out a circular, which he published in a few newspapers, inviting a certain category of people. In this circular, Chirac warned his future audience that the plays they would watch were the result of a realistic application of his new realist doctrine, "of mime alternating with the spoken word." He added: "We have overcome difficulties such that during a scene depicting the act of [sexual] possession between the beggar and the daughter of the woodsman, the curtain will not fall."

The printed program repeated the contents of the circular, stating that in *The Abortion* there would be a mimic expressing abortive maneuvers. These ads that promised surprises to viewers attracted a large crowd that far exceeded the number of guests that Chirac had invited, as well as those who paid to see the plays.

According to contemporary accounts, attendees literally crushed each other in the hall. A reporter from the *Figaro* later heard a witness say: "the congestion was such that I could hardly make it to my seat. Women had climbed onto chairs and I could only partly follow the possession scene. Protests arose on all sides, with some complaining that they saw too much and others saying they did not see enough." The day after the performance, an article entitled

"Scandal" appeared in *Le Soir*, denouncing the production of the Realist Theater as really being in contempt of public decency.

On the same day a chronicle appeared in the *XIXe Siècle* in which a journalist gave his impressions as an eyewitness, stating that the play *The Beggar* was primarily a pornographic show. He wrote: "We saw a young woman come dressed in a skirt and blouse, so loose that her breasts could be entirely seen; then she lay on the ground and the beggar, lifting her skirt, lay down with her."

In *The Abortion*, the scandal was such that the audience demanded that the curtain fall before the end of the play. Immediately warned of what had happened, the police commissioner was convinced, rightly, that it was not a private meeting and therefore returned to the prosecutor to have the facts examined by the courts for violation of Article 330 of the Penal Code. Indeed, the press had immediately reported that the show had strayed far from its private character. In fact, "the first passerby was able to enter the theater by paying for his seat."

In addition, it became clear that Chirac had rented out a certain number of chairs for the performance at 7 francs each, and was said to have sold so many tickets at that price that there were 800 people in the auditorium. Chirac would have sold these tickets to anyone who was ready to pay for a seat. Thus, in relation to the requirements of Article 330, there was no doubt whatsoever about the publicity of the show.

During the trial, it was learned that in *The Beggar*, Myriane, the daughter of a forest ranger, falls in love with a tramp after her father decides to offer him hospitality, and incites him to be intimate with her. As indicated in the manuscript, to overcome the scruples of the beggar: "She spreads open her camisole violently and reveals her breasts, saying: 'Well, beggar, here is my flesh, plant your kiss on it.'" As the beggar hesitates, Myriane becomes increasingly urgent, embraces him, and both fall to the ground, lips sealed together. "Take all of me so that I feel you in my body; I had enough trouble getting you to decide, now don't deprive me this moment of possession," she commands. The beggar agrees, and the two characters hug, mimicking the sexual act, until Myriane's father arrives and curses them.

According to the court, the actress who played the role of Myriane did so with the "advertised expressive gestures." Opinions differed on whether or not the actress had shown one of her breasts. However, everyone agreed that mimicking the sexual act had really occurred. According to the court, the immorality of the situation had raised so much murmuring in the auditorium that the show had to be stopped for a moment, before resuming after Chirac asked the audience to remain silent.

In *The Abortion*, Marcelline, a prostitute, pregnant with her pimp's child, finally makes the fatal decision after some hesitation. She takes off her jacket and petticoat, and throws herself on a bed, ready to undergo treatment proffered by the widow Mathieu, who performs the intervention. The widow approaches the bed, puts on a white apron and operates on the patient, who moans at intervals. The abortionist says, gesticulating: "Look, I have it. Yet another one who will no longer move." Then she sets a bowl full of alcohol on the table and wipes her hands, red with blood, on her apron. It was at this moment that the spectators, far too patient until then, violently protested. "The entire room was standing, trembling with indignation and shouting the epithets m … f … at Chirac!" Given this explosion of public anger, the director of the Realist Theater lowered the curtain after a vain attempt to resist.

The next day in the *XIXe siècle*, Henry Fouquier insisted that he had never seen such a tumult in a theater motivated by "such disgust from the audience. The revolt was so strong that the public thought it was able to hear and see everything."[10] Unfortunately for the poor young man, no artist sought to defend his approach to call it "art," or even less see him as the victim of an ignorant justice system. Nobody affirmed that his "obscenities" were in any way "redeemed" by his art. Even his lawyer argued that his client had the "intention" of creating a work of art, which unfortunately failed, only managing to produce an act that incited corrective justice. As if the lack of talent was not enough punishment for the artist, it had to be further matched with a criminal conviction.[11]

The Criminal Court of Paris condemned Chirac and one of the actresses to fifteen months in prison and a fine of 200 francs, and the other two actresses to one and two months respectively. The court stated that, "despite the morbid curiosity of the spectators, the defendants are guilty of the offense of contempt of public decency."[12]

The most interesting legal issue raised by this case was that of the clear consent of the public. Can one complain about the content of a performance when it has been described in advance? Can the content of certain scenes nullify the previously given consent? But these questions could only be posed if the show were private and not public.

However, the courts convicted Frédéric de Chirac of a public spectacle by using the concept of "morbid curiosity" that applied to the private world. "Morbid curiosity" was used to invalidate the publicity of an assault committed in a private space because the witness of a scene had knowingly sought it out. "Morbid curiosity" could not be applied when a scene was enacted in public because everyone was supposed to be able to watch it.

So, why did the court put forward this notion while Chirac's show was undoubtedly public? The show's audience on 22 December 1891 knew that they would witness "hot" scenes. However, while they had shown a "morbid curiosity," they could not imagine that the show would be "so repugnant." Therefore, the expression "despite their morbid curiosity" emphasized the court's disapproval, as if it had wanted to mean that whether the show had been private or public, it would have been in contempt of public decency. But in fact, this was a matter of style. For if the performance had been private, Frédéric de Chirac would not have been convicted despite the disgust of the public, because everyone had been warned in advance of what they would see.

Nevertheless, this formulation led liberal scholars to think that if the audience had not responded in such a manner, the show could not be held in contempt of public decency—an idea that completely contradicts mainstream juridical interpretations. With the condemnation of the Realist Theater, these scholars sought to advance the opinion that a spectacle that does not cause disapproval despite its sexual content should not be considered in violation of Article 330. This is the argument that Pierre Louÿs, one of the main protagonists of the famous war of the nude in the 1910s, advanced.

Louÿs lauded the "considerable movement in the direction of the freedom to be nude in theater,"[13] and wrote that "this movement is even stronger due to the fact that it is anonymous and spontaneous." For Louÿs, the consent of the people followed the favorable opinion of the artistic circles themselves to the extent that "for some time in Paris, over 2,000 theatrical shows with nude actresses have been performed without causing a scandal, not a single one." Except, of course, the one put on by Chirac. But was his spectacle really a "theatrical show?"

In 1953, the *Journal of Criminal Science* [*Revue de science criminelle*] published a short piece entitled "Can nudity in a performance be in contempt of [public] decency?" written by a legal scholar whose opinions in sexual matters were so conservative that he did not even dare sign his name to the much cited article. In this anonymous opinion on the Chirac case, the author wrote:

> [...] when a producer of a show promotes contempt for himself and his audience, along with the most vile greed to the point of performing the bestial act of coupling on stage with curtains drawn up—as was the case at the Realist Theater on 22 December 1891 in Paris—only to be followed by the revolting illusion of abortion along with gestures, cries and blood, the public's conscience can only rise vehemently against such unspeakable exhibition. And besides, this public, which was initially disposed to hearing and seeing everything, revolted *en masse* with such an explosion of disgust in response to the vile representation to which critics' memory attributes the most formidable turmoil that ever erupted in the theater. So, there it is, the most patently clear evidence that the sense of modesty of this public, which had initially expressly assembled to watch the said indecent acts, had indeed been outraged. And whatever school or doctrine that such shows espouse, they do not fall within the realm of the theater critic but that of the criminal justice system.[14]

This theory, which sought to legalize certain kinds of public performances, could not accept that the simple consent of spectators was enough to make lawful sexual exhibition. The fact that they so enthusiastically applauded Chirac's conviction was aimed at taking away such power from individual consent. In contrast to such "extreme" libertarian streaks a more moderate theory—which was nevertheless based on the consent of spectators, not as individuals but as a collective [*foule*]—was floated.

The authors of the latter theory seemed to suggest in essence that if the consent of the spectators sufficed to avoid the application of Article 330, the article should not override what this impersonal collectivity—the public—ought to be able to see. It is for this reason that the consent of the public was to be given twice. Once, before the arrival, as for private performances; and again, at the end of the show, either to be demonstrated by approval or by silence. For if the crowd shouted, gathered, protested, created a scandal, it meant that it did not consent to see what it was shown, and that the first consent had been falsely extorted.

Yet, given that it is evident that one cannot consent to past acts, this second consent is not an act of will but more a moral or aesthetic judgment. This implies that spectators should be the masters of the fate of the performance, and also confuses the quality of a show with its legality. Would it not be better under these conditions for the director to know in advance that he cannot stage certain plays instead of indulging the whims of a crowd posing as the concrete representation of the public?

Certainly, one had to go beyond the standards of the classical theory to liberalize public performances. However, attempts made to establish such shows after the Realist Theater case were not able to provide any judicial security to those performances. Thus, as often happens in terms of freedom of artistic expression, the hateful condemnation of Frédéric de Chirac did not expand freedoms, at least in theory, for anyone at all.

It was not until the 1950s and 1960s that legal scholars developed more rational theories meant to liberalize performances based on the consent of spectators. But that would have been unthinkable had the Court of Cassation not changed its own doctrine of consent. In the 1950s, for the first time since the Ponce decision, the court endowed the consent of witnesses with the power to restrict publicity in sexual scenes enacted in certain public spaces.

IV Consent and publicity: the Court of Cassation rulings of the 1950s

If the last quarter of the nineteenth century saw the extension of publicity to private spaces, the 1950s marked publicity's decline. The Court of Cassation changed its doctrine and outlined a series of rulings that established the new rules regarding publicity that are, indeed, still in force.

The monopoly of sight

Shortly before the court began the process of "privatizing" public spaces, a seemingly innocuous decision of an appellate court—to which legal scholars have assigned different dates in their copious comments[15]—introduced a change, or at least a clarification of great importance to publicity. The events that motivated this unpublished decision, delivered on 29 January 1949 [sic] by the Court of Appeals of Dijon, had taken place sometime in 1949 in the toilet of the station of that city. A man and a woman had locked themselves inside it to make love.

A person passing by thought he heard "moaning in the cabin" and imagined that they were the groans of "a sick lady in the toilet." Anxious to help her, that person alerted an employee who, in turn, called the service agent. The two men hoisted themselves above the door and, through the opening between the door and its frame, saw what they should not have seen. As a result of this quid pro quo, the two lovers were prosecuted for contempt of public decency but were acquitted by the Court of Dijon.

Louis Hugueney wondered, while approving the court's decision: "given the enclosed space, on what grounds can one qualify as public this contempt of decency committed in a closed space? Was it because the act had been seen? But that had been the case only after some real gymnastics in which the agent and the employee had engaged to come to the lady's rescue. As the Court of Dijon noted, by locking the door, the lovers had taken 'all normal precautions to avoid publicity, given the layout of the said space,' and it is only in the absence of adequate precautions to keep the act secret, that the doctrine and jurisprudence agree to recognize the indecent act to be in contempt of public decency." In the absence of visual perception, Hugueney states that there was only what the Court of Dijon called "auditory perception, sound heard by the passerby." But could this perception be sufficient to constitute publicity?" For Hugueney, "the court did not believe so because the passerby had not understood correctly; he took the moans to be those of a sick lady rather than an expression of sexual satisfaction. He was thus an unconscious witness who was no more harmed than a baby in its cradle who witnesses a scene of debauchery but hears nothing."[16]

This decision explicitly changed the doctrine of the Court of Cassation, which had repeatedly ruled that it was not necessary to see a scene, but it was enough to use any of the senses of perception for there to be contempt of public decency.[17] However, since the late nineteenth century, there has been no ruling in which the court had taken into account any sensory perception other than sight to determine the constitution of the publicity of indecent exposure. Thus, a jurisprudential movement was pieced together to "protect" the exhibitions produced in enclosed spaces. From then on, at the expense of hearing or touch, sight would be the only sense called upon to constitute publicity, thus contributing to its limitation: only scenes that could be seen would qualify as public.

Consent and virtual publicity by accessibility

The first decision of the Court of Cassation, which ushers in the period of privatization of public spaces, dates from 11 November 1952. It rules on the publicity of exposure in an enclosed space that was not a home but a space to which many people had access. That is, it was public due to the fact that it was accessible.

Until then, according to the jurisprudence of the court, the only way to prevent such a space from being qualified as public under Article 330—in addition, of course, to its invisibility from the outside—was if the door were locked. I have previously mentioned a 1938 Court conviction for an exposure that took place at an association's meeting place where the door was not locked. Even if no one had opened the door, the contempt of public decency was constituted by the fact that someone could have come in and seen the sex scene. However, on 11 November 1952 the court changed this doctrine.

The defendant had photographed a number of willing women, after having made them undress fully or partially in an office, the door of which was not locked, and to which many people had access. The court quashed the defendant's previous conviction because "the alleged crime occurred outside the presence of involuntary witnesses in a private room, enclosed by a door separating it from the outside and without any indication that the door was opened while a woman was in that room."

Virtual publicity is no longer sufficient *when the witnesses consent* to the exposure. For such exposure to be classified as public, the door *had to have been effectively open*, not just that *it could have been open*, or alternatively, if the door were not open, there had to be a nonconsensual witness who watched the act of exhibition.

On 5 July 1956, the Court of Cassation handed down another decision that clarified the central point. The Court of Appeals of Colmar had found a certain Mr. Adam in contempt of public decency on 12 July 1955: he had made an obscene gesture in the presence of a single involuntary witness in a hotel room with the door pushed closed or shut, but not locked. The personnel of said hotel could have thus surprised him. Adam denied the existence of publicity and appealed to the Court of Cassation. After all, had the Supreme Court not decided the other way a few years previously, in the case of the photographer? Had it not required on that occasion that the door be actually open and not just that it could have been?

But the court had then made a subtle distinction, which it clarified and emphasized in commenting on the 1956 affair: "Whereas the contested judgment notes that on 3 April 1954 Adam, an economic survey clerk, took advantage of the fact that the audit he was conducting of a hotel in Strasbourg placed him in the company of Miss Kalz, an employee of said hotel, to expose his genitals to her; the earlier decision states that Ms. Kalz witnessed Adam's actions and that the event took place in a room where the door was only pushed shut and where anyone could enter; whereas these statements sufficiently establish the existence of the publicity necessary to constitute the crime of contempt of public decency in that they establish both that the offending act was seen by an *involuntary witness* and *that it was possible that it could have been seen* by others; given that these material facts and the failure to hide them have been thus noted, far from misreading the laws referred to, the lower court's decision represents an exact and correct application of the law."[18]

Thus, these two cases show that virtual publicity in publicly accessible spaces exists only when the witness is involuntary. If his or her presence is voluntary, publicity must be concrete and real. This is indeed a real turnaround in the jurisprudential use of consent. It could be used not only for extending publicity to enclosed and private spaces when it was negative (the Ponce decision) but also to put a stop to publicity when it was affirmative. However, this new rule was only valid for locations *accessible* to the public and not for those *visible* from the outside through a window or any opening connecting to the outside or to another private space.

This is what a 7 December 1960 ruling of the Supreme Court shows us,[19] confirming a decision of the Court of Appeals of Limoges on 14 January of the same year. A certain Marcel Talabot was sentenced for contempt of public decency for engaging in obscene acts with a young lady who was consenting, in the sheep pen of his farm. But it turns out that the pen's wall had a small hole leading to another barn belonging to the same owner. This is how Marcel Talabot's son had witnessed the scene by putting his eye to this little hole.

This time, the Supreme Court did not consider the consent of his partner, and held that Mr. Talabot should have blocked the small hole so as not to be seen. From this it concluded, "that no precautions had been taken to avoid the publicity of the scene, and that by looking through a hole in the wall separating the two stables, the young Talabot had witnessed the act. [...] Indeed, an indecency becomes public even when enacted in a private space if it can be seen by others, if adequate precautions are not taken by its perpetrator."

As in the past, in the case of publicity due to accessibility, when the door was actually opened, the consent of the witness continued to play no role. If two consenting lovers are in a private space accessible by a door, and the door opens, publicity as understood by Article 330 continues to be constituted. This is what a much later ruling of the Court of Cassation (from 14 December 1971) shows, as I mentioned in Part I.[20]

While in the dining room of his girlfriend, Ms. Ollivier, Marcel Delcluze asked her child and one of his friends to go play in the next room. Then, he closed the door to this room without locking it, and was engaged in sex with his girlfriend when the children opened the door and took them by surprise.

This poor man's neglect earned him a conviction of six months in prison from the Court of Appeals in Paris. The Supreme Court upheld the conviction because "the act of the accused presented the characteristics of publicity and fell under Article 330 of the Criminal Code. In effect, the indecency becomes public when enacted, as here, in a private space, where, for having failed to take adequate precautions, it could be seen unintentionally by others."

New rules for indoor publicity

The last decision from this period relates to the conditions of publicity in private spaces neither visible nor accessible from the exterior. This decision is very important because it transforms the doctrine that had been established by the Court of Cassation in 1877 with the Ponce ruling, and the way of thinking about the triangulation between "the exhibitor,* the public, and the affronted witness."

* Translator's note: the term *exhibeur* (exhibitor), rarely used in the French language, is sometimes employed by the author to distinguish from the more current form, *exhibitionniste* (exhibitionist). In the context of this discussion, the former can be understood to designate culprits under the old law (Article 330) who did not necessarily seek to derive pleasure from transgressing the law itself (i.e., rendering it into an object of sexual pleasure). Rather, they were held in contempt of public decency for having (in)voluntarily exposed themselves. In contrast, exhibitionists, as will be explained in detail in Part III, especially as understood within the current framework of the new law, are those culprits who do derive pleasure from transgressing the law itself and as such render it into a sexual object.

Since the Ponce decision, for there to be indoor publicity, it was sufficient that at least three people were gathered in an enclosed space and that one of them did not consent to what was shown to him or her.

Thus, in a 1932 ruling, the Court of Cassation condemned a young man who had photographed the sexual organs of a woman—who was herself perfectly willing—in the presence of another woman who protested the scene that she witnessed.[21]

As I mentioned earlier, of these two individuals who were watching, the girl who had consented filled a spatial function while the other, who did not consent, filled a social function. Together, they were thought to incarnate this spatial and social reality that is the street, that is, a space where there is free passage day and night and in which one ought not to be accosted by a scene of a sexual nature.

However, in a ruling of 15 June 1954, the Court of Cassation changed this doctrine.[22] The case revolved around some obscene acts performed by a couple in the presence of a 10-year-old child in a closed bedroom. The defendants had appealed their conviction for contempt of public decency.

The Supreme Court upheld the conviction under the principle of justified punishment, because the incriminating acts constituted the crime of enticement of minors to debauchery. But it took care to point out why this act could not be held as contempt of public decency. The court stated that "in contrast to indecent assault, prevention of contempt of public decency is not primarily intended for the suppression of indecent acts as committed against a specific individual but for the reparation of scandal caused by such acts, given the nature of publicity they entail." In this case, there was no publicity according to the court, even if there were three people, one of whom was nonconsenting.

Thereafter, in order for the space containing three individuals to become public, it was necessary for two of the individuals who were watching the exhibitor to be nonconsenting. Thus, the scene that affronted one witness had to also affront the other. It is only when both see the same sexual scene as an imposition that the conditions for publicity are met.

According to this "scenario," indoor publicity cannot be established when two people voluntarily engage in sex in front of a third person inside a closed room. The voluntary partner who is engaged in a sexual scene cannot act as a witness to the offense of the third party present. The new scenario therefore involves one exhibitor imposing a sexual spectacle on two persons.

In the first two judgments of the Supreme Court, the question was the following: how can publicity be present in a space, accessible by a door, and in which there are at least two persons? The answer was as follows: it can occur if at least one of these people is not consenting. This nonconsent along with a door that can potentially be opened together produce publicity. In contrast, the consent of the person who is inside a room of which the door is not open interrupts the publicity of a space that is otherwise public by accessibility.

In the latter case, the question concerned publicity in a confined space that was not accessible by any door. The answer was that for there to be publicity at least two persons from among those who watched the scene had to be nonconsenting, not just one of them.

As the judges had signaled with the Ponce decision, indoor publicity was a *derivative* of a private space that became public by accessibility. In a nonaccessible and nonvisible location, the gaze of two witnesses faced with an exhibitor would thus "replace" the presence of an open door, that is to say that these two eyes became the functional equivalent of an opening to the outside. But since, hereafter, the conditions to consider as public a space accessible by a door were liberalized, the conditions under which indoor publicity could be cited also had to change.

These rulings had not only posed more stringent requirements to construe a private space as public (indoor publicity) but they had restricted the publicity of certain publicly accessible spaces. Would they support the process of rendering private all public spaces, or at least those involving the consent of the spectators? Ought we not to think of theaters as private spaces, despite the presence of a public, due to the consent given by the audience members?

While some scholars thought so, we see that as soon as the Court of Cassation had the opportunity to comment on these matters, it disappointed those with such expectations. And this is not due to any puritanical malice on its part but rather due to its willingness to clarify the modification in emerging forms of publicity that it had introduced in the 1950s. Indeed, if the rules defining the publicity of publicly accessible spaces had been modified, nothing had changed regarding public performances. Although theaters are not spaces either accessible or visible from the outside, their publicity is not related to the nature of space but how spectators had been gathered together.

The new importance that the court bestowed on the consent of witnesses did not govern the public in theaters. Although they had paid for their seats, the spectators were nonetheless like passersby that Article 330 sought to guard from seeing scenes of a sexual nature.

Until the Court of Cassation ruled on these points, legal scholars as well as public prosecutors saw in those cases from the 1950s the emergence of a new legal theory in which the consent of the public was going to play a new role: privatizing public entertainment spaces. This likely explains why, from the 1960s on, prosecutors tolerated more shows with high sexual content.

V The influence of the new case law on theaters: *Hair* and *Oh! Calcutta!*

Until the late 1960s, the theory of chaste nudes, that is to say, nudity redeemed by artistic goals, had prevailed. This theory and practice had distinguished visible from nonvisible areas of the body and required that the behavior of people nearly naked not be obscene. According to the courts it was under this condition alone that nudity was devoid of its sexual content, and therefore could be seen by the public without infringing Article 330.

But the appearance of these chaste nudes signaled the failure of the production of a new political philosophy of space. Since the attempt to transform public performances into private ones had failed, one had to settle for a territorialization of the body into authorized or prohibited zones and the restriction of its movements.

However, the new importance given to consent in restricting publicity of spaces accessible by a door allowed for a new perspective on these issues. It was postulated that public performances could be rendered private due to the consent given by spectators. As a result, not only total nudity but also lascivious gestures could be permitted because one could see them performed both in public and private shows.

This is how we can understand the absence of prosecutions, despite numerous complaints, against the famous show *Hair*, which was produced in Paris at the Théâtre de la Porte-Saint-Martin in 1969. Not only were actors, both men and women, completely naked on stage but they also made gestures traditionally deemed obscene. The show ran with a full house for fifteen days before the premiere and its success continued undiminished for three years.

Some time later, it was the same with the show *Oh! Calcutta!*, which played until 1974 and whose "filthy" character, as the moralists put it, was much more serious. In *Hair*, full nudity only appeared in one scene, whereas in *Oh! Calcutta!*, the actors appeared naked from the beginning and the nudity in this play was consciously sexual and erotic.

The director, Kenneth Tynan, asked some well-known authors, including John Lennon, to write skits about their own sexual fantasies or about those they had observed in their contemporaries. According to the dance historian Jean-Pierre Pastori, "with *Oh! Calcutta!*, the nudity on stage was deliberately suggestive; some would even say pornographic."[23]

Tynan also seemed to fully embrace this position. When asked to justify the nudity he staged, he replied: "If it's used to symbolize something else—student revolt, psychic liberation, anti-Vietnam protest—then it comes under the heading of nudity with an ulterior motive, in which case it is very unlikely to be erotic. But if the aim were to communicate pleasure, it would be pretty surprising if nudity—selectively used—were not an effective means. The fundamental question here is: do you believe it is justifiable to use artistic means to produce erotic pleasure?"[24]

So "veiled" nude scenes were a thing of the past, as was the will to de-eroticize them in order to make them into displays of chastity or authenticity. Once one agreed to enter a theater, what was presented ought only to depend, at least in principle,[25] on the performance's own specific artistic constraints.

A columnist at *Le Figaro* asked himself: "What I do not understand is why the act of stripping off one's clothes must be accompanied by dirty deeds ... Is there no other way to get naked?"[26] Yet, complaints lodged by associations and individuals were never, like with *Hair*, pursued by prosecutors. Thereafter, a new implicit theory of performances was implemented by the music halls, nightclubs and small shows in which the content of representations no longer had limits *fixed* by their public nature.

In 1968, Robert Vouin wrote in his *Manual of Special Criminal Law* [*Manuel de Droit pénal spécial*]:

> If contempt is attributed to a dancer, who, for example, presents herself naked before an audience that was attracted to the show specifically by the announcement of such a performance, I would argue that we ought to consider the audience, in this case, as voluntary witnesses of an affront committed in a private space [...]. The voluntary witness—that is to say, voluntarily present and consenting—does not constitute the publicity required by law, regardless of whether the act is accomplished in the presence of several individuals, passive or participating in the act.

And this last remark, "passive or participating in the act," paved the way for the legality of swingers clubs or gay saunas, that is to say what was considered to be dissolute spaces.

According to Roger Doublier, until 1973, institutions announced their programs in Parisian weeklies dedicated to theater, indicating the nature of their performances. But these details have since disappeared. Announcements are now made on the walls of an establishment or auditoriums that are fairly well-known (for example, the Mayon or the Crazy-Horse), so that audiences cannot say they did not know in advance what they would see.

VI Implicit theories vs. explicit doctrine

What was the basis of the implicit theories of public performance deduced from the Supreme Court rulings of the 1950s? In reality, there was none. It was sufficient for there to be favorable cases for judges to apply the official theories. And let us remember that, according to them, an enclosed space became public insofar as a nonindividuated audience had access to the space.

The official doctrine had the opportunity to be heard from the late 1970s on. Some decisions leaning in this direction have been strongly criticized by commentators who certainly cannot be suspected of promoting libertarian ideas. On 5 November 1976, the Criminal Court of Paris handed down the first of these decisions relating to sexual scenes that took place in a swingers club.[27] The question that judges had to rule on was the public nature of the space and how the public had been assembled there. What weight was to be given to their consent in order to neutralize publicity under Article 330 of the Penal Code?

The court ruled in the clearest manner possible: "If a club is not restricted only to its members, and if the public, largely informed by advertisements in magazines about the kinds of meetings that are possible in such places, has easy access to it, it is a public space. Due to the public nature of the space, there cannot be any distinction made between witness, whether voluntary or involuntary, and other customers in this bar. Prevention of contempt of public decency does not fundamentally have as its object the repression of immoral actions committed against a specific person, but it is intended, in a special way, to facilitate the reparation of the scandal caused by such acts to public morality. Thus, it is immaterial that the witnesses of these acts that are contrary to public morals are voluntary when publicity exists in the space in which they were committed."

The same court had the opportunity to reiterate its doctrine on 5 December 1978[28] in the case on events that took place in a gay sauna. It stated that "the defendants who engaged in sodomy in a bathhouse open to the public are guilty of the offense of contempt of public decency, since the act was seen or was likely to be seen, the morality or immorality of any witnesses having no influence for the purpose of committing the offense."

More important still was not a decision of the lower courts but one handed down by the Court of Cassation itself—a decision it nevertheless decided not to publish. On 31 January 1978,[29] the court upheld the conviction of a theatrical performance in which the actors enacted real or simulated sex: "the owner of a theater and artistic director of the institution have been rightly convicted for contempt of public decency and complicity in this crime, as they admitted to enacting—or having enacted—erotic scenes in the presence of a public in which the actors performed or simulated sex or other lewd acts." The commentator for this ruling states that, "despite their frequency, obscene exhibition in theaters and cabarets still constitutes the crime of contempt of public decency. They characterize the material indecent act, and although they are enacted before consenting spectators, they have the element of publicity required by Article 330."[30]

It became clear that, since the Supreme Court would not change its classical doctrine and join the new theories of public spaces, legal reform was essential. This reform was completed in 1992. However, the reform does not adopt the theories according to which the consent of the participants interrupted publicity. In reality, it is through another more sophisticated legal construction that we now accept that we can exhibit unchaste sexuality in front of a consenting audience, in a space not visible from the exterior.

VII Spatial politics and the politics of sex on the eve of the moral revolution

The long period stretching from the late nineteenth century to the 1992 reform was distinguished by two institutional processes of great importance. The first is the emergence of a fledgling new regime of visibility of sexuality, in which publicity begins to be "neutralized" through a less fixed interpretation of nudity, as well as the increasing importance attributed to consent. The second is related to a change in the hegemonic structures that control sexuality. Since the mid-nineteenth century, these structures were organized by a spatial logic and they slowly began to be replaced from the 1950s on by other structures based on [an ideological framework that I will call] Sex.* That is why this period marked the beginning of the decline of the offense of indecent exposure, while, at the same time, there has also been a rise in sexual crimes in France.

A new spatial regime of sexuality

The explosion of sexuality in public spaces can be interpreted as a consequence of the Ponce decision. The loss of sexual spaces outside the purview of law and the extension of constraints with respect to the visibility of sexuality within private and enclosed spaces produced a relaxation of certain behaviors in both enclosed and open public spaces, such as theaters, or beaches and streets.

There are several hypotheses explaining this relaxation. One such theory is that of the "internalization of constraints." The ban on exposing one's sexuality in public spaces had as a corollary the lack of control over sexual impulses in private spaces. Once these spaces were "integrated," won over to the domain of the "rule of law," there was no reason not to liberalize the visibility of sexuality in public spaces.

This hypothesis could explain the triumph of the chaste nude and the self-control that it presumes and imposes, of which nudists and monokini wearers are very aware. In fact, this practice of

* Translator's note: This concept of Sex will be developed more fully in Part III.

public nudity implies a "civilizing" process that would reinforce the hypotheses that Norbert Elias[31] and other sociologists[32] have tried for several years to confirm. This "civilizing" process would have required the State to assume responsibility for integrating private spaces under its own purview and influence.

However, these assumptions seem to be invalidated by other data, at least from the turn of the 1950s. In this period there emerged a need to create new mechanisms to enable the visibility of nonchaste nudity. Those mechanisms affected both performances and meeting places, such as swingers clubs or gay bathhouses. Indeed, these public spaces gave access to unbridled sexual behavior, and if there was self-control, it was to engage more fully in the wildest of experiences. Thus, rather than bearing witness to the public repression of impulses in an increasingly sexual climate—as presumed by the hypotheses drawn from studies of Norbert Elias—one began to see the organization of unbridled impulses.

Thanks to the concept of consent, the State could imagine the existence of a new form of collective sexuality that would no longer be private but public and organized by the law. The producers of performances and the owners of swingers clubs owed much to the State, as did the nudists, for organizing "debauchery" by means of old tools (spaces not visible from the exterior) and new ones (consent of participants).

The resulting type of "community of debauchery" was new as well. This expression no longer designated an individualized community but an anonymous and public one. It was a group of individuals that would not be asked—as was the case for nudists—to share values, life forms, predetermined practices. They would no longer be required to be previously acquainted or to be bound by specific social networks. Since the State governed these new associations of debauchery, it was no longer necessary for them to come under the former private world, which was conceived of as a universe outside the purview of the law. Publicity would no longer be the essential element but a subsidiary part of the regulation of the distribution of sexuality in space. The new communities of debauchery could not be anything but public.

However, these spaces did not give themselves over, like beaches, to the fullest public visibility. Quite the contrary, these forms of sexuality, held to be both *deviant* and lawful at the same time, had to hide from the eyes of all, be prohibited to certain audiences such as minors, and require conditions of secrecy and specific consent. They were to be at once both hidden and public.

But these new rules did not yet have a legal basis. When the courts were questioned, they said that they did not intend to break with the long history that had rendered publicity and sexuality incompatible. Thus, it was not until the 1992 Penal Code reform that the rules could be established and clarified. This explanation can account for the stiffening of the rules of public decency that the courts had put in place since the mid-nineteenth century based on a parameter other than repression. This rigor did not reflect the will to persecute debauchery; rather it was to organize it, to regulate it within the law and to efface this enormous shadow projected by the wall of shame on private space. Thus, instead of analyzing this process as the desire to repress sexuality in private spaces, one can envisage it as the process by which the State sought to remove these spaces of lawlessness, the organization and regulating of which it had delegated to the private world.

From a spatial logic to a sexual logic

The liberalization of the public visibility of sexuality starting in the 1950s marks the passage of structures founded on space to ones based on Sex. This transition can be observed very clearly in the statistics of convictions for rape.

If, in the 1920s and 1930s, there was an annual average of thirteen to twenty-five convictions for rape of adult women, they numbered 126 in the years following World War II to 1950. This figure was more or less stable until the 1980s. Then in a rising curve, we moved from 190 convictions per year between 1970 and 1978[33] to 480 in 1984.[34] Just for the prosecutor's office of Nantes, between 1976 and 1984, there was an increase of 40 percent in complaints for rape and indecent assault, while convictions for contempt of public decency declined by 50 percent.[35]

This inversion is even more evident when comparing the statistics of convictions for contempt of public decency and those of sexual violence for a century, that is to say from the beginning of the imposition of penalties on crimes[36] until the moral revolution. In 1880, one finds eighty-five cases of rape and molestation of adults, 679 for children and 2,899 cases for contempt of public decency. In 1900, there were sixty-five cases for adults, and 383 for children, but 2,967 for contempt of public decency. It was only with the "revolution" of criminal law in the 1980s and 1990s that a significant reversal could be observed in the statistics. Thus, in 2000, 6,873 convictions were for rape and sexual assaults on adults and children, with only 1,897 cases of sexual exhibitionism.[37]

This inverse movement between the liberation of the public visibility of sexuality and the increase in the severity of crime reflects a civilization in which, rather than being subject to self-control, the impulses, are, on the contrary, subject to increasingly rigorous penal control. But this control no longer operates through space, a concept linked to the structure of contempt of public decency, but through the repression of ordinary sexual crimes and offenses.

Therefore, rendering sexuality publicly visible does not obey a process of internalization of constraints. Instead, this visibilization is the counterpart to the most extraordinary mechanisms of repression in sexual matters that France has known since the *Ancien Régime*. If the public visibility of sexuality is no longer as constrained, new state structures to control an individual's impulses have emerged, which make the criminal's *psyche* the new territory in which to intervene. Now the scandal of Sex will no longer unfold in space but in the minds of those who do take their pleasure within the purview of the law.

Notes

1 Polydore Fabreguettes, *Traité des délits politiques et des infractions par la parole, l'écriture et la presse*, 2e édition, 1901, t. l, p. 89.

2 H. Perrée, *La Publicité du spectacle (Étude juridique du théâtre de société)*, Doctoral thesis submitted to the School of Law [La faculté de droit], l'université de Paris, 1911, pp. 22–23.

3 *Ibid.*

4 *Ibid.*

5 Cass., 14 April 1892. D. 1893. 1. 239.

6 For more on this subject, see pp. 46–49.

7 *La Gazette des tribunaux*, 21, 27, July 28 1908.

8 *La Gazette des tribunaux*, 25 November and 2 December 1908.

9 During the nineteenth century, Article 330 was not used much for performances because of the system of prerequisite censorship, and the powers granted to the administration either to authorize certain performances, or to prevent them when they were likely to disturb public order and morality.

The administration exercised this set of powers differently over shows, depending on the type of performance. We can distinguish three different regimes of control. The first was the so-called private shows, which were protected in the same way as private spaces, and were closed without the obligation of accounting for the type of show that could take place within. Then there was the public theater, considered the most noble of all, which, according to Victor Hallays-Dabot, a famous critic of the Second Empire, was supposed to have the ability to penetrate the spiritual and political realms and the domain of thought and thus threaten or strengthen the "constituent bases of any society." Finally, there were other public performances, defined in contrast to theater, and dubbed "curiosity shows," which covered music halls and cafés-concerts, among others.

Since the Revolution, the legal regime showed a marked preference for theater at the expense of curiosity shows, so much so that one could indeed speak of a dual legal system.

While Article 4 of Title XI of the Law of 16–24 August 1790 stated: "public performances can only be permitted and authorized by municipal officers," the law of 13–19 January 1791 abolished censorship on performance of dramatic works. Thus, the regime for control as prescribed by Article 11 of the Declaration of the Rights of Man and of the Citizen of 26 August 1789 opposed a common law based on prior authorization applicable to all other public performances.

Although, from this date, theater experienced periods of censorship and periods of greater freedom, the legal system that governed it often remained separate from that of other types of performance.

The decree of 8 June 1806 established strict censorship in theaters. Article 15 excluded other types of shows from its scope, which were to be subject to special rules and could "no longer hold the title of theater." The Law of 9 September 1835 established that "no play or show of any kind can be produced without prior authorization from the Ministry of the Interior."

While maintaining the censorship of dramatic works during the Second Empire, the imperial decree of 6–18 January 1864 "relating to freedom of theaters," allowed the construction and operation of a theater as long as it was reported, while requiring that other types of shows remain subject to the previous licensing requirement.

The municipal law of 5 April 1884 gave the mayor "the authority to maintain good order in spaces where there are large gatherings of men," including "performances," in order to "ensure order, security and public safety."

But while this regime might have seemed at first to be favorable to theater, in reality, given the important role the theater was supposed to perform, the regime was not very beneficial.

Victor Hallays-Dabot observed that, given the imperative to protect the "three great ideas" that are "the life and strength of a nation: the religious sense, the moral sense, the patriotic spirit," theatrical censorship was justified. Other shows, however, had no other purpose than entertainment and were the object of a purely negative control. Cf. Christophe Fouassier, *Le Droit de la création cinématographique en France,* Paris, L'Harmattan, 2004, pp. 28–31.

This great political importance of theater justified the fate of censorship after the fall of the Second Empire. On 30 September 1870, a decree issued based on Jules Simon's proposition had abolished the Review Board of dramatic works. But less than a year later, on 18 March 1871, the Marshal de Mac-Mahon restored censorship under the powers he inherited from the state of siege. The end of the siege nevertheless did not end the rule of censorship. On 1 February 1874, a decree confirmed its existence and the law of 24 February 1875 transferred special funds to the Ministry of Public Education to ensure the functioning of the Inspection of Theaters.

According to Maurice Boy, during this period theater censorship was "odious and ridiculous." There was protest against its excesses on all fronts. But it is also due to its existence that prosecution for contempt of public decency was extremely rare during this period. The requisite censorship undertook to prevent the production of works that were deemed immoral, as was the case in 1891 for the play *The Girl Elise* [*La fille Élise*], adapted by Jean Ajalbert from Goncourt's novel (see, Maurice Garçon, *Histoire de la justice sous la Troisième République*).

10 *La Gazette des tribunaux,* 14 January 1892.

11 Here's how Chirac's lawyer, Mr. Labori, presented the defense of his client: "Gentlemen, I have no intention of justifying Mr. Chirac's theories. I am not advocating a literary trial; we are all in agreement on this point. Such is the feeling of the court, it is the feeling of the prosecutor, it is that of general opinion and it is mine. But this is not the sense that M. Chirac has and we are forced to consider his position. He acted with a conviction that was at once cynical and naive. With the ardor of puberty driven by a compelling mania, he followed it to its logical conclusion. And from his chimera, he fell to this bench, perhaps without being disillusioned. What he committed was a common law offense, and for it, he is now reviled, abused, beaten. Rather than take part in a literary competition, he needs the most gifted lawyers. [...] The question is this: you may find him guilty, but will you hit hard?" *La Gazette des tribunaux*, *ibid*.

12 *Ibid*. According to Maurice Boy, Chirac was pardoned after a fairly long imprisonment. "Slightly calmed, he still persisted in pursuing his projects. Sometimes in Montmartre, sometimes in the provinces, he

insisted in front of his audience that his show no longer put on what he called "real-life spectacle." He added some anti-war verses to his crude but more nuanced repertoire. Neither censorship nor the criminal court hounded him anymore, but in a garrison in the East, his audience took it upon themselves to punish him. Officers went up on stage, lowered his trousers and spanked him, facing towards the public. He died miserably in Nemours at the end of a performance. This is the only moment in which he can be compared to Molière. After the troupe's women sat in a wake over his fate at the inn, he was buried in a common grave still dressed as an apache. No one had taken the trouble to cleanse him of his makeup." *La Gazette des tribunaux*, pp. 285–286.

13 *Le Journal*, 25 April 1908.

14 R. C., "Le nu au spectacle peut-il outrager la pudeur," RSC, 1953. 362–366.

15 In his article "Observations sur l'outrage public à la pudeur (à l'occasion de l'ouvrage de M.C. Laplatte)," de la RSC, 1969. pp. 839–851, Robert Vouin remarks on the variation in citations of this ruling, which is attributed to the criminal tribunal trial of 21 June 1949 by Laplatte, p. 40, and by P.A. Pageaud in Juris-classeur pénal, art. 330–333, 1965, n° 4. Whereas Lambert refers to the trial at the Court [of Dijon] on 21 June 1949, Lambert, *Traité de droit pénal spécial,* Paris, 1968, p. 611.

16 RSC, 1949. 345.

17 For more, see the examples cited in Chapter 3.

18 GP, 1956.2.222, and Bull. crim., 1956, n° 555.

19 Bull. crim., 1960, n° 573; D. 1961. 1. 94.

20 See p. 68.

21 Crim. 10 November 1932, D. 1933. 1. 133 note Mlle Vandamne.

22 Cass. crim., 15 June 1954, D. 1954. 1. 701.

23 Jean-Pierre Pastori, *A corps perdu: histoire de la danse nue au XXe siècle,* Paris, PM Favre, 1983.

24 Kenneth Tynan, "Pornography? And is that Bad?," in *The New York Times,* 15 June 1969, cited by Jean Pierre Pastori, *ibid.*

25 Of course, "in principle" is the operative term in this context. In the conclusion of his book on the history of nude dance in the twentieth century, Jean Pierre Pastori writes: "[...] the few choreographers or companies that have tried to develop a nude repertoire are hardly successful [...] nudity—both in ballet and theater—inevitably stumbles on the notion of eroticism. Despite the profound transformation of attitudes with respect to morality, nudity on stage is still interpreted as an appeal to the senses. [...] of course, dance itself is an art of erotic nature. The rendering nude of the dancers makes this eroticism particularly explicit, to the point that, in many cases, in the minds of spec-

tators, it ends up prevailing over all other considerations of artistic nature."

26 *Le Figaro,* 13 January 1970, "Tout nu!," cited by Doublier, *Le Nu et la Loi*, p. 67.
27 Tribunal correctionnel de Paris, 17e chambre, GP, 25 January 1977, pp. 56–58.
28 JCP 1979. U. 19.138.
29 GP, 1978. 2 somm. 380.
30 *Ibid.*
31 Normbert Elias, *La Civilisation des mœurs,* translation of the second German edition by Pierre Kamnitzer, Paris, Calmann-Lévy, 1973. For a very interesting contestation of these hypotheses, see Hans Peter Duerr, *Nudité et pudeur. Le mythe du processus de civilisation,* preface by André Burguière, translated from the German by Véronique Bodin, Paris, Éditions de la Maison des sciences de l'homme, 1998.
32 Most importantly, see J.-C. Kaufmann's study on nude breasts, *Corps de femmes, regards d'hommes.*
33 Cited by Bordeaux et al., *Qualifié viol.* pp. 21–22.
34 Cited by Vigarello, *Histoire du viol.* p. 258.
35 Cited by Bordeaux et al., *Qualifié viol.* p. 70.
36 See Chapter 4.
37 *Annuarie statistique de la justice*, éd. 2006.

Part III

The politics of spaces in the era of Sex

The protest movements of the 1960s and 1970s never stopped proclaiming that the personal was political too. It is likely that they did not realize what they were doing by insisting on such an equivalence. For, in substance, they were transforming into a "victory" everything that the State sought to impose by force with the impressive revolution in legal codes that began in the early 1970s. The main consequence of such legislative tumult was the substitution of marriage—whose shortcomings the slogan "the personal is political" sought to expose—with a new master under whose regime we now live: Sex.

One can indeed think of the sexual revolution, and the dramatic reversals it has caused in the ways we enjoy, love, procreate, look and see or break and obey laws, all as the result of substituting marriage with Sex. Marriage, with all its attendant opacities, organized lies and declared impunities, would make room for the transparency, truth, and exemplary punishment produced by Sex. Now, nothing could be more political than the private. In order to codify this revolution in language, the 1992 reform eliminated the words "morals" and "modesty" from the Penal Code, only to speak of "sexual" assault, injury or exhibition.[1]

The new moral order, which emerged in part due to the contributions of revolutionary minorities, first appeared in the early 1970s, following a series of reforms which, without going so far as to abolish marriage, disabled its former functions. It became a legal institution whose main function was to guarantee economic solidarity between spouses. And even that guarantee was not to be its exclusive domain, for, in the decades that followed, other frameworks such as cohabitation or legal civil union, called the Pacte Civil de Solidarité [PaCS], have played a similar role. The institutions that depended on marriage, such as laws about lineage and the law that repressed sexual offenses, were completely restructured.

The 1970s and 1980s were decisive in the formation of these new rules. Reproductive and filiation rights were reorganized around the primacy of the sperm and the reproductive power bestowed upon fertile women,[2] and Sex became the legal property most jealously guarded by the penal order.

Judges are no longer required to have recourse to a minor and subsidiary misdemeanor, such as contempt of public decency, in order to soften the sex crime penalties thought to be too severe, or to create new offenses that sanctioned such conduct not covered by the penal order. Nothing was to be considered too severe to punish perpetrators of sexual offenses. No violent behavior, intimidation, harassment, corruption would be forgotten by criminal law. The new offense of sexual exhibitionism, which replaced contempt of public decency, could finally punish specific and targeted behaviors without taking into account the regulatory functions of the entire system. It is clear then that this offense was punished less than in the past, but also much less present in criminal statistics.

The new offense marked the end of a juridico-political technique of spatial surveillance of sexuality in which publicity was to be free of any display of sexuality. The crime of sexual exhibitionism is now an offense for which publicity is at once both an essential and subsidiary element. Essential, for we continue to make the distinction between public and private: only public exhibitions are repressed; subsidiary, because the issue of publicity only becomes operative in constituting the crime if the acts have been imposed on a concrete and precise individual who did not want to see the sex scene s/he saw. Publicity, while being essential for the constitution of this offense, is no longer sufficient in and of itself. Public spaces are no longer places where the display of sexuality must be banned under all circumstances. The new offense does not seek to repress all sexuality that appears in public per se but targets any that is imposed on others in public.

However, the law implicitly "recognizes" visual relationships as specific, legally permissible manifestations of sexuality—without forgetting that this is an eroticism that is "dissolute"—and thus merely punishes its "deviant" forms. The new penal law organizes debauchery within narrow bounds, while it tracks down perversions with great insistence.

These shifts have led to the penal order's great interest in exhibitionism, a form of sexual perversion which was formerly treated with great indulgence but now considered the first stage of a dangerous illness that can lead to graver crimes. For, in this new world, which turned the old order on its head to free us from the shackles of the past, libertines have become more tolerable than perverts.

7

The new criminal law on sexuality

The end of marriage as the juridico-sexual ideal, heretofore the primary feature of the framework of misdemeanors and crimes against morality, necessitated a clarification of the social values that these offenses were now supposed to protect. Of course, we know that the previous order did not only protect marriage but also other values, such as consent, sexual normality and a certain notion of purity or integrity when minors were involved. However, these values in the Code were subordinated to marriage, which appeared as the dominant element of the overall system.

With the fall of marriage, what could then take its place as the linchpin of all values, that fundamental element of a system that would prevail and give meaning to all others? The sexual revolution, which presented itself as a liberation of desire and pleasure, could have instead privileged personal liberty, the freedom to accept or to refuse to share with others activities deemed "sexual," the content and meaning of which could have remained open-ended. Yet, this is not how we answered that question.

Criminal law put Sex over personal freedom and decided that the latter was to be subjected to the former.[3] First and foremost, rather than assuring freedom, the State would protect "sexual integrity," that sort of invisible skin that was supposed to guard people against an atrocious evil which, according to the penal order, was as serious as, if not worse than, death itself.

If the puritanical Napoleonic Code had stripped sexual activities of the transcendent power that they had enjoyed during the *Ancien Régime* and coaxed them into servicing the domestic domain, the sexual revolution restored their lost aura.

Having rendered Sex into an object of legal protection is certainly not comparable to being the guardian of freedom, that is to say protecting the formal capacity to act or not act, as is the case for the expression of ideas or the practice of religion. Criminal law protects content more than form, presumed realities more than opportunities to act. It knows better than anyone, and more than any individual, what is good or bad, healthy or unhealthy, destructive or redemptive in this field. However, what is this curious institutional construction that criminal law so grandiloquently protects and calls Sex?

I The Sex of the State

Drawing from some broad interpretations of psychology and psychoanalysis, criminal law constructed the concept of Sex-as-law as a reality of psychological nature. But far from conceiving of this reality in the same way as other psychological phenomena—that is to say, as symbolic phenomena and therefore subject to individual variation—the law treated it as if it were a physiological process analogous to digestion or circulation, and therefore governed by fixed, stable, collective, predictable and inevitable causalities.

If criminal law instituted such interpretations, it is not because it might have been obsessed with scientific truth. This implicit knowledge of Sex created by juridical constructions is presented as a set of functional and strategic statements that aim to justify new powers to intervene in this specific aspect of interpersonal relationships that the State had more or less ignored since the Old Regime. The Sex of the resulting new criminal law appears first in every individual, not as something positive but as a weakness. It can be compared to a flaw that everyone carries within oneself, which could destroy, corrupt or kill, if not physically at least psychologically. The particularity of this painful fault is to leave individuals entirely at the mercy of one another. The more this flaw is perceived as likely to endanger the survival of the individual, the more expansive and limitless the role of guardian that the State has allocated itself. In this area, criminal law has made it possible to override a large number of rules germane to the rule of law, such as the principles of legality, nonretroactivity of criminal law, fair trial and the proportionality between crime and punishment.[4] Nothing seems sufficiently severe to prevent and punish sex crimes and misdemeanors. The stakes are such that the State feels authorized to be less and less respectful of formal rules that require it to restrain and limit itself. This is particularly evident when furnishing proof and often leads to terrible miscarriages of justice. Indeed, despite the severity of penalties for defendants, psychological tests and the victims' testimonies now replace material and rational proof.[5]

This overreach of State power is not necessarily comparable to that of authoritarian regimes, in which overreach occurs and is justified through a direct relationship with each individual in order to preserve the State's power in the face of those who dare challenge it. Rather, in this context, the State exercises an exceptional power in its capacity as a third-party arbitrator and not as the master of the freedom of its subjects. This exceptional power is justified and exercised in order to avoid the devastation that each individual can produce on others. And Sex and sexual integrity have become the first and most powerful justifications.

That mysterious "sexual integrity," which the new penal order protects, is far from being just another form of well-being. When we speak of sexual assault today, we speak freely of "psychological murder." The sexually abused are supposed to be "destroyed." The result is significant, because rather than the risk being linked to the victim's moral or social future, as was previously the case, it is now more than ever predicated on the very existence of the victim, as well as his or her emotional and mental future.

These infractions cause lives to be "arrested" and not merely "debauched." Failure at school, confinement in psychiatric hospitals, suicide, such is the lot of victims of sexual violence. Victims of this offense are not comparable to others because their psyches have been forever compromised. They have become ill and nothing can completely cure them. But the consequences are even more disturbing for it is predicted that today's victims will become tomorrow's abusers, just like vampires who transform their prey into the very agents of evil to which they were subject.

The gravity accorded to sexual violence has effects on the time frame within which the State may be called to intervene. Thus, this knowledge about Sex claims that there is often a time lag between the violence to which the victim was subject and the damage that it engenders. Moreover, the forms of action on the victims' psyche could amount to a kind of time bomb. Thus, one can never be sure that sexual abuse does not continue to be the cause of disasters decades after the fact. This has justified a more and more dramatic increase in penalties[6] and the possible establishment of longer periods of incarceration for these misdemeanors and crimes.[7]

This ideological construct that allowed the State to grant itself such power in areas that were previously relatively inaccessible also necessitated the casting of the enemies of Sex in a very special way. If the old moral order conceived them as the enemies of a certain morality, that is to say, of a set of practices related to a conception of right and wrong in sexual matters, under the current regime they are designated as psychiatric patients. If the libertine was the obverse of the marital ideal, the pervert is the obverse of the ideal of Sex.

Those who violate the standards of the world of Sex are not like other criminals and offenders. They are supposed to be, above all, sick, and most importantly, incurable patients. Indeed, institutional knowledge of Sex claims that those who commit an offense of this nature, even if it is a minor offense, or if it does not implicate them as a subject of any particular desire—for example, those who trade in forbidden images—could not have a normal psyche. Just the fact of engaging in certain antisocial pleasures appears as proof that at the time of their formation as sexual subjects, they were subject to irreparable damage. All we can hope is that these individuals repress their perverse impulses, that they restrain themselves and make a conscious and even physiological effort to avoid wreaking havoc on others.

This inability to transform oneself that is attributed to the psychology of the sexual criminal explains the new punitive mechanisms that have gradually been put in place, which simultaneously assume both sickness and flaw.[8] The figure of the sexual pervert is at once thus sexual and moral, and articulates both a mental illness and evil joined in a profile composed of psychological models old and new, secular and religious, through which discourses meant to be scientific or demonological can be heard.

The strange institutional nature of Sex seems essential to understanding the importance accorded to consent in the new order. Previously, consent had a secondary role, because it was part of a system that had less value than the power of marital relations. In the present order, consent has become subject to the imperative of Sex. Indeed, the current order in no way assumes that everyone wants the same things in looking for sexual happiness. Quite the contrary, the law acknowledges the huge variations in the propensities and corporeal or relational techniques to achieve that end, but allows for a much narrower frame than individual consent might define. For, it is not the consent mechanism that governs the new Sex order. Rather, it is Sex that accords consent a place within a system of knowledge of which the law is meant to be the jealous guardian, which explains its specific instability and insecurity.

Indeed, consent is not intended as a banal act of will but as a very serious decision insofar as it is capable of engaging the very fate of an individual. Consent is, therefore, less the manifestation of a freedom than that which appears as essential for the person not to suffer any damage. Some adults may perceive themselves as having been victims of a crime, even though they had consented to sex with their supposed attacker. Because the consent given may not have been pure, authentic, even if it took on the appearance of an act freely determined. Thus, certain consents are suspected to have been extorted from victims who would not have realized it at the time it was given.

It is from this issue of consent in the world of Sex that new discourses denouncing prostitution, pornography and promiscuity take root. The dominant hypothesis posits that those who engage in such acts voluntarily, especially women, do not *really* give consent. The quasi-metaphysical research on the assertion of will and real authenticity is linked to the subordination of consent to Sex, that is to say, to all the postulates that teach us so-called different healthy and normal ways to engage in sexual relations.

In the world of Sex, the notion of consent is related to the political hypothesis that weak subjects are not capable of self-determination and that the State is supposed to help them retroactively, to save them from extortions of which they might have been victims.

The psychological nature of Sex also seems essential to understand that infractions may protect the sexual imaginary of the public against certain types of messages that can, depending on the assumptions of the law, excite or incite certain types of behavior. For a psychological injury to occur, one does not need to physically hurt the body of the victim. It can be constituted by words, pictures or the sight of certain scenes.

So it is by means of *psychological toxicity* that we have returned the old offenses to public morality. These are not presumed to lead to debauchery but to perversion, either because they disrupt the sexual development of children or because they are likely to awaken dormant criminal impulses in adults.[9]

With regard to minors, new infractions have been maintained or even created to punish the act of subjecting them to certain scenes or specific messages in order to preserve their *purity* until adulthood.

Regarding the general population, it is assumed that there would be a minority that is conscious or unconscious of its own extremely dangerous and perverse impulses (that is to say, all of us, because who knows what we seek to repress and ignore), for whom the sight of certain images could lead to the transgression of censorship mechanisms and promote committing the act.

Finally, Sex according to the law is characterized by the vagueness of its borders, because this three-letter word in whose name we punish encompasses a world of infinite acts. No conduct by its very objectivity can escape being classified as sexual. The criminal justice system began to think of the illegal sexual being as a boundless body, thus allowing the State to grant itself an arbitrary and constantly expanding power. Every bodily contact, every gaze, every request can now be deemed sexual.[10]

These uncertainties about the "territorial" limits of sex posed very serious problems when it came to judging specific behaviors. Offences that refer to penetration, assault and "sexual" violations lend themselves, in effect, to all sorts of metaphorical and analogical interpretations. Is placing one's hand on someone's leg to be considered sexual? Can a photograph of a child naked in a bathtub be described as pornographic?

In applying these rules poorly defined for practical situations, the courts had no other recourse but to appeal to the motives of the accused, that is to say the type of interest or desire that drives an individual to perform certain actions, rather than stick to the nature of the acts themselves. The interest in the perpetrators' motives and thus in the type of enjoyment they seek has become essential for the judiciary, to the detriment of the quest for the intent behind the committing of specific acts. The sexual is now more in the mind than in the acts themselves. But we know that, when venturing into the uncertain enterprise of ascribing sexual motives to others, what prevails are the fantasies of those who judge and not some reality that could have inhabited the mind of the accused when the acts were committed. Who had a pornographic motive, the photographer who took a snapshot of her son in a tub to present it at an exhibition or the judges who convicted her of violating Section 227-23 of the Penal Code?

Through these techniques of interpretation, judges appear to exercise a kind of power over our conscience, which creates confusion between morality and law, family upbringing and State-sanctioned punishment, between medicine and law. Yet, far from seeking techniques that could reduce the arbitrariness and legal uncertainty it creates, this State, which began governing Sex so clumsily, seems to be emerging as more radical. Since the revision of the criminal code was made in the name of modernity, to protect the weak against the strong, women against men, children against adults, this order is conceived as the victory of Good against Evil. Thus, any criticism leveled against it becomes suspect. For who else but pedophiles, pimps, rapists and misogynists may fear the purifying wrath of the new order of Sex?

The new structure of sexual misdemeanors and crimes

The logic behind the new structure of sexual crimes is directly responsible for the dismantling of the hegemonic role that marriage had held for almost two centuries. This "dismantling" is manifested in two major transformations, the first of which was the subordination of sexual intercourse between married persons to the rule of consent. Heralded as the end of barbarism and a transition to civilization, the subordination of marriage to consent implies, more than anything else, the entry of the State into an area of interpersonal relationships that was previously subject to other norms. Indeed, the subordination of marriage to the rule of consent implies the end of an institution that created an exceptional space of sexual impunity within the framework of crimes against morality.

This change also brought with it what could be called a "denormativization" of sexuality, that is to say, the decline of heterosexual intercourse as the paradigm of sexual relations and "recognition" by the law of the most strange and varied forms of erotic relationships in order to make them either lawful or illegal. However, in the new paradigm of Sex, the denormativization of erotic practices permits the State not to be disinterested in them when the partners are willing. Rather, it permits the State to regulate them, prioritize them, draw them out of the darkness in which they used to take place in the past.

The subordination of marriage to consent

We have seen that in the past intercourse within marriage did not require mutual consent of the spouses. It could be required by force, because *it was* a duty owed by the spouses to one another. Thus, there could never be a rape between spouses, that is to say, that this crime, which was the most serious crime of the penal order, was incompatible with sexual relations in marriage. The 1980 law on rape was the first to break this impunity in an implicit manner. The sole criterion for measuring sexual relationships between adults became consent, including when they occur within a marriage.

However, such a reversal could not remain implicit. Much of the courts' doctrine did not reflect it. For everyone to be convinced, the jurisprudence of the Court of Appeals had to create precedent with two cases: those of 5 September 1990[11] and 11 June 1992.[12] The doctrine set forth in those cases is now the rule: "The presumption of consent to sexual acts between spouses in the intimacy of marriage is only valid until proven otherwise."

To complete this change in order, the law of 4 April 2006 introduced some modifications which made clear that marriage was subordinate to consent. In Article 222-22 of the Penal Code, which defines sexual assault in general, it added the following paragraph: "Rape and other sexual assaults occur if they were imposed on the victim in the circumstances described by this section, regardless of the nature of the relationship between perpetrator and victim, including when they are united by the bond of marriage. In this case, the presumption of consent between the spouses to sexual intercourse will only be valid until proven otherwise."

Second, and perhaps most importantly, with this law, being in a coupled relationship with the rape victim makes it an aggravating circumstance of the crime, just as when a crime causes disfigurement or permanent disability. Thus, Article 222-24 stipulates that rape is punishable by twenty years of imprisonment "when committed by a spouse or cohabitant of the victim or by a partner joined in civil union [PaCS] to the victim" (paragraph 7).

Marriage has thus lost not only its impunity with regard to rape but it has become an aggravating circumstance. To its detriment, aside from the reversal of its former privileges, with regard to rape between partners, marriage was treated in the same manner as other spousal arrangements such as cohabitation and PaCS. This "symbolic humiliation" was, however, necessary to equalize arrangements regarding interpersonal relations between partners by following the logic of civil law.

Nevertheless, couplehood as an institution continues to be an association of individuals that enjoys a special status with regard to sexuality, not so much because it can produce impunity but because it can be penalized more than any other relationship; not so much to create a space into which the State cannot enter but to open such spaces up to gain permanent control. Thus, the couple would be recognized and differentiated from other groups of people as a structure within which we must respect, more than anywhere else, partner consent, even more than on a deserted street or in an unheated garage.

Formerly, it was because people had decided to inscribe their sexuality within an institution as particular as marriage—which involved a very restrictive set of duties—that, in return, the State provided them with impunity, darkness, the opportunity to live on an island of nonlaw with respect to the inter-couple relationship that they could build. Today, this model has almost reversed. In exchange for the benefits that living as a couple affords, including the creation of economic solidarity established both within the couple and in the eyes of the State, the State requires that such unions be models of good sexuality. The partners are not bound by any sexual exclusivity but they have, more than anyone else, the duty to respect the consent of the other in their sexual relationships. Criminal law no longer focuses on adultery, while the failure to comply with the formal partner's consent has become one of the most serious crimes on the books. Marriage as an institution is no longer protected by the State, as before, against those who could threaten it from the outside, as evidenced by the existence of the crime of adultery or the differential status of children born out of wedlock. The couple as institution has become a machine that provides partners with tools to take action *against one another,* in order to impose the reign of the sexual ideal that the State ceaselessly promotes.[13]

II The denormativization of sexuality

The phenomenon that I call "denormativization" of sexuality is connected, at least in principle, to the new position occupied by consent in the framework of sexual crimes and misdemeanors.

What makes sexual relations lawful is the fact of consenting to them regardless of the type of acts to which we consent. The apologists for the current order repeatedly stress it: no matter what we do, what truly counts is that we agree with what we are going to do. The essential thing is not what we will do but under what conditions of autonomy we decide to engage in a sexual relationship.

However, if we observe this phenomenon more closely, we will understand that this denormativization is more apparent than real. Indeed, it suffers the same fate as consent in the new order of Sex. Under the guise of equality of all sexual practice, criminal law has created a new category of abnormal acts that are permissible only under certain conditions, even when they are consented to. The State's knowledge [savoir] of the nature of Sex necessarily implies the distinction between various sexual practices, either because they are presumed not to allow for the normal development of adolescents, who are thus forbidden to engage in such practices, or because consent may be contested more easily when applied to a relation seen as "abnormal."

Normal acts and those that are not so normal

If formerly, spouses could be forced to perform sexual services for each other, the content of such relations was very clearly specified. Only a certain type of sexual act enjoyed this status: the classic heterosexual intercourse in which the couple was forced to engage by conjugal duty. Other sexual acts, however, if imposed, could be punished not as rape but as violent indecent assault. Thus, even between spouses, these sex acts had to be the object of a timely and explicit consent each time they engaged in such acts.

The 1980 reform challenged the traditional definition of rape, which was seen to be patriarchal. To distinguish rape from other violent acts of a sexual nature, it rejected the exclusive criterion of vaginal penetration and extended it to include any act that forcefully engaged with the body of another without having to take into account the organ-tool or the orifice that was object of the assault.

In the new version following the 1980 reform, rape is "any act of sexual penetration, whatever its nature, committed against another person by violence, coercion, threat or surprise." This shift is very important because it dethrones classic heterosexual intercourse from its role as the model or paradigm of sexual relationships. This new society, which was ready to free our desires and pleasures beyond the old confines of normality, made sexual misdemeanors and crimes a territory ripe for denormativization.

Unconventional sexuality recognized as normal or lawful immediately made its appearance in the framework of sexual misdemeanors and crimes. Thus, punishing forced sodomy or fellatio just like rape was a way of acknowledging, albeit in an obverse manner, that these acts had the same status of "sexual relation" as conventional intercourse. They could, at least in the eyes of criminal law, potentially produce "psychological wounds" of the same nature with equally serious consequences.

But the denormativization of sexuality took a distinctive route and form. While it was very liberal in allowing two persons to have different forms of bodily contact, and while it recognized the most varied orifices and tools for pleasure, this was not the case when it came to other expressions of sexuality. Indeed, in deciding that there were no right or wrong ways to approach sex, the sexual revolution has transformed the entire body of one's partner into a territory of lawful enjoyment. The whole body became a unit of pleasure without certain parts being either authorized or prohibited. Everything is potentially sexual and legal to the extent, of course, that the partners consent to those acts.

Sociologists investigating the sexuality of the French relish it. They continue to highlight the variety, certainly relative, nevertheless real, of what we call the "sexual repertoire" of couples.[14]

However, the recognition of new pleasures is not so generous when it is not about body-to-body contact between two partners but rather the staging of fantasies or certain theater productions. The specific problem posed by prostitution aside, when sexuality involves *the actual or potential presence of more than two individuals,* implying therefore the performance aspect [*mise en spectacle*] of sexuality—the possibility of being seen by others or seeing others in such an act—consent alone can no longer make it lawful in all circumstances.

Even if the law tolerates certain expressions of sexuality of this type (such as exhibitionism, sex with multiple partners, pornography), it does so reluctantly by setting strict conditions so that they do not transgress the set limits or become commonplace.

If these expressions of eroticism are tolerated for adults over 18 years of age, they are not for those who are in the age group of 15–18 years. These youths may nevertheless consent to carnal intercourse of all kinds with adults. But, although it is permissible to engage in vaginal, anal, oral sex with teenagers between 15 and 18 years, it is still forbidden to photograph them nude or invite them to watch a sex session with multiple partners, even if they do not participate in it. And these prohibitions exist with regard to both relationships between adults and minors of 15–18 years of age and between minors themselves. Therefore, the current order has traded the normality of one act for another related to the number of partners, even if the multiplicity has shifted and is only represented. These acts thought to incite debauchery are only tolerated, and they have a status more fragile and problematic than any body-to-body contact between two persons.

Thus, a new form of abnormality is established, tolerated for some in specific conditions and in exceptional circumstances, and punished when these conditions are not met. And this is especially so when it concerns young individuals, who are supposed to be protected from corrupting influences or forms of sexuality that do not match their "normal evolution."

Such activities are perpetually expected to be the expression of a debauched sexuality that in no circumstances can be held up as example. So, it is from this distinction, well within consensual acts themselves, that a new category of sexual acts emerges and is defined by its relationship to a model of sexual normality. These acts are merely tolerated, positioning them midway between lawful acts and illegal acts.

Yet, rather than seeking to avoid the creation of débauchés, the focus of the new rules, which take certain acts to be abnormal, is on perverts. In the world of Sex, a pervert can be the one who got caught in the evil sphere of the libertines. The normality, or the abnormality, of the act aims less to protect the person who is its victim than society at large. Today as before, in the framework of sexual misdemeanors and crimes, to condemn an abnormal act is not justified by the need to protect the person who is its victim but because of the risks it is likely to inflict on others. In this regard, the example of the devastating effects that watching pornographic films is supposed to have on teenagers is paradigmatic: although one has never succeeded in showing any causal link between the viewing of these images and the behavior of the youth, we continue to argue that pornography makes rapists.

But the new order can be distinguished in particular from the older one when we look at the crucial point of the balance and functioning of the entire system. Lawful acts, that is to say, those both consensual and "normal," do not enjoy the same legal certainty that they did in the past: until the end of its long legal statutory limitation, a consensual sexual act is an event that may be the object of suspicion, reversal or charge and can be termed rape *post factum.*

This continuing instability implies that the State may be called upon at any time to retroactively validate the truth and authenticity of consent. No situation is completely out of bounds for the State. Unlike in former times, its intervention is no longer impossible (as in the case of marriage) or certain (lack of avowed consent), but becomes conceivable.

If lawful sex refers to a number of increasingly varied situations and acts, it is also becoming increasingly precarious. If new forms of "debauched" sexuality have been placed under the rule of exception—as they are presumed to be "abnormal"—the State has allowed itself to organize them so they do not transgress their legal framework, and therefore has permitted itself to exercise more control over them.

The misdemeanor of sexual exhibitionism finds its rationale in these new techniques for controlling debauchery. Visible sexual relations are tolerated in specific circumstances, while their excesses are punished by the new Article 222-32 of the Penal Code.

Notes

1 See Luc-Michel Nivôse, "Des attentats aux mœurs et à la pudeur aux agressions sexuelles," *Dr. Pénal*, 1995.

2 For a detailed analysis of this evolution see *L'Empire du ventre, pour une autre histoire de la maternité*, Paris, Fayard, 2004.

3 In this regard, we can draw a parallel with how the sexual revolution dealt with the question of lineage. We know that in this area the desire to become a parent was not substituted with previous forms of filiation and the extent to which womens' body power came to be privileged over personal freedom. For more on this subject, see *L'Empire du ventre*.

4 See Iacub, *Le Crime était presque sexuel*; Marcela Iacub et Patrice Maniglier, *Antimanuel d'éducation sexuelle*, Paris, Bréal 2005; Xavier Lameyre, *La Criminalité sexuelle*, Paris, Flammarion, 2000, and numerous other works by this author including: "L'incessant accroissement légal de la répression des infractions sexuelles," *Forensic*, n°

19, July–September 2004, pp. 13–18. See also Jacques Barillan and Paul Bensussan, *Le Nouveau Code de la sexualité*, Paris, Odile Jacob, 2007.

5 On this point see Paul and Florence Bensussan Rault, *La Dictature de l'émotion. La protection de l'enfant et ses dérives*, Paris, Belfond, 2002. Despite the scandal in the wake of the Outreau case, it would seem that the arbitrary standards of proof have not changed. For the Outreau case, see Acacia Pereira, *Justice injuste. Le scandale de l'affaire d'Outreau*, Paris, éditions Philippe Rey, 2004.

6 The majority of the verdicts rendered by criminal courts affect people accused of sex crimes. In 2004, of the 2,364 convictions, 1,744 were for sex crimes, that is, forty times more than in 1989. Among European countries, France has the highest number of convicted sex criminals. The number of inmates for sex crimes in France is two to 118 times higher than those of other member nations of the Council of Europe. While, in 2003, France held the record for 8,538 convictions for rape, comprising a total of 56,806 inmates, Germany had two times fewer, Italy four times fewer, and Denmark 118 times fewer (see *Statistique pénale annuelle du Conseil de l'Europe,* 2004 survey).

7 Since the law of 10 March 2004, the statute of limitations for sex crimes committed against a minor has been twenty years from adulthood, which means that someone who has been victim of a sexual crime as a child may file a complaint until the age of 38. It should be noted that in Switzerland the statute for these crimes does not expire.

8 See Chapter 9, in which I analyze new punitive tools for sexual delinquents and sex offenders in greater detail.

9 These offenses can now be classified into two distinct groups. In the first, they seek to protect the entire public and not just minors from the corrupting influences of certain spectacles or images. They are respectively the offenses of sexual exhibitionism (Art. 222-32), which I will analyze in detail, and the use of pornographic images of minors (Art. 227-23).

In the second, they seek to protect minors from the corrupting influences of certain forms of adult sexuality. Thus, the former affront to public decency has become the new Article 227-24, which prohibits the dissemination of pornographic or violent messages that may be received by a minor. The same goes for the old offense named *excitation des mineurs à la débauche*, renewed and extended in the 1992 reform of the Penal Code as the corruption of minors (Art. 227-22).

Thus, according to legal rationale, which was drawn from the middle of the twentieth century, the idea of corruption is compartmentalized according to its public. Certain messages are deemed to corrupt all the public and others are supposed to only corrupt minors.

As we shall see, minors are supposed to be corrupted by the "spectacle" of acts that are permitted for adults, such as orgies, or even by those for which they have been authorized, like consensual sex to the extent they take place before witnesses or when they are filmed. The spectacle is considered more harmful than reality, because it implies a form of realization of the act that is not "natural" or "healthy" for them.

But adults are also supposed to be corrupted by certain kinds of performances, although now they have become very specialized. Thus, as we shall see, sexual exhibition has changed its colors because it is not the same acts that are prohibited from being enacted in public. The same goes for child pornography, which is banned for both adults and minors. Indeed, the new section 227-23 of the Penal Code—established with the 1992 reform, and which has since been revised repeatedly—seeks to protect society against the awakening of pedophilic instincts likely to be incited by certain images. The law assumes that adult perverts cannot act unless certain external stimuli push them to do so.

10 See the detailed analysis that I devote to this issue in *Le crime était presque sexuel.*

11 Crim., 5 September 1990, Bull. crim., 1990, no. 313.

12 Crim., 11 June 1992, D. 1993. somm. 13, obs. Azibert.

13 Surveys conducted before the reform of the law have linked over 47 percent of rapes of adult women to have been perpetrated by a former spouse or partner, cf. Information Report No. 229, Senator Jean-Guy Branger of 9 March 2005.

14 For a significant example of these sociological pleasures, see Janine Mossuz-Lavau, *La Vie sexuelle en France*, Paris, La Martinière, 2002.

8

The scenography of Sex

In the new world of Sex, where the State keeps such meticulous vigil over all relations, tracks coerced consents, avenges sullied purities and prevents perverted teachings, the spatial techniques that had been utilized as modes of regulation of sexual behavior have been relegated to the background. If the visibility of sexuality has been liberalized in public spaces, private spaces are no longer policed by a spatial logic but one that is purely "sexual." So we no longer punish people like that grandmother whose grandson caught her by surprise because she had forgotten to leave the key in the keyhole. On the other hand, the female primary school teacher who placed her hand on a young student's leg can be accused of having touched the student in a "sexually" suggestive manner.

The new infraction, codified in the reform of 1992, which replaced the old contempt of public decency, is the witness and vehicle for this distancing from spatial techniques in the governance of sexuality. It has disinvested itself of the functions that the old Napoleonic infraction had possessed in regard to sexuality as a whole. It contents itself with organizing a specific form of sexual relations in which people engage with the public gaze, by punishing certain forms of their "deviant" expressions.

In the logic of the infraction, the act of showing oneself in public has become an intentional sexual behavior, a form of eroticism in and of itself, which can be either lawful or unlawful according to the circumstances. However, even if it has become modest, this infraction nonetheless produces, just like in the past, rules of spatialization for sexuality as a whole. It allows for a public space and a private space to subsist, each with its specific constraints.

Article 330 of the Penal Code was replaced with the new Article 222-32, which states the following:

"The spectacle of sexual exhibition imposed on others in a space accessible to the public gaze is punishable by imprisonment of one year and a fine of 15,000 euros."

Despite its apparent simplicity, this text hides a labyrinth of subtleties that carve out the scenography of contemporary pleasures. We need nothing less than a chapter to analyze the meaning of this short sentence. Rarely has this school of precision that is law required so much effort on the part of the interpreter. Let us first try to define our terms in a relatively abstract manner; examples will clarify the divisions that this sentence created between the legal and the illegal. Readers will be rewarded for their attention, for this analysis will allow them to understand that, in a world where the law wants to see everything, a new figure of evil has been invented and, rather than hide itself, wants to benefit from being seen.

I The new infraction: "I show to the public that I impose on someone the spectacle of my sexuality"

The new infraction lightened the punishments envisaged by Article 330 and restrains forbidden behaviors. It no longer seeks to punish, as it formerly did, the act of *making public* a *generic* sexual behavior but to repress a *specific* behavior that entails *imposing* on others the spectacle of a sexual scene. It is not all of sexuality that must be hidden from public view but a form of *exhibitionism* that could be qualified, at first glance, as *aggressive*. However, contrary to what one might believe, rather than pursuing all sexual violence done to others, this infraction only seeks to punish violence committed in public.

Indeed, as strange as this might appear to some, the act of imposing the spectacle of sexuality in private—that is to say, *upon a single* person and in a space *invisible and inaccessible to the exterior*—is still not punishable. The new infraction only applies when the acts take place in a space accessible to the public gaze. In this way, despite the central importance that consent claims to have acquired in the contemporary regime of Sex, it appears here to be an element of lesser standing than the private or public status of the space. It is necessary to highlight the curious character of this lack of punishment in a world that seems so preoccupied with avoiding any form of sexual trauma for any individual. Sexual exhibition is the only act of sexual coercion that can be either legal or illegal according to the configuration of the space in which it occurs. What characterizes the space is the still operational distinction between the public and the private.

But, if the definition of the public–private divide has not changed with the new reforms, the nature of acts labeled as "obscene"—which are thus able to constitute an infraction—has nevertheless been profoundly transformed. The novelty introduced by the reform of 1992 is to require that there exist at least one person whose "gaze has been violated," in order to ask if a punishable act has taken place in public.

Let us remember that in the past one could be found to be in contempt of public decency even in deserted spaces and without witnesses. The mediation of an individual in these spaces, such as roads, was not essential for an infraction to occur. And if there were a witness, the fact that s/he had or had not consented to viewing the sexual scene was not taken into account. It is only in private, nonvisible spaces inaccessible to the exterior that the existence of the nonconsenting witness had become pertinent since the Ponce decision. But the function of this nonconsent was not to describe an act of sexual violence toward the victim of the exhibition but only to extend the notion of publicity to private spaces.

Likewise, starting in the 1950s, a witness's consent, or the absence thereof, became key in matters of virtual publicity in enclosed spaces into which a door permitted public access. In order for this type of space to be qualified as public—even if no one had opened the door—the witness who found himself inside had to be nonconsenting. If s/he were consenting, the virtual publicity disappeared. Consequently, whether it was an accessible public space or a closed and nonaccessible one, consent was not so much pertinent to qualify the nature of the forbidden act but rather to determine the status of the space. The obscene act of indecency could be a consensual or imposed exhibition.

In the new infraction, consent becomes an essential element in constituting the obscene act, which is only subsequently qualified further by whether it took place in private or in public. In other words, if a sexual act is shown to a consenting individual, in principle, it is not an obscene act that has taken place in public.

The act forbidden by Article 222-32 can henceforth be summarized thus: "I show to the public that I impose on someone the spectacle of my sexuality." Transgressive behavior is therefore defined by the articulation of two concurrent acts regarding *the performance of sexuality*: first, the act of imposing on someone, and second, that of exposing this spectacle to the public.

The forbidden act is new, for it consists of imposing the spectacle of one's sexuality on others, but the victim of the infraction is, always already, the public. This is why the infraction requires that exhibition be realized in certain spaces accessible to the victim's gaze. Because of this, in an indirect manner, Article 222-32 of the Penal Code has made *visual sexual relations committed in public* an object of *autonomous* State regulation, of which it only punishes certain forms.

Indeed, in the new sexual order resulting from the liberation of desires and pleasures, the infraction of sexual exhibition is the slippery slope of an act that we no longer forbid: that of showing one's sexuality to a public without imposing it on anyone, as is the case in theaters, swingers' clubs or gay bathhouses. Thus, we consider a new form of sexual relation that is the act of using the public gaze as an object of pleasure. In this way, if this infraction punishes certain forms of public sexual exhibition, it authorizes and indeed even indirectly organizes others that the old Article 330 punished.

The infraction of sexual exhibition distinguishes public debauchery, which is tolerated *under certain conditions*, from perversion, which is condemned, and of which this infraction is supposed to constitute, as we will see, the first stage.

But the public debauchery that the new Article 222-32 implicitly authorizes does not have the same status accorded to "normal" sexual acts. Criminal law contents itself with "tolerating" this scopic sexual enjoyment in certain exceptional conditions, such that these practices cannot in any case become commonplace but, above all, so that certain practices, such as orgies, cannot be carried out by adolescents. Yet, the new infraction implies a fundamental change in the function that qualifies a space or a situation as public.

Indeed, in the past, such qualification had the goal of limiting the expression of sexuality. Henceforth, the public is also a body whose purpose is to set limits to certain expressions of sexuality, but it is mostly what the law erects as a sexual object for the offender. For the sexual act that it prohibits is the act of relying on the public gaze to display a sexual scene imposed on others. That which the exhibitor abuses in the new infraction is the gaze of this impersonal being that is the public. This gaze was formerly the frontier that permitted the separation and control of erotic behaviors. With the new law, it becomes a full-fledged sexual object.

II Elements of the infraction: intention, the obscene act and publicity

The new offense preserved not only the structure of the old infraction but also the content of most of its constituent elements. First of all, in both cases, the two acts must be identified separately from one another so that the infraction can be constituted: the obscene act and the act of making it public. Moreover, in the old form of indecent exposure, just like the new sexual exhibition, the first act is only punishable if it has been made public. Likewise, the notion of publicity remains identical to the one that the case law had developed up until the end of the 1950s. Finally, the victim is not always an individual person but the public, this generic and impersonal sexual body that was protected by the law on contempt of public decency.

The great transformation that the reform of 1992 engendered, therefore, comes from the nature of the obscene act that one must not make public. It is only due to the fact that this is now an act of scopic imposition of sexuality—that one ought not to make public—that one could liberalize other acts that were formerly condemned, while maintaining nearly intact both the general structure of the infraction and the elements that compose it.

At the same time, through the distinctive features of this act that one could not render public, the new infraction fundamentally transformed the structure of the scopic space of sexuality. Public spaces began to function as if they were private intermittently, as long as exhibition was not imposed on anyone, and, conversely, private spaces could sometimes become public as soon as the spectacle of sexuality was imposed. The absence of any witness, or the fact that the latter is consenting, turns public places into spaces in which sexuality can be exhibited, while nonconsenting witnesses render private places into spaces in which sexuality cannot be exhibited. In the first case, the public space exceptionally loses its power to render an exhibition criminal, just as, in the second case, the private space loses for that moment its capacity to allow exhibition in a lawful manner. The distinction of the status of public and private spaces therefore remains intact, but the one can acquire in a special manner the status of the other through the mediation of consent or the absence of consent by witnesses.

To better understand these fundamental transformations in the legal topography of sexuality, it is thus appropriate to examine, one by one, the principal elements of the new infraction and to compare them in a more precise manner with those of the old Article 330 of the Penal Code.

Intent: the desire to expose

According to past case law, the offense of indecent exposure did not require that the culprit demonstrate an acknowledged willingness to carry out the obscene act in public. People were meant not only to not seek to exhibit themselves but also to do the utmost to hide themselves. Any negligence was shameful. The broad and extraordinary criteria that the courts established to qualify a behavior as negligent evidently encouraged a permanent surveillance of the self. It is based on this surveillance that our grandparents built for us this society of modesty.

But, as I have shown, it was not only a matter of taking care to conceal an act that one knew was obscene; it was further necessary to avoid committing an obscene act without knowing. Thus, in the affair of Father Bérard,[1] the court was content to convict the priest for simple negligence—the act of having unknowingly made his penis visible through a hole in his cassock—committed in public. By privileging negligence, the court cast aside intent as a criterion with regard to both the act and the space in which the act occurred.

On the other hand, the new formulation of the infraction seems, at first glance, to require an intentional character for both acts: imposing upon others the spectacle of one's sexuality and making this first act public. One of the first decisions handed down under the jurisdiction of the new law is very clear in this regard. On 25 February 1994, at around 7.50 p.m., following instructions from the chief of police of Paris' 16th arrondissement, a patrolman went to the Foch underground parking lot. He noticed the presence of two persons in a regularly parked vehicle. The officer stated that, on approaching the vehicle, he saw that the man was at the wheel and the woman was on her knees performing fellatio on him.

The Paris Court of Appeals released the defendants on the grounds that "the concerned parties had not imposed the spectacle of the sexual exhibition upon others, because the vehicle was properly parked in a parking lot, all doors closed, and that, owing to the position of the concerned parties, the sexual exhibition in which they engaged would not ordinarily have been visible from the exterior, except if one looked specifically into the vehicle's interior, as did the patrolman." Furthermore, the court added that, "on account of the repeal of Article 330 of the Penal Code on 1 March 1994, there is room to apply the more lenient provisions of Article 222-32 of the Penal Code on this date; that the wording of the incrimination of sexual exhibition is more restrictive in what it stipulates, not only that this act must have been committed in a space accessible to the public gaze but in that it requires also that the act be visible to and imposed on others..."[2]

In this way, as one observer noted, since the reform of Article 330, "even in regard to the enforcement officer, who was the sole spectator of the exhibition, it was still necessary that it be imposed." It seems therefore that this couple was released because neither of them showed the intention of imposing upon others the spectacle of their sexuality. We can easily deduce from this that, without such intention, no infraction can be constituted. But to do so would be to proceed too quickly. For if, under any circumstance, the intent of exposing oneself in a certain space—or under certain conditions of publicity—must not produce any doubt, it seems that we are able to dispense with having to observe an intention of imposing upon others the spectacle of sexuality in order to constitute an infraction, and demand constant prudence rather than good faith in this domain.

Indeed, the law punishes the imposition of an act of sexual exhibition upon others in certain spaces. It requires the presence of a third party who can say that the scene was imposed upon him or her. Without this element, the infraction cannot be constituted. Nevertheless, this does not signify that the act had been imposed upon him or her personally. What the exhibitor does intentionally is to expose himself in a certain public space, or one that is susceptible, by virtue of social conditions in which it takes place, to being a space in which a public can be constituted. On the other hand, exposure can be seen as imposed even if the exhibitor did not target a particular individual, and even if he believed in good faith that he was not visible. In this way, the "imposed" character of the scene can result from happenstance of someone passing by, depending on the manner in which that passerby interprets the scene. So, in the example of the parking lot, the court would not have decided to acquit the couple if, instead of placing themselves in a manner such that it was necessary to make an effort to see them, they had made love on top of the car, convinced that the parking lot was empty. If the officer had by chance stumbled upon such a scene, he would have been able to say that it had been imposed upon him, and the judges would have had to punish the absent-minded lovers.

In this way, the fact of a third party affirming that someone has imposed upon him or her a sexual spectacle can result from simple negligence. The lovers thought that no one would pass by, they were convinced of it, for this space was always empty but they were chanced upon by a patrolman. If the intent of making love in a garage, that is to say, in a public space, is not questionable, that of imposing the spectacle on others, on the other hand, can be the product of negligence.

Let us imagine yet another scenario where this distinction could be evident. A couple that seeks to exhibit their sexual act in front of an audience goes to a swingers' club. But, in their ardor, they take the wrong door and, in reality, enter a normal nightclub in which people dance but do not make love in front of others. Thinking that it is still early and that others will follow them, the lovers get to work and the persons present declare themselves outraged by the spectacle. The couple's intent of exhibiting themselves to an audience was evident; the fact of imposing the sexual spectacle upon someone was not. Nevertheless, the crime will still be constituted, even if the imposition of the sexual spectacle comes from pure negligence.

On the other hand, the intentional character of the act of exposing oneself in a particular space or under circumstances that can make the public coalesce is fundamental to the logic of the new infraction. Indeed, in this logic, what the exhibitionist seeks is to be seen by the impersonal being that is the public, which becomes the real object of his sexuality and from which he derives pleasure. It is as if he maintained a sexual relationship with the impersonal—that abstract individual, the first passerby; it is *this* sexual relation that is forbidden.

That which is obscene

Formerly, the two acts targeted by this infraction—to engage in sexual behavior and to make it public—were different by nature.

Only the second was concerned with visibility; the first being general sexual behavior. In contrast, with the new infraction, it cannot be emphasized enough that to exhibit in public is also a behavior that is itself linked to visibility.

In the new infraction, actual publicity takes on a completely different valence than in the past. The character of "public," applied to a certain scene, is not immediately linked to a prohibition of the sexual spectacle. From this point of view, beginning in the 1950s–1960s, in order to liberalize certain spectacles, the infraction of sexual exhibition took a different road from the one that had been suggested by the theories propounded by legal scholars. These theories had, indeed, extolled the idea that a public constituted by willing participants rendered places such as theaters or swingers' clubs into private spaces. They had therefore conceived of the public as a body that is able to dissolve by means of consent given by the individuals who composed it.

The new infraction rejected this route and thus maintained publicity in spaces in which spectators are consenting. However, if spectators are indeed consenting, nothing obscene unfolds in this public space.

Yet, we remember that the absence of consent had been one of the litmus tests employed by judges after the Ponce decision in order to qualify as public certain private, nonvisible spaces inaccessible from the exterior, in the event that more than two persons were found there and at least one among them overtly displayed their sexuality. The Ponce decision had also been used from the 1950s on to produce virtual publicity in spaces accessible by a door.

What was only relevant to define the second act—that of publicity in private spaces and in certain public spaces—becomes an essential element of the first act. It is as if, upon liberalizing public exhibitions of sexuality, two different mechanisms were sought to produce publicity, one being required for the obscene act (for nonconsent), and the other for the space in which it occurs.

We will see how important this observation is to understand the function of the infraction. In practice, the existence of a consenting or nonconsenting witness will have the same effect for the constitution of the infraction whereas, in the past, it used to be employed to create or control publicity. It was as if the legal frameworks put into place during the 1950s to suspend publicity or privatization of certain spaces (by means of the witness's consent) had been extended to all spaces, including actual public spaces. Everywhere, consent could re-characterize spaces and render legal what would have been punishable in the past. However, this scopic liberalization of space was carried out not by permitting consent to modify explicitly, as in the past, the techniques of qualifying spaces as either public or private but by making the obscenity of acts disappear.

To force one to see

If it appears quite simple to understand what the act of exposing oneself in a space accessible to the public gaze signifies in the eyes of law, it is not the same as understanding the act of imposing a spectacle on others. For instance, does the law target a situation in which an individual is *forced* to see under threat by the exhibitionist? Does the act of "imposing upon others" make reference to a situation *of force* in which the exhibitor takes hold of the victim's head and keeps his eyes open with his fingers? Certainly not.

When the law mentions "imposing the sight of a sexual spectacle," it alludes to the fact that someone is showing himself voluntarily and that another person is *surprised*, even for a brief moment, by the sight of something from which he can easily turn his gaze away. It is therefore this short instant of surprise between the act of understanding what one has seen and that of turning one's gaze away that is addressed by the expression "imposing a sexual spectacle on others." This third party on whom the scene is imposed is certainly "forced," but in a manner that is not at all comparable to the violations of freedom of action implied by other crimes and infractions of a sexual nature.

Of course, the act of visual imposition can reveal itself to be at the very least annoying, if not more violent, if the persons find themselves in a private and enclosed space. No doubt, it can be more difficult for them to leave, and the gesture addressed to them can be quite personal. Such a gesture targets a particular individual and not the first passerby. Nevertheless, as I have already pointed out, in private spaces, invisible from the exterior, this crime can only be constituted under exceptional circumstances. It requires a confluence of conditions that make this space a public space—that is to say, it demands the presence of at least two nonconsenting individuals. On the other hand, in a truly public space, the constitution of this crime is easier, even if the forced witness is no doubt discomforted to a lesser degree.

But such is not this new infraction's only oddity. The role played by these "others," on whom a scene of a sexual nature is imposed, is just as strange. Even if this individual does not consent to see what he sees, he is still not the victim of the crime, for this space is occupied, as it was before, by the public. For, as I said before, if the same act takes place in a space not accessible to the public gaze, the crime is not constituted.

Just as in the past, the victim of the crime is not precisely the subject who unintentionally sees but the impersonal, the abstract individual, the passerby, who cannot consent to being imposed upon by a sexual a scene. This individual plays the same role as that of an involuntary witness of a sexual scene enacted in an enclosed space or one that is accessible from the outside by a door. Unlike in the past, when the presence of the witness produced publicity, today, the presence of a witness establishes the obscene act.

In this way, the lack of intent to see on the part of these "others," even if it is essential to constitute this crime, is not understood like forms of nonconsent that exist in other sexual aggressions. The lack of intent comes from a human being, to be sure, but this individual is not considered to be an individual who is hurt or affected by this offense. One might even think that this lack of will is an element of the act that the exhibitionist carries out. The witness's lack of intent is only necessary to affirm that the spectacle of a sexual scene has well and truly been imposed on others. In this sense, this individual does not represent the public, for the public is indeed present, or is potentially present in spaces accessible to it, where the scene is produced. Rather, he personifies the will of the law that seeks to keep the public from seeing a certain type of sexual scene. But, note that the scenes from which the law seeks to shield the public are those that have been imposed on an individual, the scenes that such an individual did not want to be shown. *Consequently, it falls upon this individual to decide what must be hidden from the eyes of the public.*

In short, the law leaves it up to the unpredictable will of the individual to decide whether or not a scene of sexual exhibition, produced intentionally in certain spaces and which falls on their eyes, is a crime. If a person exhibits himself voluntarily on a road in front of another individual, the latter can transform the act into a crime only if he or she can affirm that the sight of this spectacle was imposed on him or her. In this way, at least as far as public spaces are concerned, the law now delegates a power that it previously guarded jealously. This is why the act of being nude, alone and on a deserted road, used to suffice to constitute a crime. In contrast, in private spaces, the law already delegated this power to individuals, even if only to extend or limit publicity.

This new aspect of the crime explains the conditions that must be met by so-called dissolute sites in order not to be accused of sheltering an illicit exhibition. The consent of the individuals who form the public must be given upon entry by positive acts that prove that these persons knew in advance what they were going to see. By means of this preliminary consent, spectators decline to avail themselves of the prerogatives that they could have had to qualify a scene as having been imposed.

This nonhuman, impersonal treatment of the individual on whom a spectacle of a sexual nature is imposed thus borrows its procedures from the very jurisprudence that had expanded the public world into the private world. Historically, this is the first moment when real "in the flesh" individuals were given the power to determine if a scene of a sexual nature had taken place in a public or private space.

Certainly, this witnessing power is no longer the power of publicity but that of being able to qualify an act as being imposed. But in practice, this power functions in the same way, that is, as a power delegated by the law to transform a sexual exhibition into a crime. In this way, under the guise of extending the rule of consent to this seemingly withered infraction, particular individuals acquired, perhaps inadvertently, a power from the State to determine if what they saw constitutes an act of violation of their gaze in any space, whether or not it is public.

Consequently, the liberalization of public spaces, other than dissolute places, is limited. For, if someone voluntarily exhibits himself in a public space such as a roadway, it suffices for an individual to claim to be offended by the spectacle for a crime to be constituted. In substance, what it comes down to is to transform public spaces into spaces from which sexual exhibition is banned—even if, as we shall see, the notion of sexuality is more limited in this crime—for potential exhibitionists expose themselves to the possibility that the first passerby will transform their act into a "scopic rape." It is possible that the culprit of the crime is not noticed or that he will find an approving public. *It is therefore not certain* that he commits a crime, as was the case in the past, but it is certain that this uncertainty does not by its very nature promote this type of behavior.

However, from the point of view of the new ideology of Sex, it is important that the sole act of exhibiting one's sexuality in public spaces is not in itself penalized, and that we have sought out this expedient that is the harmed third party as both justification and punitive technique. In this way, it is not the State that presents itself as the censor of sexual exhibition. Rather, it is the individuals who complain that a scene has been "imposed" on them. The State only appears as a third party observer of a "violent" sexuality.

What's more, this technique of punishment varies according to the type of publicity generated by an act of sexual exhibition. Publicity resulting from the method of gathering spectators can be easily mitigated by preliminary consent, as is true for theaters. On the other hand, publicity resulting from public spaces, such as roads, will be much more difficult to "deactivate," except if passersby are informed in advance that, if they approach, they risk seeing a "sexual" scene, as in the case on certain beaches. Even then, it is necessary to possess the necessary administrative permits to practice naturism.

The new infraction requires that the sexual scene be "imposed," which presumes a voluntary act of exhibition. So, for example, no longer can those Belgian lovers—who sought, one night in 1813, to hide their embrace behind a bush on a dark road—be punished. A witness who would have seen them by lighting a lantern would not be able to reproach them for having deliberately sought to impose on him the sight of their lovemaking. However, as soon as one seeks to exhibit oneself voluntarily in public spaces, the exorbitant power of the witness will very strongly limit this new liberty. From now on, the fact of requiring the imposition of an exhibition upon a witness will nevertheless be crucial for the liberalization of private spaces—especially those accessible or visible from the outside (the rules of interior publicity had been greatly relaxed since the precedent of 1954, which required the presence of at least two nonconsenting witnesses instead of a single one).

The numerous scenarios of this type of publicity had been processed by a jurisprudence that, until the beginning of the 1970s, had been distinguished by its zeal. Thus under the new infraction, the following types of individuals can no longer be punished: individuals whom one can see from the outside through a hole, or through a crack; those who are caught by surprise in their own bedroom because the door that separated it from their living room had not been locked; those who find themselves in the presence of a third party asleep next to them but able to wake up at any moment.

Paradoxically, the relative liberalization of public spaces produced by the new infraction has had a more significant impact on private spaces.

Those things we could not see

In the case law that has followed the reform of 1992, the content of scenes that must not be imposed on others in spaces accessible to the public gaze has not changed much. Three types of acts are generally considered as having a scopic-sexual content: sexual acts, nudity and obscene gestures. If sexual acts themselves give little rise to debates over interpretation in being qualified as "sexual," the same is not true for nudity or obscene gestures.

Nudity

As discussed before, since the 1930s, the case law has distinguished between two forms of nudity: chaste and obscene. The notion of chaste nudity has evolved. In its first phase, it had to be cloaked by art. Then, for nudity not to be chaste, it was necessary to exhibit obscene gestures. The development of this case law had as a corollary a ruling of the Court of Douai on 28 September 1989, which has been frequently cited.

An individual having completely disrobed on a jetty jumped into the water and climbed back out "in his birthday suit" onto the ladder of a boat whose crew called the police. The court decided that "the simple nudity of an individual without any provocative or obscene gesture does not suffice to constitute the crime of which the defendant is accused."[3]

If this decision was the object of so much discussion, it is because chaste nudity in public spaces (at least in ones that are not set up for that purpose, such as nudist beaches) could not expose actual genitals, which were automatically considered to be sexual. The judges of the Court of Douai changed this doctrine, for the individual in question was completely naked. Despite this, the supposed uncivilized nudism, when practiced on beaches not authorized by municipal decrees, is still the target of judicial prosecution.[4]

Such an evolution fell within the process of "degenitalization" of sexual acts in the framework of sexual crimes and infractions. This process has, indeed, turned the body into a unit of pleasure with no part *any more sexual* than the other. In this sense, there is no more reason that genitals as such ought to fall under a statute distinct from the one that governs other parts of the body.

The Court of Appeals, while deciding whether or not genital exhibition without obscene gestures fell under the statute of chaste nudity, found itself confronted with an alternative. It could either choose to be consistent with the premise of degenitalization, considering each part of the body as potentially exhibiting obscene nudity—which would prevent an individual from showing even his or her mouth in public—or it could decide to throw a cloak of chastity over the whole body, including the genitals, when, of course, it does not include obscene gestures.

Obscene gestures

The old case law did not just punish obscene forms of nudity; it also punished gestures of this type made even without baring oneself. Even as late as 25 January 1990, we find rulings such as one handed down by the Appellate Court of Bourges, which punished a certain Jean-Pierre C. for grasping his genitals between his hands through his trousers and saying to someone: "Hey, look! For you!"[5] But the Court of Cassation changed that stance on 4 January 2006. Starting from perfectly identical facts, it overturned the decision of the appellate court, which had declared Jean-Pierre C. guilty on the grounds "that the crime of sexual exhibition assumes that the body or part voluntarily exposed be or appear to be bared for others to see [...]."[6]

Thus, obscenity alone does not suffice; it requires that sexual organs be or appear to be exhibited. The act that Jean-Pierre C. committed was sexual and public, but it could not be understood as an exhibition in the sense of the new crime. This reflects the way that the infraction was pulled in two different directions. On the one hand, the cloak of chastity can hide forms of nudity, including that of the genitals themselves; on the other hand, obscenity alone cannot reveal them.

The public: a weakened class

Having charged obscenity with diminishing the rigors of the law, the mechanisms that produced publicity that had been set out by the case law until the 1950s were nevertheless conserved. As a consequence, we live under the same regime of publicity as before the moral revolution.

The expression "space accessible to the public gaze" from the new Article 222-32 of the Penal Code seems to have sanctioned an idea advanced by the jurisprudence and doctrine from the late 1940s, according to which there is only *visual* publicity, precluding the kinds that can be produced by other senses, such as hearing or touch.

As in the past, publicity can be purely *virtual* in public as well as private spaces. It is enough for someone to impose upon others a sexual spectacle on a street in order for a crime to be constituted, even if no one aside from the nonconsenting witness witnessed the scene.

The same is true of private spaces. It suffices that someone impose on others a scene in a space that is private but accessible to the public gaze through a door for the exhibition to be public, even if no one opened that door.

An important ruling of the Court of Cassation in 1999 serves as a good example:[7] an individual had gone to his lawyer's offices, where he was received by the latter's female colleague. During the interview, while he was sitting opposite her, the client exhibited his erect penis before putting it back in his trousers. Outraged, the female lawyer immediately kicked out the client.

In an affirmative decision, the appellate court punished this individual with six months of imprisonment with a suspended sentence and two years probation for sexual exhibition, a decision that he appealed to the higher court.

According to the appellate court, the space in which the interview between the female lawyer and her client took place was one that was accessible to the public gaze, even if no one had opened the door, because the secretary or other colleagues *would have been able to come in* at any moment. The exhibitionist's appeal in the higher court sought to assert that a lawyer is bound to take all measures to keep conversations with clients confidential. According to this argument, an attorney's office does not constitute a space accessible to the public gaze in the sense of Article 222-32 of the Penal Code.

The court refuted this syllogism by emphasizing that the confidentiality of interviews between a lawyer and his or her clients does not necessarily imply that the space in which they are located must be inaccessible to the public gaze. What counts primarily is not the sight of the attorney with his client but the confidentiality of words exchanged between them. This confidentiality can be assured, even if the interview takes place in the hallway of an examining magistrate, in a waiting room etc. In this way, according to the court, an attorney's office can assure the confidentiality of interviews while being a space accessible to the public gaze.

In matters of the rules for the production of publicity in spaces that are invisible and not accessible to the exterior, those established by the case law of the Court of Appeals in 1954 have been maintained.

Let us recall that, in 1954, the Supreme Court had decided that both of the two witnesses of a sexual scene in a space inaccessible and invisible to the exterior had to be nonconsenting (and not just one of the two), thus modifying the doctrine in effect since the Ponce decision of 1877.

This new doctrine held due to the fact that, in a series of decisions from this era, consent gave a way to put an end to the virtual publicity of enclosed spaces accessible to the public by a door. Thanks to these decisions, when an individual was consenting, the publicity of these spaces had to be real in order for there to be an infraction. In a locale accessible to the public, if a culprit found himself in front of a consenting person, for this scene to be public it was necessary that someone actually enter by opening the door and not that this just remain a possibility. It was in this spirit that, in 1952, the court had ruled on the case of the photographer who was in a space accessible by a door in the company of his young nude models.[8]

These changes introduced in virtual publicity through accessibility also modified the conditions of interior publicity. From then on, the nonconsent of individuals had to double up: each one had to be a witness to the scene imposed on the other. We can thus explain the decision of the Court of Appeals in 1954 that had required that the two witnesses of the exhibition be nonconsenting for the nonvisible and enclosed space to become public.

For the first time, these two individuals could substitute themselves for each other. Each one of them had to be able to affirm: "Someone is imposing on me a sexual spectacle of which I am witness, and they are imposing this spectacle on someone else as well." It was thus necessary that the two acts of visual imposition mirror each other identically.

Before 1954, the nonconsenting witness and the one who played the role of the public could not switch their positions. The first demonstrated to the second that he or she did not consent to witness the scene, while the second could be consenting. This configuration of interior publicity seems to have perfectly anticipated the logic of the new infraction stemming from the reform of 1992 in which it is visual imposition itself that is forbidden to be made public. In this version, each of the two witnesses is the object of an imposed sexual exhibition and serves the other as the public. Thus, there was no reason to change the requirements put forth by the case law of 1954.

A frequently cited decision of the Court of Appeals on 12 May 2004[9] confirmed the renewal of this rule. In this case, a senile grandfather had shown his penis to his two grandchildren in closed-off spaces not accessible to the public gaze. On several occasions: "the defendant suddenly undressed in front of the two children (respectively 11 and 8 years old) in his home, and in his grandchildren's home, as well as in a 'hut' and again in a 'barn', and showed them his penis, accompanying this gesture with obscene comments."

Without denying the fact that these exhibitions had been "imposed," the appeal contested the public character of the exhibition, for it had unfolded "in spaces that were by definition private." But the court rejected the appeal on the grounds that, "even though some of the acts had taken place in various private spaces, all the acts had been imposed on the witnesses involuntarily and by surprise." And there were two witnesses.

Nevertheless, we can propose another interpretation of the new infraction by focusing less on the precise formulation of the terms of the law than on the type of acts that it forbids and authorizes.

The meaning of "imposing the spectacle upon others," as we have seen, follows a logic in the new infraction analogous to the one that produced interior publicity, as well as the virtual publicity of spaces enclosed but accessible to the public through a door. In this sense, and even if the law does not say it as such, the witness on whom one imposes a sexual spectacle continues to institute the publicity of the space, since it is his or her presence that permits a crime to be constituted.

Put another way, for the publicity of a space to be established in regard to the constitution of the infraction, a nonconsenting witness has to be present in that public space. It is as if, in substance, open public places, such as roads, had become closed spaces accessible to the public through a door. All actual public spaces have acquired the same status as an office of which the door has not been locked and which people may enter at any time, as illustrated by the case with the female lawyer who was victim of an exhibitionist as judged by the Court of Appeals in 1999. Indeed, the essential difference between this type of space and a street no longer makes sense today, for the location in which a sexual scene takes place does not suffice in itself to qualify an infraction. What is further required is the presence of a nonconsenting witness.

On the contrary, we could think that the so-called dissolute places have become private by means of the consent given by all participants upon entering. Once again, even if the law does not express it in these terms, it is indeed in this spirit that it conceives of the new infraction. For, in practice, the preliminary consent given by spectators thwarts not the public status of the space but rather the possibility for the constitution of the infraction.

Thus, we could think that it is not so much the obscene action that has changed in the new infraction, as it is the nature of the space in which it takes place. It is as if, ultimately, it is always the act of displaying one's nudity, one's obscenity, one's sexual acts in public spaces that is forbidden, except that this publicity can be voided if no one has been outraged. The involuntary witness would therefore be less a component of the obscene act than an element that serves to qualify the space.

This interpretation, according to which it is not the obscene act that has changed, in reality, but rather the status of spaces in which this act takes place, seems consistent with the evolution that the notion of publicity has undergone since the middle of the twentieth century.

Even if the 1992 reform seems not to have changed publicity, it used a technique of producing publicity in order to describe forbidden behaviors: "imposition of the spectacle of one's sexuality upon others." Analysis of this expression has shown us that it alluded to the same technique as the one used to extend or limit publicity. Consequently, we can affirm that the new description of the obscene act is the one that we used to use and it is still used to produce publicity in closed spaces as a mechanism by which to limit publicity. However, unlike in the past, when this definition served to make publicity exist or disappear, it is rendered operational for the constitution of an infraction.

However, there were two contexts that were not modified by the change in case law brought about during the 1950s: the first was the constitution of the virtual publicity of private spaces through accessibility, and the second was that of interior publicity.

The most important transformation is that of veritable public spaces. These spaces have been made to function as if they were enclosed spaces accessible to the public through a door. We can thus compare them to offices or to the toilets in a train station. Nevertheless, in these closed spaces that become public by means of accessibility, we can lock the door to avoid the constitution of the crime of sexual exhibition. Nothing like this is evidently possible in open public spaces such as streets. By definition, these latter spaces cannot be locked, and nothing can stop the arrival of a passerby on a street or in a public park. Thus, since the 1992 reform, the following is no doubt the best definition for what a public space has become: it is a space that is closed but accessible to the public through a door that one cannot lock.

III The meaning of the infraction: one must not take advantage of the law

Publicity has always had two distinct meanings in the context of contempt for public decency. On the one hand, the term designated the spatial or social conditions in which a sexual scene took place and, on the other hand, the nature of the victim. The victim was not a precise and concrete individual but the public, this impersonal and abstract authority. Case law has often emphasized it: contempt of public decency never takes into consideration the exact individuals harmed by this type of act but the scandal that this type of act can produce within the *public*.

Thus, publicity did not define an act in which the victim is an individual, as was the case with other infractions, e.g., defamation. Even though the crime of defamation can only be committed in public, the victim is the slandered individual and not the public. In contrast, with contempt of public decency, publicity was both simultaneously constituted as an element of the crime and what was affected by the crime.

In classical theories, the law sought to protect the public from viewing certain scenes to prevent desires or aversions linked to sexuality from being awakened within it. Nevertheless, as we have seen in the case of theaters, the public could not choose to see or not to see. Its consent was, by definition, perfectly immaterial. The public was the audience to which one should not show certain scenes.

However, in the past, the public gaze did not used to be an object of desire or pleasure as such. During their quest for pleasure, exhibitionists were accused of having been indifferent as to whether the public saw them or whether it could have seen them. The public was meant to be untargeted but nevertheless, in a certain manner, an indirectly affected victim. It is from this point on that we find a wide variety of criteria that judges used to affirm that the culprit of an exhibition had been imprudent or negligent when circumstances showed that the exhibitionist had not in any way sought to be seen by the public.

In the new law, the position of the public with regard to the exhibitionist's intent has clearly changed. The public does not mark the boundary of sexuality in general but rather that of a targeted exhibition directly addressed to it. It is the act of displaying one's sexuality to the public that is targeted by this infraction. The intent that the law seeks to define is that of voluntarily exposing oneself in certain places, while the third party on whom the exhibition is imposed is the one who is given the power to have the exhibitionist punished. Therefore, as opposed to the infraction targeted by Article 330, the intent of the culprit is to expose himself deliberately in a place, or under conditions in which the public may appear. What is forbidden is to transform the public gaze into a sexual object, to derive pleasure from what must stop us from so doing, to take pleasure precisely from these limits. Since the reform of 1992, the public is harmed because, instead of considering the public an impassable boundary for the act of exposing oneself, exhibitionists deliberately address their act, considered to be sexual, to the public.

The new infraction forbids us from taking advantage of the watchful eye that controls us, from transforming a limitation into a tool of enjoyment. We might then presume that the rule created by the new crime dictates that we may not take pleasure from the law—that it is created to govern behaviors and not to arouse and satisfy desires. It is as if the law foresaw that it could itself be the victim of sexual abuse.

In contrast, exhibition in dissolute spaces is not a form of enjoyment of those limitations, for the public in this instance no longer fulfills its function because of the absence of an involuntary witness.

In this way, the law conceives of dissolute spaces as an imitation, a sham, a staging of a limitation that is juridically "deactivated."

The new infraction's function is not only to continue to distribute sexuality within space but also to target the first stage of "deviance." As we will see in the next chapter, the crime of sexual exhibition punishes the least offensive act of deviance to be found at the border between normality and sexual perversion. Indeed, of all the infractions for which post-penal monitoring has been devised in order to avoid recidivism or the commission of graver acts, the crime of sexual exhibition is the one that is punished with the least heavy sentences and the only one without real or potential victims. To be sure, we could include in this category other crimes without specific victims, such as pornography distributed to minors, or child pornography. But, in these scenarios, the law seeks to avoid the corruption of an entire category of the population by viewing certain images as susceptible to inflicting damage upon others. In the first case, society judges that youths can be corrupted, and in the second, that the mechanisms used to censor pedophiles can be lifted.

But none of these justifications is applied to sexual exhibition. Unlike in the past, the law does not fear that exhibitionist behaviors push people to debauchery, or that they contribute to corrupting the social framework. In short, society is not afraid that guilty exhibitionists will create imitators or criminals. As the authors of a commentary on the Penal Code wrote in 1996, "at this point, the law seeks less to repair the public scandal caused by the offense than to protect the person from the deviance of the sexuality of others,"[10] that is to say, from perverse fantasies that are exhibited. It is as if the exhibitionist has become an antisocial being because of the relationship he or she has maintained with his or her own pleasure, even if this relationship harms no identifiable, individualizable victim.

How can we characterize the act of deviance of the person who exposes himself (or herself) in an illegal manner? In the world of Sex, the enemies of Order are no longer the dissolute but the perverts. These enemies are taken to be dangerous because they have not accepted the law and because they experience pleasure despite its illegality. But, while other perverts hide themselves to commit their crimes, exhibitionists seek precisely to expose themselves to those who are charged with constraining them, for it is from this very act that they derive their pleasure. And if they do not commit any wrongdoing on real or potential victims, they are seen to abuse the law itself.

In this world of Sex where all impunity is abolished, where all barriers that protected individuals from the gaze of the law—be they that of marriage, of buildings or, to a certain extent, of consent—have become illusory, the new crime of sexual exhibition takes on the appearance of a quasi-formal framework based in part on principle, which obliges each and every individual to take their pleasure within the limits of law, and never beyond those limits. What is certainly forbidden is *to take pleasure from the law itself*.

IV The minors' gaze

Even when a sexual spectacle has not been imposed on others, and even when it has not taken place in public, it is still subject to an exception clause. Indeed, if so-called dissolute spaces where these sexual relations take place have been legalized, scopic sexual relations have not been, as such, subject to the same system of consent as others.

Although the age of witnesses had never been an applicable criterion to qualify indecent exposure as a crime, despite some dissident opinions on this subject, a 1946 law had indirectly introduced in this regard an important modification. Articles 334 and 335 of the Code of 1810 punished the incitation of minors younger than 21 years of age as debauchery and corruption. But for this violation to be constituted, the act had to be repeated. That is, only several repeated acts, and not just a single instance, would suffice for the violation to be constituted. The law of 13 April 1946 included an alternative to Article 334 that punished acts of incitation of minors to debauchery, even when such acts were occasional, if committed upon minors younger than 16 years old, and left intact the requirement of repeat violation for minors up to the age of 21 years.[11]

This change considerably modified the reach of contempt for public decency. Indeed, certain forms of sexual exhibition in enclosed spaces, which were formerly considered to be public indecencies, could fall under the heel of more severe punishments for incitation of minors to debauchery. This can explain, in part, the relative retreat that publicity has experienced since the 1950s.

How was this violation transformed during the 1992 reform? How would it come to be made compatible with the new crime of sexual exhibition, which was more restrictive apart from giving very prominent importance to the consent of witnesses?

Even though the initial legislative bill sought to strike this incrimination from the books, for it had been judged obsolete on account of the "evolution of morality," the 1988 draft of the Penal Code considered substituting it with a restrictive violation that precisely targeted the boundary with sexual exhibition. The idea was indeed to limit this violation to the act of an adult organizing licentious relations in the presence, or with the participation, of a minor.[12] If, on the one hand, it was accepted that "the dissolute" could calmly quench their "vices" in spaces designated for such use, there was no question, on the other hand, of letting minors enter such spaces, or of letting them attend orgies organized in private homes.

Minors older than 15 years could enter into sexual relations with an adult without the adult risking any punishment, but it was not conceivable that this adult would introduce minors to certain sexual practices, which, though authorized, necessitated special conditions of space and consent. *Natural* sex between two individuals without spectators was one thing; group or exhibitionist sex, that sought to quench vices—but which constituted neither good example nor models of morality—that society could no longer punish as such was another. In this new world created by the moral revolution—so preoccupied by the "natural" development of erotic urge—these forms of sexuality were thought to distort and corrode the immature psyches of adolescents, traumatize them or turn them into potential dangers for society.

After lively debate, Parliament decided to modify the bill. The senators were in favor of maintaining incrimination under its previous form, even if it meant alleviating the severity of the required sentences. It was clearly indicated in the course of parliamentary debate that they did not want to risk compromising the harmonious development of the personality of the minor by weakening the penal protection of the minor in a particularly delicate domain that directly affected sexuality.[13]

In contrast, the Members of the National Assembly joined in support of the government's position, which was also in favor of limiting this violation to precise actions, i.e., only the prohibition of orgies. The question was finally resolved in a very extensive and curious manner by the joint committee, which favored the Senate's position. The old incrimination was renewed, but while this required repeated violation for minors between 16 and 18, the new Article 227-22 no longer requires it.

So Article 227-22 states in its first paragraph:

> The act of encouraging or attempting to encourage the corruption of a minor is punished with five years of imprisonment and a fine of 75,000 euros. These sentences are extended to seven years of imprisonment and a fine of 100,000 euros when the minor is less than 15 years of age.

As if to satisfy the government, this article contains a second paragraph that directly targets live erotic performances, that is to say, the domain of sexual exhibition. The text is formulated in the following manner:

> The same sentences are particularly applicable to the act, committed by an adult, of organizing gatherings comprising exhibitions or sexual relations that a minor attends or in which he or she participates.

As commentators have emphasized many times, this new arrangement appears redundant, for the first paragraph of the article already globally covered situations that it incriminates in a special manner. Other authors have thought that the word "particularly" was only set out by way of example, but this interpretation cannot hold, for this paragraph applies an age restriction for the person who organizes such gatherings.

The corruption of a minor in the first paragraph concerns acts of which minors can become guilty just as adults; in contrast, the second paragraph only targets gatherings organized by adults. Minors therefore would be able to organize this type of gathering without falling beneath the heel of the law. But if, instead of organizing them, they invite their friends who are minors to go there, they would be accused of corrupting minors. So here is the strange confusion provoked by the traditions of the debauched, as demonstrated by the worries of certain deputies, such as M. Pezet and M. Toubon.[14]

Thus, the spectacle of sexual acts, that is, this particular form of sexual relations, comes with an exception clause and is not subject to consent alone. If the crime of sexual exhibition does not apply with regard to minors in these scenarios, it is because neither the public nor private character of these licentious gatherings is of interest. All that counts is the mark that these gatherings can leave on the spirit and morality of youths. Thus, the spatial logic has yielded its place to a purely sexual logic.

But without doubt the most important consequences are those that the new arrangement extends to private spaces, neither visible nor accessible from the outside, where a consenting public is gathered. Such consequences can be seen as a sort of counterpart of the relative liberalization of public spaces.

If, until the middle of the twentieth century, architectural configurations permitted one to organize this type of gathering with consenting minors without the possibility of the State's intervention, this rule has since had to make room for a first exception when minors are present. However, with regard to minors from 16 to 18 years of age, for those who could have legal sexual relations with adults, the prohibition was only applicable as an exception, as it required that such practices be repeated. Since the reform of 1992, a single occurrence has sufficed for this serious violation to be constituted. Thus, one exception clause that required proof of regularity was replaced this time by another one of a permanent type.

Notes

1 The same criterion of negligence was used for the matter of the G-string of the female dancer from the Bagdad café, see pp. 96–98.
2 Criminal law 1995. n. 89 obs. Véron.
3 Douai, 28 September 1989, D. 1991, somm. no. 65, obs. Azibert.
4 See pp. 109–10.
5 CA Bourges, 25 January 1990: juris data no. 1990-046729. We find similar decisions already in the nineteenth century, for example, that of the Court of Appeals on 3 March 1898, Bull. crim. 1898, no. 93.
6 Cass. crim., 4 January 2006, Bull. crim. 2006, no. 3; Dr. p. 2006 no. 33, obs. Véron.
7 Cass. crim., 31 March, Dr. p. 1999, no. 127, obs. Véron.
8 See p. 129.
9 J. Bull. crim. 2004, no. 119, pp. 463–464. See comments by Gabriel Roujou de Boubée, who linked the notion of publicity that emerged from this case law to the decisions from before the reform of 1992, D. 2004 somm. no. 38, commented, pp. 2750–2751.
10 Gabriel Roujou de Boubée, Jacques Francilion, Bernard Bouloc, Yves Mayaud, *Code pénal commenté, article par article,* Books I–IV, Paris, Dalloz, 1996, p. 231.
11 For a history of this violation and its relationship with the history of the

notion of pimping, see Marie-Laure Rassat, Juris-classeur pénal Art. 227-22, "Fait de favoriser la corruption d'un mineur," 2002, p. 3.

12 Art. 227-17 of the draft bill.

13 In the words of the reporter of the Senate Commission on Laws: "we estimate that the current text is of great importance and all efforts that have been made, particularly by the government, [...] to try to rewrite it, inevitably lead to limiting its reach in a very delicate domain in which situations of exceptional gravity can occur." (*JO Sénat*, 1991, p. 2652).

14 JO AN, 22 June 1991, p. 3563. During this session, Mr. Toubon had deemed that "the law in place at that time, and the well-established jurisprudence that it had produced would have offered solutions closer to reality." One deputy, Mr. Marcus, was even worried about the risks of extending a law of this nature to television signals, as this could entail making the president of the TV network responsible. The law of 17 June 1998 modified this violation by creating a new aggravating circumstance wherein the minor comes into contact with the culprit through the use of a telecommunications network, or wherein the acts have been committed inside a scholarly or educational establishment, or close to the student entrances or exits of such an establishment. The law of 9 March 2004 raised the sentences to ten years of imprisonment and a [maximum] fine of one million euros when the acts are committed by organized groups.

9

Perverts and the dissolute

It is possible to imagine that the rigors of public modesty were shot down in a manner that favored those who are called "exhibitionists" today. However, under the aegis of Article 330 of the Penal Code, judges did not seek to punish this "minority," which society believed to be grotesque, inoffensive and ridiculous. The courts required the system to apply sentences intended for contempt of public decency to those that it believed to be "debauched" but not to the "diseased" who deserved, in their eyes, either pity (and thus mitigating circumstances), or acquittal for irresponsibility.

This logic of division between debauchery and mental illness was entirely reversed by the reform of 1992. Indeed, from that point on, the description that the Penal Code gave the new crime of sexual exhibition seems to be based on a textbook of psychiatry, as if it had been conceived to punish exhibitionists in a specific manner. Because the law has since punished only those who *knowingly* seek to make their sexuality public in front of non-consenting witnesses, exhibitionists have become, in principle, the most affected. In contrast, even though dissolute persons are not considered to be incarnations of collective sexual ideals, and the penal order regards them with distrust and even a certain disgust, they have nevertheless attained the right to reserve public spaces in which they can indulge in their vices and customs without fear of any penal sanction.

To be sure, the new crime of sexual exhibition does not only have to do with exhibitionists. Certain persons are punished for sexual exhibition even though they have never been affected by a psychological disorder: they are those who knowingly choose to transgress the boundaries that separate public space from private space. But these "rebellious" exhibitors who are sound of mind—as opposed to exhibitionists suffering from psychological disorders—are not affected by the frameworks of control and post-penal surveillance that, since 1998, have been implemented for culprits of sexual crimes and offenses. In fact, these measures were conceived to track disturbed psyches who, because of their condition, are susceptible to repeating the acts for which they were first sentenced.

In order to evaluate the changes in the treatment of exhibitionists introduced since 1992 by the penal system, we should briefly consider their fate under the aegis of the old Article 330. These reminders will show us how these inoffensive creatures, who from time to time exposed for a brief second their flaccid members in front of some nun in a church, have been metamorphosed into alarming individuals against whom our society feels the imperious need to protect itself.

I Exhibitionists and Article 330 of the Penal Code

We can find the first descriptions of this "perversion" in the writings of Lasègue in 1877—incidentally, the inventor of the neologism[1]—then in those of Magnan[2] at the direct request of the magistrates, who strove to show themselves to be merciful toward these strange individuals who, unlike debauched persons, did not seem to constitute a danger toward the social order.[3]

Understood to be "poor inoffensive fiends" who exposed their flaccid members without reason in public spaces, these exhibitors embodied exactly what the courts did not want to punish since they had decided, around the middle of the nineteenth century, to begin their crusade against vice and debauchery.

The augmentation of sentences for contempt of public decency that were enacted in 1863, as well as in the law of 1885[4] on relegation for cases of recidivism, explains that French society sought to understand this "kind of madness" in order to help these "sick individuals" to avoid being imprisoned—for persons harmed by such curious compulsions were most often those who found themselves to be repeat offenders.

Exhibitionism pushed judges to make doctors intervene in order to apply mitigating circumstances to defendants in the case of "mental disorder." This process constituted a genuine watershed moment in judicial practices. For decades before, magistrates had shown the greatest suspicion toward the intervention of doctors to evaluate the responsibility of defendants of crimes and offenses when they were not truly mad.

Indeed, Article 64 of the Penal Code of 1810 had established that "there is neither crime, nor offense committed, when the defendant is in a state of insanity at the time of the action, or when he has been propelled by a force that he cannot resist." But there was no provision in the law to pursue the "half-mad," or individuals with psychological disorders, and the Code treated them as normal people. Psychologists were summoned by judges to justify the application of mitigating circumstances to individuals with mental troubles, and exhibitors were the first people to be affected.

It was only in 1905 that the Minister of Justice, Joseph Chaumié, sent to the Attorneys General a simple memorandum ordering them to modify the Commission of Experts. Judges not only needed to ask experts if a defendant was in a state of insanity at the moment of the act but, in cases where a defendant was not determined to be insane, their investigations needed to ascertain whether the defendant suffered from physical, psychological or mental anomalies enough to serve as mitigating circumstances. This practice survived until the reform of the Penal Code in 1992.

In the 1957 edition of his famous work, *Code pénal annoté*, Émile Garçon refers to these efforts at the end of the nineteenth century to extol and recall the spirit of gentleness that must have inspired judges when they were confronted with these individuals who laid bare their sexual parts in public spaces:

> Often such acts appear still to be explicable as lechery, such as those committed by exhibitionists who expose themselves on the streets in front of women or children. In such cases, magistrates act prudently and order assessment by a medical-legal expert. Without wanting to suggest that all exhibitionists are, without exception, irresponsible, it is scientifically established today that these abnormal and inexplicable acts are often one of the first manifestations of certain forms of insanity and especially of general [mental] paralysis. Neither the social condition of the defendant, nor his state of recidivism, his apparent reason/lucidity, nor the awareness that he appears to have of his own morality ought to allow for the dispensation of this measure of judicial process, which alone can avoid regrettable judicial errors.[5]

Psychiatrists and exhibitionists

Responding to this generous call from the judiciary, psychiatrists set themselves to describing in detail, sometimes with great eloquence, these strange creatures that Article 330 allowed them to examine during their assessments. According to Lasègue, these sick persons were beings who, "not having ordinarily crossed the extreme limits of reason, still feel the need to have a semi-satisfaction. So, defiant or intimidated, their actions partially give in to the ideas that subjugate them." In order to "increase understanding of this strange kind of fleeting madness," Lasègue offers the first medical description of exhibitionism in the case of a 30-year-old man in the following terms:

> [...] from an honorable family, [the young man] enjoyed an enviable life as a secretary to a politician of that period. He was cultured, and his education brought him into the orbit of the elite. The authorities had been informed, by multiple complaints, of a scandal that was occurring in churches, always around nightfall. A young man reportedly presented himself suddenly in front of women praying alone in church, at a time when it was rarely visited; he exposed his genitals without uttering a word and disappeared shortly thereafter into the shadows. Surveillance was difficult due to the number of locations where it would have had to be set up. One night, however, this strange fantasist was arrested in Saint-Roch, in the midst of his act in front of an elderly nun who screamed out loud and caught the attention of the watchman. The offense was so unique that the public prosecutor's office requested a medical examination. I had a number of long interviews with the defendant from which I could only gain a few clues. The impulse was irresistible, reoccurred periodically at the same hour, never in the morning; it was preceded by an anxiety that he attributed to a sort of interior resistance. The investigation was pursued with due diligence but did not produce any foolproof evidence. Everything was irreproachable except for the act that had led to the arrest.[6]

But, in his famous essay, Lasègue reported other cases that, rather than deserving mitigating circumstances as this one did, instead fell under the purview of Article 64 because they did not involve any criminal culpability.

This is also true for cases of epilepsy and senile dementia, but also when acts of exhibition are only symptoms of total mental paralysis or a state of recognized insanity. Still others were in contempt of public decency because they were affected by chronic genital and urinary tract infections. Lasègue writes, sometimes, exhibitionism is like the final fit of frenzy of a worn-out organism that is close to dying.

This was also true of "this man, of elevated intelligence, correct manners," a 65-year-old retired superior officer, who had lost his wife a year prior. He found himself being detained for indecent exposure because:

> every second day, with bizarre regularity, he stands in front of the gate of a house where young girls live, in the same locality as his own residence. There, he exposes his genitals; then, after some minutes, he rebuttons his pants and continue his regular walk [...]. The accused seems to be in full possession of his faculties; he responds perfectly well to questioning; however he denies the charges without much conviction, considering the offense as improbable rather than refuting it outright.

Now, since the death of his wife, this man had been "subject to fits of dizziness with mental confusion and sometimes even sub-delirium. He wandered around in his garden during these fits, uttering disjointed sentences, came back into his apartment and went to sleep in an armchair [...]. No follow-up was given to the affair, and the patient, paralyzed on one side, has since died [...]."[7]

Other cases of this type, that is, free of any criminal culpability, because they fell under Article 64, were described in 1896 by Raphaël Lalanne in his thesis, *Les Exhibitionnistes*.

For example, this 33-year-old patient, a shoemaker, married and father of two children, who was examined by Lalanne in Saint-Lazare:

> believes himself to be the victim of many of his wife's lovers who pursue him and, to humiliate him, come at night to assault him and forcibly insert their penises into his anus while still covered in his wife's vaginal fluids. This last detail in particular is what infuriates him; he considers it the cruelest of the affronts. Under the influence of his anal hallucinations, he has become a rear-end exhibitionist. In fact he wants everyone to acknowledge the well-founded nature of his complaints. So, he pulls down his pants, in the grip of a great rage, and exposes his anus. If we refuse to look at him, he becomes violent.[8]

Or the 39-year-old male nurse working at the Broussais hospital, who thought himself to be so irresistible that he imagined that the only desire of the female nurses "was to see his genitals, which, judging by the rest of his body, had to be marvelously beautiful." And since "it was up to a gallant man to satisfy them, he satisfied them. As he would have it, the spectacle of his genitals had striking effects on them: they ran away in ecstasy. He went anywhere he could find them alone in the hospital to bring them this inexpressible pleasure."[9]

Lalanne concluded that the "physician must consider both sickness and vice: we must not let all these debauched persons escape the just severity of the laws and the public's contempt—a veritable plague of society; we could not punish them with too much severity."[10] This triage between sickness and vice was, according to Lalanne, the very goal of the expert. The sentences provided for by Article 330 had to be reserved for those who had transgressed through *lechery*.

In 1893, a controversy erupted in the medical field when Chevalier called into question the right to mitigating circumstances for exhibitionists. Whether to punish, detain or commit, no half-measure could be tolerated, for, as Lalanne writes, the irresponsible ones "could not achieve their goals without corrupting those close to them; in addition, aside from some cases where the power of suggestion could yield some results, it is essential to put them out of harm's way."[11] But these debates had no consequences for the legal discipline.

Until the mid-1950s, the few studies led by psychiatrists in regard to this question did not yield any great new findings, compared to those from the end of the nineteenth century. Thus, for example, in 1950, the well-known psychiatrist Henry Ey gave some practical advice for assessments on the matter of exhibitionism. "For dubious cases," he wrote:

> when it comes to a first offense, it would be best to declare those exhibitionists who can benefit from the possibility of a suspended sentence to be guilty so as to allow them to pull themselves back together. This 'practical rule' acknowledges that for exhibitionists there exists a certain susceptibility to intimidation and that the 'sword of Damocles' suspended over their head would most likely reinforce their moral censure. If, on the contrary, we are dealing with unrepentant recidivists, we must still consider such recidivism to be an important feature of the clinical evidence of the neurotic structure of criminal behavior: nonaccountability and institutionalization. Finally, in the

> most delicate cases, after a first recidivism by an individual difficult to sort into the category of psychoneurotics, we could invoke attenuated responsibility as an exception [...].[12]

But, in any case, for Dr. Ey, "the very practice of evaluation easily allows us to determine whether we are dealing with a sick person, a pervert or a faker."

Furthermore, Ey establishes typologies that range from masochistic exhibitionism to sadistic exhibitionism in order to show how this symptom is not a precise and unequivocal sign of any one particular form of mental illness, but that it actually fits within many different psychological structures. Nonetheless, Henry Ey introduced a new consideration in the domain of French psychiatry. He affirmed the act of exposing oneself as a normal behavior, just like seeking to watch. Thereby, he rejected the continued use of the category of "debauchery" to designate individuals with a particular moral vice, because he recognized the importance of a certain form of exhibitionism that was based on neither sickness nor guilt.

This new position in psychiatry in relation to scopophilic pleasure is very important, for, at the same time, the 1950s saw the emergence of a relative liberalization of public spaces due to a greater tolerance on the part of public prosecutors. To look at, and to see, would resort to forms of *normal pleasure* not reserved just for the perverted and the lecherous.

At the same time, jurisprudence began to separate sight from the other senses as the single form for constituting publicity in Article 330. As we have seen, in a series of widely noted rulings, the Court of Cassation introduced significant changes to the notion of publicity, giving a completely new place to the consent of witnesses. Little by little, new rules regarding the exhibition of sexuality began to be conceived and would find their affirmation in 1992 when only exhibitions *imposed* in certain spaces would be understood to be criminal. The more the case law liberalized the public visibility of sexuality, the more it *tended* only to punish behaviors close to those of exhibitionists. Admittedly, these more liberal rules did not set their sights at all on punishing exhibitionists. Rather, their goal was to limit the crime of indecent exposure by limiting publicity to certain very specific cases.

In 1967, in his thesis in medicine, Jacques Stéphany[13] proposed a typology of exhibitionists, in which he retained only the "semi-mad"—that is, those convicted of criminal sanctions—while discarding cases caused by delirium or epilepsy. In that first category, he distinguishes between two large groups: neurotics and perverts. Stéphany points out that, because the latter are impervious to sanctions, in place of being punished, they ought to be subject to imprisonment. However, even just short sentences for neurotics could have a negative impact on their healing process.

This notion of "perverts," which designates a category distinct from that of "perversion," and characterizes a certain type of exhibitionism as similar to other forms of sexual deviance, finds its origin, according to Georges Lanteri-Laura, not in end-of-nineteenth-century psychiatry nor in psychoanalysis but in later works. It is the psychiatrist É. Dupré who in 1912 for the first time presented this new nosological category, which supplanted the category of offenders and sexual criminals.[14]

According to Dupré, beyond sexual perversions, there exists a perverse condition that expresses itself from childhood in aggressive conduct and with a deplorable malignance. These weaknesses reveal themselves as inherent, independent of any external influence, before any sort of learning. In substance, it would be a matter of a tendency of preferring bad behavior over good behavior. Sexual perversions are just one aspect among others comprising the perverse condition. For Dupré, this is indistinguishable from the born-criminal proposed by the anthropologist Lombroso. According to Dupré, "the moral amelioration of perverts is an illusion." The perverse condition is thus primary and present before sexual deviance, and it guarantees the existence of a whole series of flaws and vices that are ready to manifest any day.

In his thesis, Stéphany reprises these postulates to apply them to a certain type of exhibitionism; in them he highlights a feature that will later characterize the manner in which the law imagines all criminals and sexual offenders: "by virtue of his instinctual agenesis and his basic abnormality, he [the pervert] cannot be immoral; he is amoral. His sexuality is certainly fouled, but resolves itself for him in a natural way through his action; in fact as an individual, rather than opposing our morals in a voluntary manner, he positions himself apart from them."

According to Stéphany, perverted exhibitionists are protected "from all internal conflict, and the total integration of their sexual conduct with the very source of their inner being [*leur moi*] makes them ignore others rather than hide themselves."[15] Furthermore, for him, unlike simple neurotics, perverted exhibitionists "respond to a raw, urgent and thus immediate need for genital satisfaction, experienced by the subject on a purely organic level. From this we see the apparent impulsivity and the absence of any emotional process."[16]

Stéphany employs psychoanalytical explanations, as opposed to the quasi-demonological type espoused by Dupré, to describe the etiology of perverts, particularly for the development of certain mental conditions whose hypothetical advent can be traced back to very early childhood. This would explain the strange relationship with morals that makes these subjects as dangerous as they are incurable. However, for Stéphany, to the extent that this small group of individuals has not been responsive to penal sanction, it has to be treated as a case of insanity. Perverted exhibitionists did not have to be subject to conviction but to a measure of security with hopes of protecting society.

This concept of the pervert as a subject outside of the law would have a long future, due less to psychiatry than to the law. In the penal system under the aegis of Sex, wherein there is no place for any pleasure outside of the law, and legal transgressions, mental illnesses, and moral faults are all to be confused with one another, the pervert embodies the prototype of the sexual delinquent, going from exhibitionist to rapist-murderer of children.

The notion of the pervert thus represents the obverse of the full face of State control that has made all forms of sexual relations—verbal, visual, physical, conjugal, extra-conjugal, normal, abnormal, consenting, nonconsenting, real or virtual—subject to its control until the end of the long sentences that it metes out for offenses and crimes.

II Exhibitionists in the world of Sex

Since the reform of 1992, the position of exhibitionists within the judicial system worsened in successive stages without any measures having targeted them in particular. Exhibitionists were the victims of a system whose rationality necessitated excluding and punishing them.

If the sentences given to exhibitionists for the violation were in principle less harsh in the 1992 Penal Code, the new definition of the prohibited act nevertheless affected them directly. But, above all, the same reform that installed a new regime between justice and expertise immediately turned against them. If in prior years mental health issues elicited clemency from magistrates for exhibitionists, from now on they will be invoked as the best reason to punish them.

Finally, the law of 1998, which implemented social and legal supervision, brought exhibitionists into the category of potentially dangerous sick people whose faults could be interpreted as the first step along the path to a life of crime.

Exhibitionists and the new definition of the violation

In the 1988 draft of the new Penal Code presented by Robert Badinter, exhibitionism is clearly designated as a target of the new violation:

> Contempt for public decency will only be assessed a *fine*. However, *sexual exhibitionism*, voluntarily inflicted upon others, in spaces open to the public gaze, constitutes a form of aggression against others and especially against children. It remains a crime punishable by a year of imprisonment.[17]

However, this idea disappeared from parliamentary debates that preceded the 1992 reform, and legal scholars were unanimous in affirming that this violation not only targeted exhibitionists but all those who transgressed the boundaries of the visibility of sexuality between the public and private worlds.

Even though the intention of the legislator was not just to punish exhibitionists, the liberalization of the violation seems to have gone hand in hand with the prioritized targeting of this minority of individuals who make these borders meant to put them under surveillance into sources of pleasure. Indeed, the process of liberalization of this violation, which began in the 1950s, has had the consequence of restricting prohibited behaviors to those who expose their sexuality to nonconsenting witnesses. This process began by narrowing the notion of publicity. In this way only exhibitions produced in certain spaces, through which individuals imposed a sexual spectacle on others, were understood to be public. But these restrictions were only applied to closed spaces accessible to the public through a door, or in cases of interior publicity. Consequently, the 1992 reform extended this technique of "privatization"—even if, to accomplish this, it did not directly use the notion of publicity—to all spaces, among them veritable [open] public spaces. The change introduced by the 1992 reform that most affected exhibitionists is no doubt the transformation of exhibiting one's sexuality in certain places into an intentional act. With the application of the new norms, society has excluded the behaviors of a heterogeneous group of persons by two mechanisms: by restricting publicity to cases where there would be nonconsenting witnesses and by linking intentionality to exhibition. This was also the case for foolish and hot-headed individuals such as nudists who exposed themselves on beaches, producers and artists of certain types of performances, as well as those who like to expose themselves and see others engaged in the sexual act. The new law has become blind to offenders and tolerant of the dissolute.

Exhibitionists are the only ones who have shown themselves to be uncontrollable and stubborn, by definition, and fit into none of these categories. They do not make themselves visible through carelessness or impetuousness, and do not derive pleasure from the act of putting themselves in spaces where it is legal to see nudity or others' sexuality, for, in those spaces, the border that they attempt to transgress does not exist.

Certainly, without being exhibitionists, some individuals will fall under the heel of the violation either by challenge, or because of the relative vagueness that the law creates in the matter of exhibition in public spaces. The law leaves it to individuals, as we have seen, to feel affronted and thus transform an exhibition in a public space into a crime. This will discourage the majority, but will give to some individuals the feeling that they do not risk being seen and therefore being punished. Whatever the case may be, given that only exhibitionists act precisely because someone will be able to see them in certain places, they become the primary subjects affected by this violation.

It seems rather paradoxical to go to so much effort to turn this violation into an intentional crime when in truth it only targets exhibitionists, that is, those who act less through reason than by compulsion and illness. It is precisely in this way that the 1992 reform continues to prosecute them. Indeed, the absence of their internal liberty is no longer considered in lightening their culpability. On the contrary, such an absence constitutes the principal reason to increase their guilt.

III Experts and the law

The reform of 1992 introduced significant changes in the domain of penal responsibility of persons affected by mental disorders. According to the first paragraph of the new Article 122-1, "a person who was affected by psychological or neuropsychological disorder at the time of his or her action is not criminally responsible, having lost discernment or control of his or her actions." The final code uses the words "not criminally responsible," but, during the debate of the bill, psychiatrists had proposed that the formulation "nonpunishable criminally" be used; the offender would have been declared guilty, but exempt from punishment. According to the new "therapeutic theories," for a sick person, the fact of being held responsible would be healthy, for this would permit him or her to think that he continues to be a part of the community.

As far as half-mad persons are concerned, the Chaumié memo of 1905 declared them responsible, but granted them the benefit of reduced responsibility. The reform of 1992 completely changed these practices. According to paragraph 2 of Article 122-1:

> a person affected by a psychological or neuropsychological disorder at the time of his or her actions, having impaired his or her discernment or hindered control of his or her actions, remains punishable; however, the jurisdiction considers these circumstances when it determines the sentence and establishes the system.

This text seems to confirm the practice laid out by the Chaumié memo. However, compared to the Chaumié memo, it does not expressly provide for a reduction in responsibility. It leaves to the judge all the power of appraisal, for the weight of the sanction as well as for the enforcement of sentences.

Since then, the practice of the tribunals has shown that psychological disorders do not lead to lighter sentences but instead to heavier ones. This can be attributed to two reasons. First, a "dangerousness" is attributed to these mental disorders. Second, there is the fact that the same sentence is meant to be therapeutic, according to the fashionable new theories on the meaning of punishment. Sickness strengthens sentences instead of reducing them or replacing them with therapeutic treatment. Thus all violators have to pay both for the mistakes made and for the fact of being a pervert or a psychopath who has not learned the significance of the law; and they pay all the more, since one is not likely to heal from this type of illness.

This new type of criminal creates a division in the heart of the subject of law—between the reasonable part and the insane part, where the former must pay for the latter. It is as if the sick part was only an instrument of the healthy one, as if the criminal had voluntarily allowed his mental disorders to commit the reprehensible acts in the same way as someone who deliberately gets drunk before driving his car onto a highway.

But, if this way of considering psychological disorders is inherent to all criminals, those who have committed sexual violations are subject to new measures that also affect exhibitionists. The law of 1998 launched a long series of increasingly harsh legal texts, and implemented a new practice of punishment that is now called socio-legal supervision.

Exhibitionists and socio-legal supervision

The history of exhibitionists saw a true turning point with the passage of the law of 17 June 1998. This law did not just content itself with imposing socio-legal supervision for those who took responsibility for sexual violations or certain crimes involving endangerment of minors.[18] It also constructed a typical profile for these violators by assigning them their fate.

As the memorandum below elaborates:

> For several years our society—like those of several foreign countries—has become aware of the breadth of the problem caused by acts of violence of a sexual nature, particularly those directed against children.
>
> The repressive system punishing such violations against individuals already has great impact [...]—and the severity of the punishments handed down has not stopped increasing.
>
> However, the legislative arsenal applicable to these crimes and offenses appears today to be insufficient to prevent recidivism to a sufficient extent.
>
> Indeed, even if they are judged criminally responsible for their acts, the culprits of these violations suffer from mental disorders in most of these cases; these disorders persist after their punishments are carried out, and by their nature increase the odds of carrying out the act again.
>
> It is therefore advisable, beyond the handing down of a sentence

> depriving them of liberty in a manner proportional to the gravity of the acts committed, to make it such that these persons can, upon regaining their freedom, be subject to follow-up measures—including compulsory care when necessary—designed to prevent recidivism [...].
>
> This is why the first objective of the first article of the present draft of the law is to institute [...] a measure of socio-judicial supervision that will be applicable to culprits of crimes or offenses of a sexual nature, and which will permit society to better prevent these violations [...].[19]

This draft went on to be revised several times, introducing all the more stringent measures with each successive revision.

The analysis conducted by Georges Vigarello in his *Histoire du viol* published sometime before the promulgation of this draft law permits us to understand why exhibitionists have suddenly become perceived as dangerous individuals.

This law was inspired by a truly demagogical spirit—as has become the custom in these domains in the last fifteen years or so—and was voted on without taking into account the numerous testimonies of experts who had nevertheless been summoned to give their advice. This demagogical stance sought to echo the popular belief, largely advanced by the media, that sexual offenders and criminals cannot but fall into recidivism and commit crimes that are ever more atrocious. The fascination with rape and child murder inflects all sexual violations, sharpening the gaze on their dangerousness, making all sexual assailants into potential murderers.[20]

Socio-judicial supervision meets the needs of popular expectations by instituting a requirement to submit all criminals to measures of surveillance and assistance,[21] under the aegis of the judge responsible for the enforcement of sentences, for the period determined in the verdict, after the convicted person has served his or her prison sentence (Article 131-36-1 of the Penal Code).

That this follow-up can be applied as much to rapist-murderers of children as to exhibitionists or pornographers can be explained by the fact that committing insignificant acts is seen to be the first stage before committing graver acts. They can reveal a perverted personality that could show itself to be much more dangerous after the fact. Because of this reasoning, small crimes such as exhibitionism can provide an opportunity to stop a future criminal itinerary in time.

The length of follow-up surveillance is ten years in the case of an offense and twenty years in the case of a felony. But the law of 9 March 2004 decided that, "in correctional matters [as is the case for the offense of sexual exhibition] this length can be increased to twenty years by special decision justified by the jurisdiction of the verdict."[22] This 2004 law also intended for punishments in cases of noncompliance with these decisions, which range from two to three years in case of an offense, and from five to seven years in case of a felony. Socio-legal supervision can include compulsory medication, which, in substance, consists of psychiatric treatment and possibly medication to induce chemical castration.[23] According to Article 131-36-7, in penal matters having to do with exhibitionism, among others, "socio-legal surveillance can be prescribed as the principal penalty."

For this reason, the small penalties that the 1992 reform had set out for exhibitionists take on a whole other importance. The act of committing this offense is not only seen as a form of pollution of public space but also a sign of social dangerousness. Rather than being threatening due to the possibility of recidivism (new acts of exhibition), the danger arises due to the fact that the mental physiology of the category of perverts to which the exhibitionist is likely to belong could bring the culprit to seek satisfaction for ever increasing criminal desires.

Expert assessments, which, in the past, had allowed exhibitionists to benefit from mitigating circumstances, and even not to be held responsible, have been put to perfectly opposite use. The more the exhibitionist is sick, the more he must become subject to punishments as well as measures for security, for all persons whose symptoms manifest in sexual deviance are perceived to be extremely dangerous.

The spatial boundaries that separate public space from private space and that are transgressed by exhibitionists thus become traps that allow for the separation not only of two systems of sexual visibility but also for two forms of psychic function in regard to the law—one for normal people and one for perverts. This derives from the fact that sexual exhibition, which is the most minimal, weakest and most inoffensive of all sexual violations, nevertheless throws its culprits into the category of the damned.

Even if it comes down to a small offense, it is understood to be sufficient in demonstrating the relationship that the offender has with the law, which is the first criterion that the penal system uses to recognize a pervert. The first demonstration of noncompliance with the law is the act of transforming it into an object of enjoyment. Exhibitionists neither take their pleasure within the purview of the law, as honest people do, nor outside its purview, as other sexual offenders and criminals do, but instead they enjoy the law itself, as if they decided not to obey or to break it, as if they had chosen to remain on its border, fascinated by the eye that controls them.

Admittedly, the current violation will always reserve a place for those other exhibitors who are not exhibitionists *per se*, but they will only be punished for having transgressed publics and spaces that, with certain restrictions, have been given over to the dissolute.

Notes

1 "*Our medical language lacks any expression to describe the many numerous states that exist as intermediaries between reason and madness. In this report, as in so many others, the vernacular is richer; however, despite the richness of its vocabulary, we are forced on occasion to resort to neologisms. It is this necessity that will excuse the title that I believed I must give to this short study*," Charles Lasègue, "Les exhibitionnistes," in *L'Union médicale*, 1877, published in *Études médicales*, Vol. 2, Paris, Asselin et Compagnie, 1884, p. 692.

2 V. Magnan, *Des exhibitionnistes,* Paris, J.B. Baillère, 1890. According to Magnan, it was not so much the exhibitionist gesture that signified an illness but the fact that clinical examinations revealed signs of mental degeneration, namely obsessions and impulses. Among the rare studies on exhibitionism published in French during this period, we can cite Dr. Pribat, *L'exhibitionnisme chez les épileptiques*, Paris, 1894; Lalanne, *Les Exhibitionnistes*, Paris, 1896; Dr. Georges, *Considérations sur les exhibitionnistes impulsifs*, Paris, 1899; H. Chuwen, *Contribution à l'étude de l'exhibitionnisme*, Paris, 1936; E. Gelma, "À propos de l'exhibitionnisme impulsif," *Annales médico-légales*, 1925, Vol. V, p. 305 ff.; Abely and Truche, "Exhibitionnisme conscient et sans caractère érotique," *Annales médico-psychologiques*, February 1931; R. Benon, "Exhibitionnisme et médicine légale," in *Bulletin médical*, 1934, Vol. 48, p. 569 ff.; A. Francheteau, "Sur quelques aspects médico-légaux de l'exhibitionnisme," in *Bulletin médical*, 1938, Vol. 52, p. 107 ff.

3 Georges Lanteri-Laura, "L'expertise psychiatrique en droit pénal français : une rétrospective parmi tant d'autres," *L'Unebévue*, *Revue de la psychoanalyse*, Robopsy, "Des lois pour les âmes, des âmes pour les lois," no. 20, autumn 2002, pp. 29–38. See also his excellent and

indispensable study on the history of sexual perversions in psychiatry, *Lecture des perversions, histoire de leur appropriation médicale*, Paris, Masson, 1979.

4 See Chapter 1.

5 Garçon, *Code pénal annoté*, no. 16, p. 174.

6 Lasègue, "Les exhibitionnistes," pp. 694–695.

7 *Ibid.*, p. 697.

8 Raphaël Lalanne, *Les Exhibitionnistes,* thesis in medicine, Paris, 1896, p. 40.

9 *Ibid.*, pp. 35–36.

10 *Ibid.*, pp. 62–63.

11 *Ibid.*, p. 63.

12 Henry Ey, *Études psychiatriques, aspects séméiologiques*, Vol. 2, Paris, Desclée de Brouwer, 1950, pp. 222–223.

13 Jacques Stéphany, *Contribution à l'étude de la personnalité exhibitionniste,* Paris, Masson, 1967.

14 Érnest Dupré, "Les perversions instinctives," 22nd session of the Convention of Psychiatrists and Neurologists of France and Francophone Countries, 1–7 April 1912. Dupré's report was published by Masson in 1912, who published the Conference proceedings a year later, cf. Georges Lanteri-Laura, *Lecture des perversions*, p. 102 ff.

15 *Ibid.*, p. 49.

16 *Ibid.*, p. 50.

17 Draft of the new Penal Code, presentation by Robert Badinter, Paris, Dalloz, 1988, p. 37.

18 Social and judicial supervision is mandated in this law for persons who have taken responsibility for violations laid out by Articles 222-23 to 222-32 of the Penal Code, that is: rape, sexual assault, sexual exhibition except for sexual harassment, and 227-22 to 227-27, that is, crimes involving endangerment of minors: corruption of a minor, exploitation of child-pornographic images, pornography and sexual abuse of a minor.

19 Draft of law relating to the crackdown on sexual violations as well as the protection of minors, presented by Mme Elisabeth Guigou, Attorney General, 3 September 1997, JO AN, 1997, no. 202.

20 Vigarello, *Histoire du viol,* pp. 277–278.

21 Art. 132-44 of the Penal Code.

22 For crimes punished with a thirty-year prison term, the length of supervision is thirty years; when the crime is punishable by life imprisonment, the criminal court may decide that the socio-judicial surveillance will apply indefinitely, subject to the possibility for the court to end the penalties at the end of a period of thirty years (cf. Art. 131-36-1 of the Penal Code).

23 According to Article 3711-3 of the Code for Public Health: "The referring physician is empowered, with written consent renewed at least once a year by the convicted person, to prescribe the convicted person with a treatment using medication [...] according to a list set out by decree of the Minister of Health, which will bring about a reduction in libido, even if the authorization to bring said medication to market has not been given for this prescription," cf. law of 12 December 2005. Even though only this law introduced them in the Code for Public Health, these treatments existed before within the framework of socio-legal surveillance.

Works cited

Legal sources

Aix, January 20, 1965. JCp, 1965. II. 14. 143 bis.
Aix Court of Appeals, 22 November 1854, D. 1856. 2. 302.
Robert Badinter, Draft of New Penal Code, Paris, Dalloz, 1988, p. 37.
Bourges Court of Appeals, 25 January 1990: juris data no. 1990-046729.
Bourges Court of Appeals, Bull. crim. 1898, no. 93.
Jean-Guy Branger, Information Report No. 229, March 9 2005.
Bull. 1897, no. 158, Pandectes 1898. 1. 453.
Bull. crim., no. 289, p. 651.
Bull. crim., 1813 no. 58, p. 144.
Bull. crim., 1828, no. 48.
Bull. crim., 1956, no. 555.
Bull. crim., 1960, no. 573.
Bull. crim., 1971, no. 352.
Bull. crim., 2004, no. 119, pp. 463–464.
Cass., 30 Nivôse, Year 11, *Journal du Palais* (3rd edition), Volume 3, p. 116.
Cass., 1 December 1848, S. 1849. 1. 543.
Cass., D. 1869. 1. 305.
Cass., 18 March 1858, D. 1958. 1. 561.
Cass., 23 December 1858, Bull. crim. 1858 no. 317.
Cass., 11 March 1859, D. 1959. 1. 626.
Cass., 28 November 1861 (cited by É. Garçon, *Code pénal annoté*)
Cass., 1 May 1863, D. 1864. 1. 147.
Cass., 6 October 1870, D. 1870. 1. 433.
Cass., D. 1873. 1. 176.
Cass., 5 June 1874, Bull. crim. 1874, no. 158, p. 293.
Cass., D. 1877. 1. 287.
Cass., D. 1877. 1. 288.
Cass., 15 May 1879, D. 1879. 5. 30.
Cass., 4 March 1880, S. 1881. 1. 44.

Cass., 28 April 1881. Journal du Ministère public, 1882, p. 49.
Cass., 28 April 1881, D. 1881. 1. 447.
Cass., 14 April 1892. D. 1893. 1. 239.
Cass., 7 May 1897, Bull. 1897, no. 158.
Cass., 3 March 1898, D. 1899. 1. 59.
Cass., 8 February 1900, D. 1900. 1. 279.
Cass., 21 July 1911, Bull. crim. 1911, no. 372.
Cass., 29 October 1926, cited by É. Garçon, *Code pénal annoté*.
Cass., 20 October 1955, D. 1956. 1. 117.
Cass. crim., 7 April 1859, D. 1859. 1. 239.
Cass. crim., 28 April 1881, S. 1881. 1. 389.
Cass. crim., 19 March 1910, Bull. crim. 1910, no. 265.
Cass. crim., 18 July 1930.
Cass. crim., 27 October 1932, Bull. Crim. 1932, no. 220.
Cass. crim., 18 February 1938, DH. 1838. 293.
Cass. crim., 19 April 1939.
Cass. crim., 15 June 1954, D. 1954. 1. 701.
Cass. crim., 31 March, Droit pénal 1999, no. 127, obs. Véron.
Cass. crim., 4 January 2006, Bull. crim. 2006, no. 3; Droit pénal 2006 no. 33, obs. Véron.
Code for Public Health (*Code de la santé publique*).
Collection Duverger, 1825, p. 150, and 1830, p. 278.
Le Courrier français, June 25 1893.
Crim., June 25 1857, S. 1857. 1. 711.
Crim., 10 November 1932, D. 1933. 1. 133 note Mlle Vandamne.
Crim., 18 February 1938, OH, 1938. 1. 294.
Crim., 22 December 1965. JCP., 1966. II. 14. 509.
Crim., 5 September 1990, Bull. Crim., 1990, no. 313.
Crim., 11 June 11 1992, D. 1993. somm. 13, obs. Azibert.
Criminal law 1995. n. 89 obs. Véron.
D. 1933. 1. 133 and note Vandamne.
D. 2004 no. 38, commented, pp. 2750–2751, Gabriel Roujou de Boubée.
Decision of 6 April 1903, D. 1904. 1. 395; S. 1904. 1. 273.
Dijon Court of Appeals, 20 April 1859, D. 1859. 5.37.
Douai Court of Appeals, 28 September 1989, D. 1991, Summary. no. 65, obs. Azibert.
Garçon, Émile. *Code pénal annoté* (2nd edition, updated by Marcel Rousselet, Maurice Patin, Marc Ancel). Paris: Sirey, 1956, art. 330, p. 173.
Gazette du Palais 1911. 2. 259.
Gazette du Palais 1939, 855 and DH, 1930. 462.
Gazette du Palais 1956. 2. 222.
Gazette du Palais 1978. 2. 380.

Gazette des tribunaux, 10 August 1865 and 21 August 1878, cited by Emile Male, *Code pénal annoté, Volume II* (art. 295-401), p. 196.

Gazette des tribunaux, 14 January 1892.

Gazette des tribunaux, 24 June 1893.

Gazette des tribunaux, 20 and 27 July 1908.

Gazette des tribunaux, 21, 27, 28 July 1908.

Gazette des tribunaux, 25 November and 2 December 1908.

Gazette des tribunaux, December 2 1908.

Grasse criminal trial court [Tribunal correctionnel de Grasse], 23 September 1964, JCP, 1954. II. 13. 1974, note À Rieg.

Guigou, Elisabeth, Atty. Gen. [Garde des Sceaux]: Draft of law relating to the crackdown on sexual violations as well as the protection of minors, 3 September 1997, JO AN, 1997, no. 202.

Le Journal, 25 April 1908.

Journal des tribunaux, 15 January 1966.

Journal Officiel AN, 22 June 1991, p. 3563.

Journal Officiel du Sénat, 1991, p. 2652.

Juris-classeur périodique 1979. n. 19.138.

Juris-classeur périodique 1965. II. 1423, note A. R.

Limoges, 1 April, 1887, D. 1890. 2. 24.

Les Lois criminelles de France dans leur ordre naturel, Paris, Merigot le jeune, 1780.

Montpellier, 8 August 1859, S. 1859.2.490 and D. 1860.5.29.

Paris Court of Appeals, D. 1909.5.18. 3 March 1909.

Paris Court of Appeals, 13th chamber, 26 February 1936, S. 1936. 2. 137.

Paris Criminal Tribunal [Tribunal correctionnel de Paris], 17th Division, *Gazette du Palais*, 25 January 1977, pp. 56–58.

Penal Code of 1988, Art. 227-17 of the initial draft.

Poitiers, 18 February 1858, D. 1959. 5. 37.

Revue de science criminelle et de droit pénal comparé, 1965. 422, Hugueney's commentary.

Riom Court of Appeals, November 16, 1937, DH, 1938. 109.

Riom Court of Appeals, DH, 1938. 109 and RSC, 1938. 301.

Saint-Lô Tribunal, 8 November 1950. D. 1951 Somm. 21 and RSC, 1951. 273 obs. Hugueney.

Unpublished Decision of the Court of Appeals, Poitiers, 27 July 1892, cited by Laplatte, pp. 208–209.

Secondary sources

Abely, X. and Truche. "Exhibitionnisme conscient et sans caractère érotique," *Annales médico-psychologiques* 89 (February 1931): pp. 141–145.

Aebi, Marcelo F. SPACE I: Annual Penal Statistics: Survey 2004. Strasbourg, Council of Europe: 2005.

Alac, Patrick. *La Grande Histoire du bikini.* New York: Parkstone Press, 2002.

Barillan, Jacques and Paul Bensussan. *Le Nouveau Code de la sexualité.* Paris: Odile Jacob, 2007.

Barthe-Deloizy, Francine. *Géographie de la nudité: Être nu quelque part,* Paris, Bréal, 2003, pp. 142–143.

Baubérot, Arnaud. *Le Naturisme et la société française, histoire sociale et culturelle d'un mythe (fin du XIXe siècle–années 1930).* Doctoral thesis in history. Paris: University of Paris XII, Créteil, 2002.

Benon, R. "Exhibitionnisme et médecine légale." *Bulletin médical* 48 (1934): p. 569 ff.

Bensussan, Paul and Florence Rault. *La Dictature de l'émotion. La protection de l'enfant et ses dérives.* Paris: Belfond, 2002.

Bologne, Jean-Claude. *Histoire de la pudeur.* Paris: Olivier Orban, 1986.

Bordeaux, Michèle, Bernard Hazon, and Soizic Lorvellec. *Qualifié viol* (Geneva: Éditions Médecine et Hygiène). Paris: Méridiens-Klincksieck, 1990.

de Bordeu, Théophile. *Recherches sur l'histoire de la médecine,* 1768.

C., R. "Le nu au spectacle peut-il outrager la pudeur?" *Revue de science criminelle et de droit pénal comparé* (1953): pp. 362–366.

Casares, Adolfo Bioy. *L'Invention de Morel.* 1940.

Chauveau, Adolphe and Faustin Helie. *Théorie du Code pénal.* Paris: Edward Legrand, 1843.

Chuwen, Henryk. *Contribution à l'étude de l'exhibitionnisme.* Paris: L. Rodstein, 1936.

Courteline, Georges. "L'Article 330." In *Théâtre, contes, romans et nouvelles, philosophie: Écrits divers et fragments retrouvés.* Paris: Robert Laffont, 1990.

Darmon, Pierre. *Le Tribunal de l'impuissance : virilités et défaillances conjugales dans l'Ancienne France.* Paris: Seuil, 1979.

Daubert, Pierre. *Du port illégal de costume et de décoration.* Thesis in law. Paris: Arthur Rousseau, 1904.

Doublier, Roger. *Le Nu et la Loi.* Paris: Nature Éditions and L.G.D.J., 1976.

Duerr, Hans Peter. *Nudité et pudeur : Le mythe du processus de civilisation,* preface by André Burguière. Translated by Véronique Bodin. Paris: Éditions de la Maison des sciences de l'homme, 1998.

Dufay, Pierre. *Le Pantalon féminin.* Paris: Charles Carrington, 1906.

Dupré, Érnest. "Les perversions instinctives." 22nd session of the Convention of Psychiatrists and Neurologists of France and Francophone Countries, 1–7 April 1912.

Elias, Norbert. *La Civilisation des mœurs* (2nd edition). Translated by Pierre Kamnitzer. Paris: Calmann-Lévy, 1973.

Ey, Henry. *Études psychiatriques, aspects séméiologiques,* Vol. 2. Paris: Desclée de Brouwer, 1950.

Fabreguettes, Polydore. *Traité des délits politiques et des infractions par la parole, l'écriture et la presse* (2e édition). Paris: Chevalier-Marescq & Cie, 1901.

Feydeau, Georges. *Mais n'te promène donc pas toute nue.* Play in One Act. Paris: Librairie théâtrale, 1911.

Le Figaro, 13 January 1970, "Tout nu?"

Flobert, Paul Laure. *La Femme et le costume masculin*, lecture given at the Archaeological, Historical and Artistic Society, 28 March 1911. Lille: Printing Lefevre-Ducrocq, 1911.

Fouassier, Christophe. *Le Droit de la création cinématographique en France.* Paris: L'Harmattan, 2004.

Francheteau, A. "Sur quelques aspects médico-légaux de l'exhibitionnisme." *Bulletin médical* 52 (1938): p. 107 ff.

French Ministry of Justice. *Annuaire statistique de la justice* (2006 edition).

Garçon, Maurice. *Histoire de la justice sous la Troisième République,* Vol. II. Paris: Fayard, 1957.

Gelma, E. "À propos de l'exhibitionnisme impulsif." *Annales médico-légales* 5 (1925): p. 305 ff.

Georges, Adolf. *Considérations sur les exhibitionnistes impulsifs.* Paris: G. Carré & C. Naud, 1899.

Grand-Carteret, John. *La Femme en culotte.* Paris: Flammarion, 1909.

Iacub, Marcela. *Le Crime était presque sexuel : et autres essais de casuistique juridique.* Paris: Flammarion, 2002.

Iacub, Marcela. *L'Empire du ventre : pour une autre histoire de la maternité.* Paris: Fayard, 2004.

Iacub, Marcela and Patrice Maniglier. *Antimanuel d'éducation sexuelle.* Paris, Bréal, 2005.

Kaufmann, Jean-Claude. *Corps de femmes, regards d'hommes, Sociologie des seins nus.* Paris: Pocket, 2006.

Lacassagne, Alexandre. *L'Affaire du père Bérard.* Bibliothèque d'anthropologie criminelle et des sciences pénales, Lyon, Storck éditeur, Paris, Steinheic, 1890.

Lalanne, Raphaël. *Les Exhibitionnistes.* Thesis in medicine. Paris, 1896.

Lambert, *Traité de droit pénal spécial*, Paris, 1968.

Lameyre, Xavier. *La Criminalité sexuelle.* Paris: Flammarion, 2000.

Lameyre, Xavier. "L'incessant accroissement légal de la répression des infractions sexuelles." *Forensic: Revue de psychiatrie et de psychologie légales* 19 (2004): pp. 13–18.

Lanteri-Laura, Georges. *Lecture des perversions, histoire de leur appropriation médicale.* Paris: Masson, 1979.

Lanteri-Laura, Georges. "L'expertise psychiatrique en droit pénal français : une rétrospective parmi tant d'autres." *L'Unebévue : Revue de psychanalyse* 20 : Robopsy, Des lois pour les âmes, des âmes pour les lois (2002): pp. 29–38.

Laplatte, Claude. *L'Outrage public à la pudeur et la contravention d'affiches indécentes.* Troyes: Éditions de la Renaissance, 1967.

Lasègue, Charles. "Les exhibitionnistes." In *Études médicales*, Vol. 2. Paris: Asselin et Cie., 1884, pp. 691–700.

Laver, James. *Histoire de la mode et du costume*, translated from the English by Michèle Hechter, Christine Chareyre and Christian-Martin Diebold. Paris: Thames & Hudson, 2003.

Le Peletier de Saint-Fargeau, Louis-Michel. "Rapport sur le projet de Code pénal fait au nom des comités de constitution et de législation criminelle." Sessions of 22 March and 23 May 1791, in Pierre Lascoumes, Pierre Lenoël and Pierrette Poncela, *Au nom de l'ordre : une histoire politique du Code pénal.* Paris: Hachette, 1983.

Louÿs, Pierre. *Le Journal*, 25 April 1908.

Magnan, V. *Des exhibitionnistes.* Paris: J.B. Baillère, 1890.

Maillefaud, Abel. *De l'outrage public à la pudeur.* Doctoral thesis, University of Lyon, 1896.

Makowski, Elizabeth M. "The Conjugal Debt and Medieval Canon Law." *Journal of Medieval History* (1977): pp. 99–114.

Mendes, Valérie and Amy de La Haye. *La Mode au XXe siècle.* Paris: Thames & Hudson, 2000.

Monseignat, "Rapport au corps législatif," 17 February 1810, in the old Répertoire Dalloz, *Attentat aux mœurs : Répertoire méthodique et alphabétique de Législation, de Doctrine et de Jurisprudence, 1846–1864.*

Montesquieu. *De l'esprit des lois.* 1748.

Mossuz-Lavau, Janine. *La Vie sexuelle en France.* Paris: La Martinière, 2002.

Nivôse, Luc-Michel. "Des attentats aux mœurs et à la pudeur aux agressions sexuelles." *Chroniques de Droit Pénal* (May 1995): pp. 1–3.

Normandy, Georges. *Le Nu à l'église, au théâtre et dans la rue*, preface by Gustave Kahn. Paris: Paul Dupont, 1909.

Pageaud, P.A. Juris-classeur pénal, art. 330–333, 1965, no. 4.

Pastori, Jean-Pierre. *À corps perdu : histoire de la danse nue au XXe siècle.* Paris: PM Favre, 1983.

Pereira, Acacio. *Justice injuste : Le scandale de l'affaire d'Outreau.* Paris: Éditions Philippe Rey, 2004.

Perrée, H. *La Publicité du spectacle : Étude juridique du théâtre de société.* Thesis in law. Paris: University of Paris, 1911.

Perrot, Philippe. *Les Dessus et les Dessous de la bourgeoisie.* Bruxelles: Complexe, 1984.

Poughon, Louis. *De la séduction envisagée au double point de vue civil et pénal.* Doctoral thesis, Paris, Librairie ancienne et moderne, 1911.

Pradel, Jean. *Droit pénal général.* Paris: Éditions Cujas, 2000–2001.

Pribat, Henri-Joseph. *L'exhibitionnisme chez les épileptiques.* Paris, 1894.

Rassat, Marie-Laure. "Fait de favoriser la corruption d'un mineur." Juris-classeur pénal art. 227-22, 2002.

Roche, Daniel. *La Culture des apparences : Une histoire du vêtement XVII–XVIII siècle.* Paris: Fayard, 2006.

Roujou de Boubée, Gabriel, Jacques Francilion, Bernard Bouloc and Yves Mayaud. *Code pénal commenté, article par article,* Books I–IV. Paris: Dalloz, 1996.

Steinberg, Sylvie. *Le Travestissement de la Renaissance à la Révolution.* Paris: Fayard, 2001.

Stéphany, Jacques. *Contribution à l'étude de la personnalité exhibitionniste.* Paris: Masson, 1967.

Tynan, Kenneth. "Pornography? And is that bad?" *The New York Times,* 15 June 1969.

Vigarello, Georges. *Histoire du viol XVIe–XXe siècle.* Paris: Seuil, 1998.

Vouin, Robert. *Droit pénal spécial.* Paris: Précis Dalloz, 1968.

Vouin, Robert. "Observations sur l'outrage public à la pudeur (à l'occasion de l'ouvrage de M.C. Laplatte)." *Revue de science criminelle et de droit pénal comparé* (1969): pp. 839–851.

Witkowski, Gustave-Joseph and Lucien Nass. *Le Nu au théâtre depuis l'Antiquité jusqu'à nos jours.* Paris: Daragon, 1909.

Index